Gertrude Himmelfarb

THE DE-MORALIZATION OF SOCIETY

Gertrude Himmelfarb taught for twenty-three years at Brooklyn College and the Graduate School of the City University of New York, where she was named Distinguished Professor of History in 1978. Now Professor Emeritus, she lives with her husband, Irving Kristol, in Washington, D.C. Her previous books include *On Looking into the Abyss: Untimely Thoughts on Culture and Society*; *Poverty and Compassion: The Moral Imagination of the Late Victorians*; *The New History and the Old*; *Marriage and Morals Among the Victorians*; *The Idea of Poverty: England in the Early Industrial Age*; *On Liberty and Liberalism: The Case of John Stuart Mill*; *Victorian Minds* (nominated for a National Book Award); *Darwin and the Darwinian Revolution*; and *Lord Acton: A Study in Conscience and Politics*.

THE

DE-MORALIZATION

OF

SOCIETY

———————

From Victorian Virtues to Modern Values

GERTRUDE HIMMELFARB

VINTAGE BOOKS

A Division of Random House, Inc.
New York

To my Grandchildren
Rebecca, Anne, and Joseph Kristol
Maxwell and Katherine Nelson

FIRST VINTAGE BOOKS EDITION, FEBRUARY 1996

Copyright © 1994 by Gertrude Himmelfarb

Portions of the following chapters have been previously published: chs. I and V in the *American Scholar*, Spring 1988 and Summer 1990; ch. VI in *Commentary*, February 1989; the Epilogue in *Forbes*, September 14, 1992, and in an expanded adaptation in *The Public Interest*, October 1994; and the Postscript in the *Wall Street Journal*, January 12, 1994.

The Library of Congress has cataloged the Knopf edition as follows:
Himmelfarb, Gertrude.
The de-moralization of society: from Victorian virtues to modern values /
by Gertrude Himmelfarb. – 1st ed.
p. cm.
Includes index.
ISBN 0-679-43817-3
1. Social values–United States. 2. Social values–England. 3. United States–Moral conditions. 4. England–Moral conditions. 5. United States–Social conditions. 6. England–Social conditions.
I. Title.
HN59.2.H56   1995
303.3'72–dc20   94-12365
CIP
Vintage ISBN: 0-679-76490-9

Manufactured in the United States of America
10 9 8 7 6 5 4 3

CONTENTS

	Acknowledgments	*vii*
Prologue	From Virtues to Values	3
Chapter I	Manners and Morals	21
II	Household Gods and Goddesses	53
III	Feminism, Victorian Style	88
IV	"The Mischievous Ambiguity of the Word *Poor*"	125
V	"Gain All You Can. . . . Give All You Can"	143
VI	The Jew as Victorian	170
VII	The New Women and the New Men	188
Epilogue	A De-Moralized Society	221
Postscript	The "New Victorians" and the Old	259
	Notes	*265*
	Index	*307*

ACKNOWLEDGMENTS

In my earlier books, I was happy to acknowledge the assistance of librarians and archivists who made available to me documents and manuscripts on the Victorians. Now it gives me great pleasure to thank the friends who introduced me to the statistical sources and monographic literature on the contemporary United States: William Bennett, Douglas Besharov, Edward Himmelfarb, Daniel Patrick Moynihan, Charles Murray, Michael Novak, Peter Wehner, and James Q. Wilson. I especially want to thank Irwin and Cita Stelzer, who provided me with valuable statistical data, clippings from the English press, a critical reading of the final chapter, and much appreciated moral support. I am also grateful to Josephus Nelson of the Library of Congress, who facilitated my research there; Karlyn Bowman, who prepared the graphs and instructed me in the arcana of that art; Elizabeth Martell and Elizabeth Anderson, who scoured the libraries for books and journal articles; and the library staff of the Woodrow Wilson Center, who served as a conduit for books from other libraries. Ashbel Green, my editor, has been as encouraging and helpful as ever, and Melvin

Rosenthal, my copy-editor, as meticulous. For the first time I have enlisted the services of an agent, and I am grateful to Glen Hartley and Lynn Chu for making this so agreeable an experience.

Finally, and once again, I am at a loss to express my debt to my husband, Irving Kristol, who knows much more and has thought more deeply than I about the contemporary subjects I have now ventured upon, and who has been endlessly patient in reading about the Victorians, of whom he now knows more than he ever wanted to know.

THE DE-MORALIZATION OF SOCIETY

From Virtues to Values

———————◆———————

The discussion of "values" has become so commonplace in the last few years that one may well forget how recent it all is. It started in England in the election campaign of 1983, when an interviewer of Margaret Thatcher observed, rather derisively, that she seemed to be approving of "Victorian values"—to which Mrs. Thatcher enthusiastically agreed: "Oh exactly. Very much so. Those were the values when our country became great."[1]

"Victorian values" promptly captured the headlines and became an election issue, with many journalists, professors, and Labour Party members frankly contemptuous of so retrograde a notion. Mrs. Thatcher herself was undaunted. One historian later explained that she had stumbled on the expression "by accident, conjuring the phrase out of nowhere, and launching it on its public career."[2] However she came to it, she happily exploited it. In the course of another interview, she explained that she was grateful to have been brought up by a Victorian grandmother who taught her those "Victorian values."

We were taught to work jolly hard. We were taught to prove yourself; we were taught self-reliance; we were taught to live within our income. You were taught that cleanliness is next to godliness. You were taught self-respect. You were taught always to give a hand to your neighbour. You were taught tremendous pride in your country. All of these things are Victorian values. They are also perennial values.[3]

Almost a decade later, in another election campaign, the term "family values" was introduced into the American vocabulary. Used first by the Republicans, it became a bi-partisan slogan the following year, when President Clinton, on the anniversary of his election, spoke in the church in Tennessee where Martin Luther King, Jr., had delivered his last sermon. Inspired by the place and the occasion, he made one of the most eloquent speeches of his presidency. What would King have said, he asked, had he lived to see this day?

He would say, I did not live and die to see the American family destroyed. I did not live and die to see thirteen-year-old boys get automatic weapons and gun down nine-year-olds just for the kick of it. I did not live and die to see young people destroy their lives with drugs and then build fortunes destroying the lives of others. This is not what I came here to do.

I fought for freedom, he would say, but not for the freedom of people to kill each other with reckless abandon; not for the freedom of children to have children and the fathers of the children walk away from them and abandon them as if they don't amount to anything. I fought for people to have the right to work, but not have whole communities and people abandoned. This is not what I lived and died for.

After describing what his administration was doing to curb drugs and violence, the President concluded that the government alone could not do the job. The problem was caused by "the breakdown of the family, the community and the disappearance of jobs," and unless we "reach deep inside to the values, the spirit, the soul and the truth of human nature, none of the other things we seek to do will ever take us where we need to go."[4]

The English idea of "Victorian values" is both more and less comprehensive than the American "family values." More comprehensive because it includes the family as well as hard work, thrift, cleanliness, self-reliance, self-respect, neighborliness, patriotism. One reason why the discussion of family values has been so unsatisfactory in the United States is that it has been narrowly interpreted, focused almost entirely on such matters as illegitimacy, abortion, and homosexuality. It does not belittle these subjects to suggest that they can be better understood in the larger context of Victorian values—of character, conduct, and the social ethos.

The expression "Victorian values," however, has its own limitations, for it would seem to be time-bound and place-bound—and, critics might add, gender-bound, race-bound, class-bound, culture-bound, and whatever other flaws are now commonly assigned to the past in general and to the Victorian period in particular. Values identified with the England of a century and more ago may be thought to have little or no relevance to England today, still less to other parts of the world.

Mrs. Thatcher herself has given those values a more venerable and varied lineage. On one occasion she described them as "perennial values," on others as Christian, Judaic-Christian, Puritan, Methodist, or (for the benefit of a Scottish audience) Scottish-Tory values.[5] She might also have credited them to Evangelicalism, which, together with Methodism, was the primary inspirer of the "moral reformation" movement that laid the groundwork for Victorian values. That movement emerged in England in the late eighteenth century, half a century before Queen Victoria came to the throne. It was in 1787 that George III issued a proclamation for the "Encouragement of Piety and Virtue, and for the Preventing and Punishing of Vice, Profaneness, and Immorality." A "society" was promptly established to carry out that directive, and others soon followed, dedicated to the "Preservation of Public Morals," the "Suppression of Public Lewdness," the "External Observance of the Lord's Day," and other such worthy causes.

It was not George III, however, who seemed to symbolize the new spirit as much as Mrs. Grundy, a character in a play in 1798, whose neighbors were wont to worry about "what will Mrs. Grundy say?"[6] And more important than Mrs. Grundy (who in the play was a figure of mockery) was Mr. Bowdler, a real person and a more considerable character, who assumed the self-appointed role of literary censor. The first volume of the "bowdlerized" *Family Shakespeare,* purged of sexual indelicacies, appeared in 1804, the last in 1818, after which Bowdler performed the same service for the Old Testament and Gibbon's *Decline and Fall of the Roman Empire* (in the latter case, removing impious passages as well as indecent ones).

But there was another side to the moral reformation movement. In addition to societies for the promotion of piety and virtue, others were established for the relief of the poor and infirm—for destitute orphans and abandoned children, aged widows and penitent prostitutes, the deaf, dumb, blind, and otherwise incapacitated. And institutions were established as well—orphanages, hospitals, charity schools, and Sunday schools. The latter were primarily intended to provide religious instruction for working-class children, but they had the incidental effect of teaching the children to read, so that long before the institution of free public education in 1870, there was a remarkably high degree of literacy among the poor. The idea of moral reformation also extended to such humanitarian causes as the elimination of flogging in the army and navy, the abolition of the pillory and public whipping, the prohibition of cockfighting, bullbaiting, and bearbaiting, and, most important, the abolition of the slave trade.

The censorial spirit was much abated in the course of the nineteenth century. Although the *Family Shakespeare* continued to be reprinted, "bowdlerization," like "Mrs. Grundy," became a term of ridicule. At the same time, humanitarian and social reforms were pursued with a new fervor under the combined aegis of Evangelicalism and Utilitarianism. Motivated by different impulses and philosophies, religious and secular reformers collaborated in the passage of such measures as mine and factory acts limiting working hours, sanitation and health reforms, housing acts, public education, penal reforms, and civic amenities (libraries, parks, bathhouses, street-cleaning, street-lighting). Less formally, but no less effectively, they promoted those manners and morals that have come to be known as "Victorian values." As Evangelicalism was the primary bearer of those values among the middle classes, so Methodism was among the working classes. And as religion became more attenuated for many Englishmen, the values themselves became secularized, divorced from their religious roots but acquiring a sanctity of their own. The "moral reformation" initiated in the late eighteenth century came to fruition in the late nineteenth century.

There is a larger context, however, in which both Victorian values and family values have to be understood. Mrs.

Thatcher was reported as describing the values taught her by her grandmother as "Victorian values." But her Victorian grandmother would not have spoken of them as "values"; she would have called them "virtues."* Moreover, they were not, as it happened, "perennial" virtues. They were surely not the virtues of the classical philosophers.

The "cardinal" virtues celebrated by Aristotle were wisdom, justice, temperance, and courage; associated with these were prudence, magnanimity, munificence, liberality, gentleness. None of these appears in the litany of Mrs. Thatcher's grandmother. Nor were her virtues Aristotle's (although some of them might be subsumed under his categories). Certainly family values do not figure among the classical virtues. Plato, of course, would have utterly rejected them, as he rejected the very idea of the family; his ideal state of "communism" was a community that shared not only property but women and children as well. Even Aristotle, who repudiated Plato's view of the family, did not go so far as to elevate what we would regard as family values to the rank of virtues. Although he did recognize the natural "bonds of union" between husband and wife, parent and child, and gave the family the distinction of being "the first community" and therefore a natural part of the state, he was more solicitous of the family for the sake of a properly ordered state than for the sake of the family itself.[7] The only specific family value he singled out for commendation was household management, which dealt primarily with the finances and property of the family.

This is not to say that the Victorians would have spurned any of the classical virtues. On the contrary, they would

---

* In her autobiography, Mrs. Thatcher says that she originally used the expression "Victorian virtues." Although most accounts at the time rendered this as "Victorian values," at least one did give it as "Victorian virtues."[8]

have approved of them. If they did not assign to some of them (munificence, perhaps, or magnanimity) a high priority, it was because they would not have thought them the most essential and urgent virtues for most people in their own times. They may even have thought them more appropriate to a heroic, aristocratic age than to a bourgeois, democratic one.

Long before the advent of that bourgeois, democratic era, those classical virtues had been supplemented or displaced by the Christian virtues of faith, hope, and charity—the latter in its original meaning of the love of God. Where Aquinas saw these religious virtues as complementing the classical ones, Augustine saw them as irreconcilable, virtues that have no reference to God being "rather vices than virtues."[9] Later secular philosophers, in the seventeenth and eighteenth centuries, subverted the classical virtues more subtly, and the Christian ones more radically. But all of them insisted upon the importance of virtues not only for the good life of individuals but for the well-being of society and the state. And all of them believed in the intimate relation between the character of the people and the health of the polity. Even those philosophers like Montesquieu who assigned different virtues to different regimes, and different *mœurs* to different societies, did not denigrate or deny the idea of virtue itself.

It was not until the present century that morality became so thoroughly relativized and subjectified that virtues ceased to be "virtues" and became "values." This transmutation is the great philosophical revolution of modernity, no less momentous than the earlier revolt of the "Moderns" against the "Ancients"—modern science and learning against classical philosophy. Yet unlike the earlier rebels, who were fully conscious of the import of their rebellion, the later ones (with the notable exception of Nietzsche) seemed almost unaware of what they were doing. There was no "Battle of the Books" to sound the alarm and rally the troops. Even the new vocabulary, which was so radical a departure from the old and which in itself constituted a revolution in thought, passed without notice.

This is all the more curious because the inspirer of the revolution and the creator of the new language was acutely aware of the significance of it all. It was in the 1880s that Friedrich Nietzsche began to speak of "values" in its present sense—not as a verb, meaning to value or esteem something; nor as a singular noun, meaning the measure of a thing (the economic value of money, labor, or property); but in the plural, connoting the moral beliefs and attitudes of a society. Moreover, he used the word consciously, repeatedly, indeed insistently, to signify what he took to be the most profound event in human history. His "transvaluation of values" was to be the final, ultimate revolution, a revolution against both the classical virtues and the Judaic-Christian ones. The "death of God" would mean the death of morality and the death of truth—above all, the truth of any morality. There would be no good and evil, no virtue and vice. There would be only "values." And having degraded virtues into values, Nietzsche proceeded to de-value and trans-value them, to create a new set of values for his "new man."

When, early in the twentieth century, shortly after Nietzsche's death, the sociologist Max Weber borrowed the word "values," he had no such nihilistic intentions, which is perhaps why he did not comment on the novelty of the term, still less attribute it to Nietzsche.* Instead he used the word

---

* Although Weber rarely referred to Nietzsche in his published work, and such references as there are are generally critical, there is no doubt that he read him and was much influenced by him.

matter-of-factly, as if it were part of the accepted vocabulary and of no great moment. For that reason, because it seemed so familiar and unthreatening, it was all the more effective, for it was absorbed unconsciously and without resistance into the ethos of modern society, as it was absorbed into the vocabulary. "Values" brought with it the assumptions that all moral ideas are subjective and relative, that they are mere customs and conventions, that they have a purely instrumental, utilitarian purpose, and that they are peculiar to specific individuals and societies. (And, in the current intellectual climate, to specific classes, races, and sexes.)

So long as morality was couched in the language of "virtue," it had a firm, resolute character. The older philosophers might argue about the source of virtues, the kinds and relative importance of virtues, the relation between moral and intellectual virtues or classical and religious ones, or the bearing of private virtues upon public ones. They might even "relativize" and "historicize" virtues by recognizing that different virtues characterized different peoples at different times and places. But for a particular people at a particular time, the word "virtue" carried with it a sense of gravity and authority, as "values" does not.

Values, as we now understand that word, do not have to be virtues; they can be beliefs, opinions, attitudes, feelings,

---

Toward the end of his life he is said to have told a student:

Today a scholar's honesty, and especially that of a philosopher, can be measured by his attitude toward Nietzsche and Marx. Whoever does not admit that he could not have accomplished crucial parts of his own work without the contributions of these two men deceives himself and others. Our intellectual universe has largely been formed by Marx and Nietzsche.[10]

habits, conventions, preferences, prejudices, even idiosyn-
crasies—whatever any individual, group, or society happens to value, at any time, for any reason. One cannot say
of virtues, as one can of values, that anyone's virtues are as
good as anyone else's, or that everyone has a right to his
own virtues. Only values can lay that claim to moral equality and neutrality. This impartial, "nonjudgmental," as we
now say, sense of values—values as "value-free"—is now
so firmly entrenched in the popular vocabulary and sensibility that one can hardly imagine a time without it.*

To speak of Victorian values (as I occasionally do in the
course of this book, out of deference to common usage) is
not merely a semantical anachronism; it is a distortion of the
Victorian ethos. The Victorian virtues were neither the classical nor the Christian virtues; they were more domesticated
than the former and more secular than the latter. But they
were "virtues" as the Victorians understood the word—not
"values" in our sense. Most Victorians even believed them
to be, as Margaret Thatcher did, "perennial virtues"—and if
not literally perennial, then, for their own time and place at
least, sufficiently fixed and certain to have the practical status of "perennial."

For the Victorians, these virtues were fixed and certain,
not in the sense of governing the actual behavior of all
people all the time (or even, it may be, of most people most

---

* The "values clarification" technique currently used in "moral
education" courses typifies the new mode of thinking. The teacher
in such a course is enjoined from any pronouncement that might
intimate that something is right or wrong. Instead the students are
assigned the task of discovering their own values by exploring
their likes and dislikes, preferences and feelings.[11] (See "On the
Usage of 'Values,' " following this Prologue, pp. 19–20.)

of the time). Plato and Aristotle did not assume that of their virtues; nor did Augustine and Aquinas of theirs. But all of them did believe that they were the standards against which behavior could and should be measured. The standards were firm even if the behavior of individuals did not always measure up to them. And when conduct fell short of those standards, it was judged in moral terms, as bad, wrong, or evil—not, as is more often the case today, as misguided, undesirable, or (the most recent corruption of our moral vocabulary) "inappropriate."

This is why so much of the discussion of Victorian values has been beside the point. In his rebuttal to Margaret Thatcher, Neil Kinnock, the leader of the Labour Party, asserted: "The 'Victorian Values' that ruled were cruelty, misery, drudgery, squalor, and ignorance."[12] But this is to confuse moral values with the social realities of Victorian life (or what Kinnock took to be such); surely no Victorian, however hardheaded or mean-spirited, espoused cruelty, misery, etc., as "values," as things to be desired or advocated. The historian who disputes the idea of Victorian values by pointing to the "educated elite"—Dickens, Trollope, Morris, Ruskin, Carlyle, Arnold—who criticized the "vulgarity, philistinism and intolerance" of their time is unwittingly confirming the very idea of Victorian values.[13] For these eminent Victorians were preeminently moralists, rebuking those who strayed from the path of virtue by committing those all too common sins of vulgarity, philistinism, and intolerance. Carlyle is the archetype of the Victorian moralist, celebrating precisely the virtues—work, discipline, thrift, self-help, self-discipline—associated with Victorian values.

Similarly, Dickens's novels, so far from refuting the idea of Victorian values, actually reinforce it. Those who cite some of his more memorable characters (Fagin or Bill Sikes) as evidence of an amoral or immoral "underclass" (another anachronistic word—"dangerous class," the Victorians would have said) miss Dickens's point, which was precisely to contrast these "low" characters to those among the very poor who made a determined effort to be moral, law-abiding, and self-supporting. If we remember Dickens for his gothic characters and scenes, we should also remember him for those other characters and scenes that meant so much to him and his readers, and that perfectly embody what we now think of as Victorian values: Mrs. Nubbles, the widowed washerwoman who managed to provide sustenance for her three children in a home that was extremely poor but had the "air of comfort about it" that comes with "cleanliness and order"; or the Cratchits in their threadbare but "darned up and brushed" clothes gathered around the hearth for their meager but joyous Christmas "feast."[14]

It is not enough, in short, for the critics of Victorian values to argue that many Victorians often violated those values—that not all, perhaps not most, washerwomen were as clean, orderly, hardworking, and devoted to her children as Mrs. Nubbles; or that the Cratchits represented an idealized family in an idyllic setting of hearth and home; or that Mrs. Thatcher's grandmother may have been an untypical specimen of her generation. What the critics would have to argue is that many or most Victorians did not accept those values *as their values*, whatever their actual behavior. And that is a much harder case to prove. It is important for historians to try to take the measure of social behavior as against moral principles, to estimate the degree to which particular groups and classes at particular times and places observed or transgressed those principles. But it is no less important to recognize (as more and more historians are beginning to do) the reality and the power of the principles themselves—the belief in family and home, respectability and character. Values remain values (all the more if they are thought of, as they were by the Victorians, as "virtues" rather than "values"), even if they are not always carried out in practice. They are what people aspire to, knowing that they will never be fully realized.

The shift from "virtue" to "values" has had other unfortunate consequences. Having displaced virtue from the central position it once occupied, as the defining attribute of the good life and the good society, we have relegated it to the bedroom and boudoir. When we now speak of virtue, we no longer think of the classical virtues of wisdom, justice, temperance, and courage, or the Christian ones of faith, hope, and charity, or even such Victorian ones as work, thrift, cleanliness, and self-reliance. Virtue is now understood in its sexual connotations of chastity and marital fidelity. One of the great mysteries of Western thought, the philosopher Leo Strauss has said, is "how a word which used to mean the manliness of man has come to mean the chastity of women."[15]

This mutation in the word "virtue" has the effect first of narrowing the meaning of the word, reducing it to a matter of sexuality; and then of belittling and disparaging the sexual virtues themselves. These virtues, chastity and fidelity, have been further trivialized by the popular conception of Victorianism as obsessively puritanical. "Victorian values" conjures up images of piano legs modestly sheathed in pantaloons, table legs (as well as human legs) referred to as "limbs," and books by men and women authors dwelling chastely on separate shelves in country-house libraries—all of which are thought to exemplify the repressive, inhibited view of sexuality that is presumed to be typically Victorian. In fact, these and other niceties of taste were not the normal (or even abnormal) practices of real Victorians but as often as not the inventions of satirists, foisted by the English on gullible Americans and perpetuated by unwary historians.* "The woman who draped the legs of her piano," one historian soberly informs us, "so far from concealing her conscious and unconscious exhibitionism, ended by sexualising the piano; no mean feat."[16] It is the historian, however, who has sexualized the piano and imposed his own sexual fantasies upon the Victorians.

One of the many ironies in the current debate about family values and Victorian values is that the word "values" has taken on something of the connotation of the older "virtues." In a thoroughly relativistic climate such as our own, even "values" may come to be seen as a retreat from relativism and a reassertion of moral principles. Critics complain that the invocation of values is an appeal to moral absolutism, an attempt to restore an obsolete and coercive morality. Others, rebutting that charge, see it as a way of counteracting a moral relativism that threatens to degenerate into nihilism, an effort to recover a modest degree of a not so remote ethos.† James Q. Wilson suggests that hid-

---

* The covered piano legs originated with a traveler to America— not England—who reported seeing in a girls' school a piano dressed in "modest little trousers with frills at the bottom of them." And the sexual segregation of books appeared in a tract issued by a religious society informing the "perfect hostess" that "their proximity, unless they happen to be married, should not be tolerated."[17] These and similar pruderies, fancied or real, provided writers in *Punch* with endless occasions for satire.

† "Victorian" sounds positively ancient today—and so it must be to a generation that finds anyone over the age of thirty (or is it now forty?) suspect. It may help put the generational gap in perspective to recall that not only Margaret Thatcher's grandmother but her father and mother as well were Victorians. The first prime minister to be born after the reign of Queen Victoria was Harold Wilson, elected in 1964.

den behind the present usage of "values" is the idea of a "moral sense," so that "values" has become a code word for "virtues."[18]

Indeed, "virtues" itself is beginning to emerge as a respectable word, and not merely in its sexual connotation. In Thomas Mann's *The Magic Mountain,* one character comments on another, the philosopher Settembrini:

> What a vocabulary! and he uses the word virtue just like that, without the slightest embarrassment. What do you make of that? I've never taken the word in my mouth as long as I've lived; in school, when the book said, '*virtus,*' we always just said 'valour' or something like that. It certainly gave me a queer feeling in my inside, to hear him.[19]

One wonders whether the million purchasers of William Bennett's *The Book of Virtues* had to overcome their initial embarrassment in order to utter that word, or whether they comfortably lapsed into an older vocabulary that corresponds to their intuitive "moral sense." In any case, it is noteworthy that this anthology of moral tales remained near the top of the best-seller list in the United States for more than a year. Even more noteworthy, the virtues the book celebrates are such familiar Victorian ones as self-discipline, work, responsibility, perseverance, and honesty.[20] (Not cleanliness or chastity, but perhaps those will appear in a sequel.)

Having written two lengthy books on poverty in Victorian England, I am painfully aware of the difficulties and inequities in Victorian life, not only those arising out of poverty, but those associated with the early stages of industrialism and democracy—class distinctions, social prejudices, abuses of authority, constraints on personal liberty, restrictions and hindrances of all sorts. But I have also learned to be appreciative of those values that helped miti-

gate the harsh realities of life, inspiring a "moral reformation" that, in turn, stimulated a variety of social and
humanitarian reforms. It was no small feat for England, in
a period of massive social and economic changes, to attain a
degree of civility and humaneness that was the envy of the
rest of the world.

ON THE USAGE OF "VALUES"

It is odd that the *Oxford English Dictionary*, the generally accepted authority for the early usage of words, cites neither Nietzsche nor Weber as the source of "values." The word, in the plural, does not appear at all in the 1928 edition. In the 1986 supplement and in the new edition of 1989, the earliest citation is from William I. Thomas and Florian Znaniecki, *The Polish Peasant in Europe and America* (published in English in 1918), a work much influenced by Weber. A German-English dictionary of the 1940s still does not give "values," *Werte,* its present sense or recognize the distinctive meaning of the plural. Even the article on "Values" in the revised edition of the *International Encyclopedia of the Social Sciences* (1968) ignores both Nietzsche and Weber. Yet Nietzsche's works were translated into English in the 1890s and acquired something of a notoriety in the circles of Havelock Ellis and George Bernard Shaw. And although Weber's *Protestant Ethic and the Spirit of Capitalism* was not translated until 1920, the German version of 1904–5 had generated a good deal of interest and controversy in England long before. Weber himself was sufficiently well known in America to be invited to address the Congress of Arts and Science in Saint Louis in 1904; his paper was one of the highlights of the session.

It is also strange that although Weber's "fact-value" distinction has generated a good deal of controversy, and although Weber himself professed to be dissatisfied with the meaning generally attached to "value-free" (*Wertfrei*), there has been little or no discussion of his use of "values" as distinct from "virtues." The editor of an English translation of one of Weber's works supplies many footnotes about the meaning and translation of German words, but does not footnote the word "values."[21] The index to another English translation has several references to "values" but only one to "virtues": "Virtues, in Chinese *Annals*."[22] Weber himself, in the *Sociology of Religion,* uses "virtues" only in the context of religious virtues.[23]

There are a few, but probably only a few, earlier usages of "values" in English, in the current sense, that escaped the *OED*. T. H. Green's *Prolegomena to Ethics* (1883) refers at one point to a "universe of values."[24] But this is an isolated use of the word. It appears in a chapter entitled "Virtue as the Common Good"; it is followed by a sentence dealing with the "impalpable virtues of the character and disposition"; and in the book as a whole (a very long book), the words "virtue" and "good" (but not "values") appear on almost every page.

Manners and Morals

———✦———

"Manners and morals"—the expression is unmistakably Victorian. Not "manners" alone: Lord Chesterfield in the eighteenth century was fond of discoursing to his son on the supreme importance of manners, as distinct from morals. And not "morals" alone: philosophers had always taken this as their special province; some had made it so elevated a subject that it had little to do with anything as mundane as manners.

It was the Victorians who combined those words so that they came trippingly off the tongue, as if they were one word.[1] Yet in this, as in so much else, they were drawing on a long intellectual heritage. When William of Wykeham, bishop of Winchester and chancellor of England, founded New College, Oxford, in the late fourteenth century, he took as its motto "Manners Makyth the Man," meaning by manners something very nearly indistinguishable from morals. So too John Milton in the seventeenth century, when he defended freedom of the press except for "that which is impious or evil absolutely either against faith or manners."[2] Or Thomas Hobbes shortly afterward: "By manners I mean not here, decency of behavior; as how one man should salute another, or how a man should wash his mouth, or pick his teeth before company, and such other points of the *small morals*; but those qualities of mankind, that concern their living together in peace and unity."[3]

If the Victorians were concerned with the "small morals" of life—table manners, toilet habits, conventions of dress, appearance, conversation, greeting, and all the other "decencies" of behavior—it was because they saw them as the harbingers of morals writ large, the civilities of private life that were the corollaries of civilized social life. It was this conjunction of "small morals" and large that made Victorian society so moralistic, in aspiration at least, if not always in achievement. When William Thackeray protested, "It is not learning, it is not virtue, about which people inquire in society; it is manners,"[4] he was speaking of "society" and "manners" in their trivial senses: the high society of *le beau monde* and the genteel manners of the drawing room. For manners and society in their larger senses he had the greatest concern, which is why he was so distressed by their trivialization.

Margaret Thatcher is reported as saying that she would be pleased to restore all Victorian values, with the exception of hypocrisy. If she did say that, she could only have been thinking of the familiar sense of hypocrisy, the deliberate living of a lie, professing beliefs one does not have and acting in such a way as to belie those beliefs. There was, no doubt, a fair amount of this kind of hypocrisy in Victorian times—although it hardly qualifies as a "Victorian value."*

---

* No satirist could have invented a character so consummately hypocritical as Dr. Pritchard, who, a few hours after poisoning his wife in March 1865 (having poisoned his mother-in-law the previous month), recorded her death in his diary:

But there was another kind of hypocrisy that was more in keeping with Victorian values, and that Mrs. Thatcher might well find tolerable. This was the hypocrisy that La Rochefoucauld commended in his famous adage, "Hypocrisy is the homage that vice pays to virtue." It is also the homage that manners pay to morals. The Victorians thought it no small virtue to maintain the appearance, the manners, of good conduct even while violating some moral principle, for in their demeanor they affirmed the legitimacy of the principle itself.

This was, in fact, what many eminent Victorians did when they felt obliged to commit some transgression. They did not flout conventional morality; on the contrary, they tried to observe at least the manner of it because they truly believed in the substance of it. George Eliot, living with a man whom she could not marry because he could not legally be divorced from his wife, reproduced in their relationship all the forms of propriety. They lived together in perfect domesticity and monogamy, quite as if they were married. She called herself, and asked others to call her, "Mrs. Lewes," and had the satisfaction of hearing the real Mrs. Lewes voluntarily address her that way. And when Mr. Lewes died, after twenty-four years of this pseudo-marriage (one can hardly call it an affair), she almost immediately took the occasion to enter a real, a legal marriage with John Cross, with all the appurtenances thereof: a proper trousseau, a formal wedding in church, and a honeymoon. A recent biographer praises Eliot for her perfect

---

18 Saturday—Died here at 1 a.m. Mary Jane, my own beloved wife, aged 38 years—no torment surrounded her bedside—but like a calm peaceful lamb of God passed Minnie away. May God and Jesus, Holy Gh.—one in three—welcome Minnie. Prayer on prayer till mine be o'er, everlasting love. Save us, Lord, for thy dear Son.[5]

freedom, the freedom from conventionality and from the "burdens of respectability."[6] But she did not seek that freedom; she wanted to be married and respectable, and if she was content with her situation, it was because she assumed the forms and manners of marriage and respectability.

So too with other notorious "irregularities," as the Victorians delicately put it: extramarital relationships (like that of John Stuart Mill and Harriet Taylor), or marriages that were unconsummated (the Carlyles and Ruskins), or long-standing but discreet affairs (Dickens and Ellen Ternan), or homosexual relationships (at least until the Oscar Wilde affair toward the end of the century). Those caught up in such an irregularity tried, as far as was humanly possible, to "regularize" it, to contain it within conventional limits, to domesticate and normalize it. And when they succeeded in doing so, they agonized over it in diaries, memoirs, and letters—which they carefully preserved, and which is why we now know so much about these scandals. Like the "fastidious assassin" in Albert Camus' *The Rebel*, who deliberately gives up his own life when he takes the tyrant's life, so these Victorians insisted upon paying for their indiscretions. They tormented themselves, one has the impression, more than they enjoyed themselves.

William Gladstone, the most eminent of Victorian statesmen (so eminent one can hardly call him a politician), was the perfect example of the fastidious immoralist—except that his immoralities, by any standards except his own, were more infirmities than vices. Like a recent American president, he lusted in his heart; and when he could not contain his desires, he indulged them in solitude. When his diaries were published a century later, reviewers greeted them as the ultimate in Victorian hypocrisy, the revelation of sexual fantasies and practices that exposed the fraudulence of the Grand Old Man who posed as the Grand Old

Moralist. One of the volumes opens with the verse: "He spake no word, he thought no thought / Save by the steadfast rule of Ought."[7] That volume, like the others, records his painful struggles to abide by that rule and his frequent yielding to what he called his "besetting sins": masturbation, pornography, and an obsession with prostitutes.

By the norms of later generations (or of his own predecessors like Lord Melbourne or Lord Palmerston), these were surely venial sins. If Gladstone gave way to masturbation, it was perhaps because of the periods of abstinence resulting from the nine pregnancies of his wife in fifteen years. (The convention of the time was to abstain from sexual intercourse during pregnancy and nursing.) The pornography for which he so bitterly castigated himself was of an elevated kind: rakish passages in Petronius or bawdy Restoration poems. And he never, so far as is known, actually slept with the prostitutes he picked up; he preached at them in the street or brought them home, where he and his wife plied them with hot chocolate and tried to persuade them of the errors of their ways. (Before his death, he assured his son, who was also his pastor, that he had never been guilty of "infidelity to the marriage bed," and there is no reason to doubt his word.)[8] He did not conceal these forays in the streets from the public; he immediately informed the police of one blackmail attempt and took the case to the courts. But neither did he conceal from himself, or excuse in himself, the "courting of evil" or "filthiness of spirit" that provoked them. Instead he punished himself by flagellation (marked in the diaries by the symbol of a whip)—an act that he and most of his contemporaries thought of as chastisement but that we, in a more sophisticated age, believe to be yet another form of sexual perversion (*le vice anglais,* as the French dubbed it).*

---

* The editor of his diaries suggests that the idea of flagellation may have come to him from John Henry Newman, who used it

Gladstone's diaries are titillating; one's eyes are inevitably drawn to those whip symbols and the little *x*'s that signified encounters with prostitutes or impure thoughts. But the diaries are also (like Carlyle's memoirs, or Mill's autobiography, or Eliot's letters) sobering. For they remind us that the eminent Victorians were not only eminently human, with all the failings and frailties of the species, but also eminently moral. They did not take sin lightly—their own sins or anyone else's. If they were censorious of others, they were also guilt-ridden about themselves. They were not hypocrites in the sense of pretending to be more virtuous than they were. On the contrary, they deliberately, even obsessively, confessed to their sins. If they did not all punish themselves quite in the manner of Gladstone, they did suffer in private and behave as best they could in public. They affirmed, in effect, the principles of morality even if they could not always act in accordance with those principles.

Indeed, they affirmed moral principles all the more strongly as the religious basis of those principles seemed to be disintegrating. There were dire predictions, after the publication of Charles Darwin's *Origin of Species* in 1859, that the theory of evolution, and the progress of science in general, would undermine not only religion but morality as well. What happened instead was that morality became, in a sense, a surrogate for religion. For many Victorians, the loss of religious faith inspired a renewed and heightened

---

himself and who described it graphically in his novel *Loss and Gain,* published in 1848.[9] Gladstone had followed, with great interest and sympathy, Newman's involvement in the Oxford Movement, which sought to restore the high-church practices of the earlier Anglican Church, and was much distressed when Newman converted to Roman Catholicism.

moral zeal. Darwin himself, asked about the implications of his theory for religion and morality, replied that while the idea of God was "beyond the scope of man's intellect," man's moral obligations were what they had always been: to "do his duty."[10] Leslie Stephen, after abandoning the effort to derive an ethic from Darwinism, finally confessed: "I now believe in nothing, but I do not the less believe in morality."[11] George Eliot uttered the classic statement of this secular ethic when she said that God was "inconceivable," immortality "unbelievable," but duty nonetheless "peremptory and absolute."[12]

The religious census of 1851 was generally interpreted as evidence of the decline of religious faith even before Darwinism appeared on the scene; on the Sunday of the census only half of those able to go to church did so. By Victorian standards, that number was disappointing; by modern standards it is impressive. On that same date, over two million children attended (or at least were enrolled in) Sunday schools—over half of all the children aged five to fifteen and three-quarters of the working-class children of that age group. And the Sunday schools were perhaps a more significant institution than even the churches in the social, moral, and religious life of the Victorians—and more particularly, in developing the ethos of respectability that became so prominent a part of working-class life.[13]

By comparison with other countries, the English were notably pious. The French writer Hippolyte Taine, visiting England several years later, went to two churches and was surprised to find them full of middle-class worshippers and, more surprisingly, with as many men as women, and many of them "gentlemen"—"very different," he commented, "from our own congregations of women, aged dyspeptics, servants, working-class people." Returning to his hotel, he read in his newspaper a proclamation of the Queen affirming her duty "to maintain and augment the service of Almighty

God, as also to discourage and suppress all vice, profane practice, debauchery and immorality." To ensure the strict observance of the Sabbath, she prohibited the playing of cards or any other games in public or private, forbade the sale of liquor or the presence of guests in taverns during services, and commanded "each and every one . . . to attend, with decency and reverence, at Divine Service on every Lord's Day." The proclamation, Taine soon discovered, was not strictly enforced; one could have a drink in the back room of a tavern. Nevertheless a sophisticated Frenchman was shocked by that "vestige of former Puritanism."[14]

It is interesting that even in issuing the command to attend church and observe the Sabbath, the Queen invoked not only the name of God but also the duty to "discourage and suppress all vice, profane practice, debauchery and immorality"; the moral imperative was at least as prominent as the religious one. Taine remarked upon this moral preoccupation of the English. In English sermons, he observed, dogma always takes a "back seat" to the "good life," and religion as such "is hardly more than the poetry which informs ethics or a background to morality." He quoted Thomas Arnold, the famous headmaster of Rugby (now more famous as the father of Matthew Arnold), who advised a man tormented by religious doubts: "Begin by looking at everything from the moral point of view, and you will end by believing in God."[15] (Arnold himself was no passionate believer in God; his faith—"Muscular Christianity," as it was dubbed—resided not so much in God as in a national church that promoted ethical and civic virtues more than dogmas or rituals. But he was a passionate believer in virtue.)

A visiting Frenchman might be astonished by the English predilection for morality without doubting it in the least.

Some recent historians are more skeptical. They charge those middle-class moralists with hypocrisy—indeed, of a double hypocrisy, paying lip service to values that they violated in their personal lives, and compounding their offense by imposing those values on the lower classes for their own ulterior motives.

This view is often advanced by historians who claim to be writing "history from below," history as experienced by the ordinary people, the working classes or "anonymous masses." From this perspective, "Victorian values" are seen not as generically Victorian but as specifically middle-class values, values that were alien to the working classes and that the middle classes sought to instill in them for purposes of "social control." This canon of values included not only the familiar ones of work, thrift, cleanliness, temperance, honesty, self-help, but also less obvious ones that were crucial to the "work ethic": promptness, regularity, conformity, rationality. It is this work ethic that is said to have been the crucial instrument of capitalism, the means by which the ruling class transformed the agricultural laborers into an industrial proletariat and exercised its "hegemony" over a docile workforce and citizenry.[16]*

One of the paradoxes of this "social control" thesis is that

---

* This "social control" thesis has been applied to manners as well—what Thomas Hobbes called "small morals" and what we call "etiquette."

> The ritual order of etiquette, by sternly guarding against slips in bodily and emotional control, assured the individual's deferential participation in the dominant social order. Instead of allowing any outward relaxation, bourgeois etiquette drove the tensions back within the individual self, providing ritual support for the psychological defense mechanisms of repression, displacement, and denial necessary to cope with the anxieties of the urban capitalist order.[17]

it professes to celebrate the working classes—to rescue them from "the enormous condescension of posterity"[18]—while demeaning them as the unwitting victims of "false consciousness." Unable to perceive their own "indigenous" values, the argument goes, Victorian workers were all too easily persuaded to accept the values of their oppressors, to be "moralized" and "socialized" against their own best interests. But is it not more condescending to attribute to these workers a "false consciousness" than to credit them, as most Victorians did, with a true consciousness of their values? Is it not more respectful to think of them not as gullible victims or dupes but as rational people acting in their own interests and pursuing their own values? If they often failed to abide by those values, is it not less patronizing and more humane to assume that that was because of the difficult circumstances of their lives and the natural weaknesses of human beings?

And if these were middle-class values, what were the indigenous working-class values? One historian has said that the reformers' schemes to inculcate the principle of self-help can be understood only through the "distorting lens of middle-class aspirations to gentility."[19] Does this mean that self-help, or independence, was alien to the working classes, in which case are we to understand that dependency was more congenial to them? Or that they were, by nature and preference, indolent rather than industrious, profligate rather than frugal, dirty rather than clean, drunk rather than sober, dishonest rather than honest?

In fact, these Victorian values were as much those of the working classes as of the middle classes. And they were the values not only of the artisan class (the so-called "labor aristocracy") but of the overwhelming majority of the working classes and even of the very poor. Describing the primitive, overcrowded cottages in some rural areas, one historian observed: "One is continually struck, when reading nineteenth-century reports of housing conditions, by the extent to which the poor strove in the almost impossible circumstances of their lives, to conform to middle-class standards of morality."[20] This was especially true in the latter part of the century, as the less skilled and unskilled workers benefited from the expanding economy, the availability of consumer goods, the growth of literacy, and the greater mobility within the working classes—the latter facilitated by the dissemination of precisely these Victorian values. Indeed, toward the end of the century, the working classes became more puritanical and moralistic as the middle classes became more relaxed and permissive.

These values were summed up in the idea of "respectability." Today this word is suspect, redolent of "Victorianism" at its worst. To some historians, it is also redolent of the middle classes at their worst.[21]* Yet the word was used as much by the working classes as by the middle classes, and while it meant somewhat different things to each of them, it was equally important for both. What it did not mean for most of the working classes (except for a small portion of the artisan class) was any desire to emulate the middle classes or to aspire to that status.[22] For them, respectability was a "value" that was thoroughly "indigenous." It did not even necessarily imply "bettering" themselves, although that was often its effect. More often it simply meant being respected by themselves and by others in their own community.

Indeed, within the working classes, among laborers and

---

* And to some contemporaries as well. Lady Wilde, Oscar Wilde's mother (and something of a bohemian in her own right), is reputed to have said, when asked to receive a "respectable" young woman, "You must never employ that description in this house. It is only tradespeople who are respectable. We are above respectability."[23]

factory workers as much as artisans, the division between the "respectable" and the "rough" amounted almost to a class distinction. And that distinction was moral rather than economic. In terms of income, some "roughs" might actually belong to a higher "class" than other workers. But in terms of behavior—being drunk, dirty, disorderly—they were viewed by other workers as of a distinctly lower order. This is not to say that the respectable were paragons of virtue; they were quite capable of getting drunk on occasion or of spending money wastefully, even of lapsing for a time into the condition of the rough. For some it was a constant struggle to maintain their respectability. But it was a struggle most of them waged, often against great odds, precisely because they valued respectability. It was, in fact, the poorer workers who valued it most, because they were the most vulnerable without it.

Respectability was a function of character. And "character" had not only the meaning it has today—the moral and social attributes of a person—but a more specific meaning as well. It was a written testimony by an employer of the qualities and habits of his employee—his industriousness, honesty, punctuality, sobriety. Today we would call it a "reference," thus obscuring its specifically moral connotation. Moreover, it was not addressed and sent to a prospective future employer but remained in the possession of the worker, often carried in his pocket so that he could read it for his own satisfaction and produce it if required. He knew what his "character" said—and what his character was.

Working-class memoirs and the evidence of oral history testify poignantly to the efforts to remain respectable, to have a good character (in both senses of that word), in spite of all the difficulties and temptations to the contrary. For men it meant having a job, however lowly, and not being habitually drunk; for women, managing a clean, orderly, and thrifty household; for children, being obedient at home and school, doing chores and contributing, if possible, to the family income. For the family as a whole, it meant staying "out of the house" (the workhouse) and off the dole, belonging to a burial club or Friendly Society so as to be spared the ignominy of a pauper's burial, having a "clean" (paid up) rent book, wearing clean if shabby clothes and, for special occasions, "Sunday best," and giving no cause for disgrace (such as being arrested for drunkenness or having an illegitimate child).

In this panoply of values, cleanliness is the one that is most difficult to credit, in view of the lack of running water and sewage systems, the dirty and foul-smelling streets, the crowded houses, and the overworked men and women (women particularly, whose job it was to keep the family clean). We envisage Victorian children as begrimed and ragged, looking like chimney sweeps fresh from their jobs. One historian, mocking Margaret Thatcher's invocation of the "cleanliness is next to godliness" adage, said that it was "so much pious nonsense" in Mrs. Thatcher's youth, let alone in Victorian England: "a dirty, smelly age in which a largely dirty, smelly population was sorely afflicted by all manner of diseases rooted in a chronic lack of hygiene at all levels." How could even the middle classes be clean, this critic asks, sweating in all those layers of thick, dark clothing and "without much in the way of regular dry cleaning!" or with all those heavy, cluttered furnishings in "the pre–vacuum cleaner age"?[24]

If anyone is guilty of imposing middle-class values upon the Victorian poor—and late-twentieth-century values at that—it is surely a historian who cannot conceive of cleanliness, either as a value or as a reality, in the absence of dry-cleaning and vacuum cleaners. (It was not Mrs. Thatcher but John Wesley who coined the motto "Cleanliness is next to godliness," more than two centuries earlier, at a time when sanitary conditions were even more primitive.) Of course, the Victorian working classes were dirty and smelly by our standards, as the early Victorians were by the standards of the late Victorians.* But what is impressive in reading their memoirs is the enormous effort made by the working classes to be clean as well as to be seen to be clean: the scouring of scullery floors and doorsteps and the black-leading of stoves and grates; the ritual of weekly baths (carefully planned so that girls and boys could be bathed separately in a tub in the kitchen); the washing of clothes and linens (which involved heating the water on the stove, transferring it in buckets to the tub, scrubbing the clothes, emptying the buckets, refilling and reheating them for the rinse, wringing out the clothes, sometimes with the help of a mangle, drying them on lines in the yard or, when it rained, as it frequently did, in the kitchen, and finally ironing them).

Even more impressive is the spirit in which these tedious, backbreaking tasks were recalled. There was no minimizing of the hardship, but there was far less resentment than one might expect, and sometimes there was positive pride. A typical recollection is that of a woman whose chore it was, as a young girl, to do the steps:

You sort of had to wash your step, then wet . . . the sandstone, like you do a pumice stone style, sand it along right on the edge and then you had to get your

---

* The situation improved greatly in the latter half of the century. The water supply became more plentiful as well as more potable; bathhouses were available in the towns, and many working-class houses acquired running water; sewage and sanitary conditions vastly improved; soap was cheaper and cotton fabric was increasingly used for clothing, which greatly facilitated washing.

fingers and go nice and smooth. . . . [I] used to love scouring those steps. It's a work of art, you know.[25]

Foreigners regarded this obsession with cleanliness as yet another English eccentricity. It was not entirely in admiration that the German historian Heinrich Treitschke observed: "The English think soap is civilisation."[26]

If cleanliness was next to godliness, work was godliness itself—or so it seemed to Thomas Carlyle:

> *Laborare est Orare,* Work is Worship. . . . All true Work
> is sacred; in all true Work, were it but true hand-labour,
> there is something of divineness. . . . No man has
> worked, or can work, except religiously; not even the
> poor day-labourer, the weaver of your coat, the sewer
> of your shoes.[27]

Carlyle, of course, can be dismissed as yet another middle-class preacher. But it is not so easy to dismiss the overwhelming testimony of workers who believed that work, if not sacred, was essential not only to their sustenance but to their self-respect. They could, in fact, have had sustenance without work—in the poorhouse, or on the dole, or from charity. But that would have put them in a condition of "dependency," which was repellent to the respectable working classes, for it was precisely their "independence" that defined their "respectability."

One of the surprising things about the working-class memoirs of the period is the extent to which children shared this work ethic. They respected their parents' work and thought it perfectly natural that they themselves should work, first by helping in the house, then by earning small sums running errands or doing chores for neighbors, finally by getting a regular job. They took satisfaction in being able to contribute to the family income and seemed not to resent giving their earnings to their mothers. (The fact that their fathers also turned over their wage packets made this a manly thing to do.) "If you could earn a copper anytime," one man recalled of his youth, "then you ought to earn a copper, and of course when you came home you turned it up."[28] Part of the ethos of work was the pride of growing up, assuming the mantle of adulthood, and with it of work. But part of it was also a sense of responsibility to the family and, beyond this, a sense that work itself was something to be proud of, a source of self-respect and the respect of others.

It is at this point that "family values" and "Victorian values" merge, for the work ethic, like so many of the other values encompassed in the idea of respectability—cleanliness, orderliness, obedience, thrift, sexual propriety—centered in the family. "Respectability," one historian observes, "became a family enterprise; its achievement depended upon cooperation from the entire membership and an understanding that collective reputation took precedence over personal preference."[29]

The Rise of Respectable Society is the title of a recent book on Victorian history by F. M. L. Thompson. The book confirms what contemporaries knew: that respectability was not only a value but a reality, and that it became more of a reality as the century progressed. When Charles Booth, in his survey of London in the last decades of the century, came up with the much-quoted figure of 30 percent of the population below the poverty line, he was well aware that if that same poverty line had been applied to an earlier period, the figure would have been much higher, and that the poor were not only less numerous but also less poor than they had ever been. He also knew that their economic improvement had been accompanied by an equally substantial moral improvement. Had there been a study such as his half a century earlier, he was confident, it would have shown "a greater proportion of depravity and misery than now exists."[30]

There had been, in fact, such a study (although not nearly as objective or comprehensive as his) conducted in the middle of the century. Henry Mayhew's *London Labour and the London Poor,* in spite of its ambitious title, focused on a small segment of the poor: the "street-folk" who made their living on the streets (street-traders, street-laborers, street-artisans, street-performers); and "those that will not work" ("prostitutes, thieves, swindlers, and beggars"). These groups were never as large as Mayhew's impressionistic work made them seem; nor were they as outlandish in their modes of life as he made them appear. But they were sufficiently conspicuous to make them appear a significant class of the poor—a "race" apart, according to Mayhew.

By Booth's time, forty years later, the "Mayhewian" poor—including the "residuum," as some were known—had so shrunk in size as no longer to constitute a "race" or even a major social problem. There were still sensationalist tales, such as *In Darkest England* by "General" William Booth of the Salvation Army (no relation to Charles Booth), of millions of people living in savage conditions like those of the natives of "Darkest Africa." But this was a missionary tract designed to focus attention not only on the destitute but also, indeed primarily, on the drunken and faithless. "Darkest England," according to this account, consisted of three concentric circles: the outer inhabited by "the starving and the homeless, but honest Poor," the second by those who "live by vice," and the third, the innermost circle, by those who "exist by crime"—the whole of the three circles "sodden with Drink."[31]

At the very time that *In Darkest England* appeared, in 1890, Charles Booth was refuting this image of a sodden, "submerged" tenth of the population.[32] One of his most interesting findings was that drink and thriftlessness combined (they were so interrelated that he could not separate them) were primary causes of poverty in only 14 percent of the "very poor" (the latter comprising only 8.4 percent of the population). Drunkenness, so far from being a major social problem in the last decades of the century, had become a much less pressing one, partly as a result of the licensing acts of 1869 and 1872, and, more important, of the influence of the temperance movement.

One historian calls the temperance movement the epitome of the "cult of respectability."[33] As early as 1841, the social reformer Edwin Chadwick had said that "it was on the temperance societies that he rested his hopes for the recovery and permanent improvement of the labouring classes."[34] By the end of the century, that movement numbered half a million activists and between three to six million members. Even if many of those who took the pledge had occasional relapses, the figures are impressive, testifying at the very least to the value placed upon sobriety. That value was not imposed upon the working classes by the middle classes; it grew out of the working classes themselves. Within the Chartist movement, in the late 1830s and early 1840s, was a group known as the Temperance Chartists, who took this as their special mission.

In 1830, Sydney Smith made his famous remark: "The sovereign people are in a beastly state."[35] Twenty years later, when the Great Exhibition was planned, Parliament debated the question of surrounding the Crystal Palace with troops to preserve order. It decided not to do so and was pleased to find that nothing was stolen or vandalized. Reporting upon the exhibition to a committee of the House of Commons, one of the chiefs of the Metropolitan Police commended the "good conduct of the people."[36] Hippolyte Taine was also impressed by the orderliness of the people: "I have seen whole families of the common people picnicking on the grass in Hyde Park; they neither pulled up nor damaged anything." This was truly admirable, he reflected, for "the aim of every society must be a state of affairs in which every man is his own constable, until at last none other is required."[37]

That utopian state had surely not come to pass by the end of the century, but there had been a substantial decrease of crime in every category, from homicide through violent and nonviolent crimes against persons and property. This may be attributed in part to the existence of the constabulary. (The metropolitan police force was established in 1829; in 1856 it was extended to the entire country.) Yet the police cannot entirely, or even largely, account for that decline, for if they deterred crime, they also discovered and recorded infringements of the law that would otherwise have gone undiscovered and unrecorded, thus inflating the numbers of crimes even as they apprehended the criminals. In spite of that inflation, however, the crime rate decreased considerably. In 1857, the rate of indictable offenses per 100,000 population was 480; in 1901, it was 250—a decline in less than half a century of almost 50 percent. The absolute numbers are even more graphic: with a population of 19 million in 1857, there were 92,000 crimes; with a population of 33 million in 1901, there were 81,000 crimes—14 million more people and 11,000 fewer crimes.[38]*

---

* One historian, belittling the idea of "Victorian values," concedes the considerable decline of crime but disparages it by arguing that the late Victorians were law-abiding only because it was in their "self-interest" to be so. The spread of "material better-

Public violence too was much abated in this period, despite some highly publicized and exaggerated accounts of riots. A Hyde Park demonstration in July 1866, held by the Reform League in defiance of official prohibition, resulted in the tearing down of some park railings and the trampling of flower beds. More serious riots forty years earlier had provoked Thomas Arnold to declare: "As for rioting, the old Roman way of dealing with *that* is always the right one; flog the rank and file, and fling the ringleaders from the Tarpeian Rock!"[39] His son Matthew Arnold quoted this approvingly in the first edition of *Culture and Anarchy*, published a few years after the 1866 demonstration, but thought better of it and deleted it from later editions. This did not prevent his twentieth-century editor, the distinguished literary critic Dover Wilson, from perpetuating the myth about the riot: "It is scarcely too much to say that the fall of the Park railings did for England in July 1866 what the fall of the Bastille did for France in July 1789. The shooting of Niagara was seen to be inevitable."[40] The "shooting of Niagara" turned out to be the passage the following year, without any untoward incident, of an electoral reform admitting a large portion of the working classes to the franchise.

Two other riots, described by some historians as incipient revolutions, occurred during the economic depression of 1886–87. The first riot, known as "Black Monday," was a mass demonstration that spilled out of Trafalgar Square into

---

ment" among the lower classes gave them a motive to protect their goods and style of life; thus they were "peaceable and law-abiding not out of fear of the consequences of transgressing, but from a clear appreciation of the benefits to be gained from keeping within the law."[41] Tocqueville would have regarded this as a prime example of "self-interest rightly understood," which he took to be an eminently respectable moral principle as well as a virtue of democracy.

Pall Mall, resulting in the smashing of windows, overturning of carriages, and looting of some shops, and ended up in the East End with the singing of "Rule, Britannia." No one was seriously hurt, let alone killed, and the four socialists who were tried were acquitted—a far cry from the *"grande peur"* following the fall of the Bastille, to which one historian has compared it.[42] The second riot, "Bloody Sunday," was more serious. This was a demonstration in support of some imprisoned Irish nationalists, one of whom had refused to wear prisoner's garb and had been deprived of his trousers (hence the rallying cry "O'Brien's Breeches"). Wanting to forestall a repetition of the earlier riot, the police tried to disperse the demonstrators. The result was scores of injuries, one to three fatalities, and the imprisonment of two of the leaders—a bloody event by English standards but hardly by continental ones (*pace* the historian who compares the violence of this decade with the "mob fury" in the revolutions of 1848).[43] Only two years after "Bloody Sunday," the London dock strike brought tens of thousands of workers marching through the streets of London day after day, some of the processions involving as many as eighty thousand people, with almost no violence, no rioting, and no casualties.

In 1901, the Criminal Registrar was pleased to report: "We have witnessed a great change in manners: the substitution of words without blows for blows without words; an approximation in the manners of different classes; and a decline in the spirit of lawlessness."[44]

The "rise of respectable society" can be measured not only by the decline of crime, violence, and drunkenness but also by the decline of illegitimacy and the increased stability of the family. As impressive as the statistics on crime are those on illegitimacy, especially by comparison with present-day figures. From 7 percent in midcentury, the illegitimacy ratio declined to 4 percent by the end of the century. Premarital pregnancy was far more common, as high as 40–50 percent in some parishes early in the century, although far lower later.[45] While such pregnancies are suggestive of sexual laxity, the large differential between the illegitimacy and premarital pregnancy figures testifies to the power of the moral code: the obligation to marry once a child was conceived. It is also consistent with Victorian "family values," since that child, and all subsequent ones, were brought up in a stable family.

The "single-parent family" in our sense—the unmarried, divorced, or deserted mother—was not a serious problem in Victorian England. (Divorces, even after the liberalization of the divorce laws, were so few as to be of no account in the lives of the vast majority of the people.) The common problem, even among the "roughs," was not the absence of a father but the presence of one who was irregularly employed and regularly drunk and abusive, or, somewhat less commonly, a mother who was drunk and slatternly. Among the respectable poor, both parents were normally present and accounted for, carrying out, however adequately or inadequately, their distinct and traditional roles. Even in families with a widowed mother (a widowed father was more likely to remarry), the presence of the father at least in the early life of his children, and his memory later, preserved the sense of family; so far from lacking a "role model," the boys in such a family felt obliged to take the place of the father, supplementing their mother's earnings by whatever they could contribute to the family income.

Respectability exhibited itself in other statistics: the number of families who regularly paid their dues to burial and friendly societies (more than 80 percent by the 1870s); or who were depositors in savings banks (the Post Office Savings Bank opened in 1861 and acquired over a million accounts in the first decade and many times that number by the end of the century, most for sums under twenty-five pounds); or whose children attended school (two-thirds to three-fourths of girls as well as boys—this before the act of 1870 providing for free compulsory education).

In a class-conscious society like England, respectability was the common denominator linking all the classes, the common virtue to which they all paid homage. If the Chartists were moved to form groups of Temperance Chartists and Education Chartists (the most famous Chartist leader, William Lovett, was passionate on the subject of education), it was because their claim to the suffrage was based on the idea that the working classes were respectable members of society and therefore worthy citizens of the polity. Political equality depended on moral equality. And this, in turn, assumed that the working classes had the same virtues, aspirations, and capacities as all other classes—that they shared a common human nature and a common civic and political right.

It is ironic that at the turn of the century, when, by all measures, the economic and moral conditions of the working classes had greatly improved, there should have arisen a new cause for alarm: the "degeneration of the race." This was inspired by the report of thousands of volunteers for service in the Boer War who were found to be physically unfit, the result, it was popularly supposed, of the unnatural and unhealthy conditions of urban and industrial life. The idea was seized upon by the growing eugenics movement, which thought it necessary to control and improve the biological nature of human beings, much as the socialists sought to control and improve the social environment. The Fabians, believing in both, were among the staunchest supporters of eugenics.

For various reasons, including the usual sensationalist journalism, the problem was much exaggerated. It could not be demonstrated that the physical condition of "the race" had deteriorated; all that could be proved was that it was less than satisfactory in the present. Nor was there any evidence of moral deterioration—of increased crime, violence, drunkenness, or illegitimacy; on the contrary, these statistics showed a dramatic improvement. The only evidence of "degeneration" was the failure rate of the volunteer soldiers (but there had never been so many people subjected to such a test) and the incidence of venereal disease, which had been a subject of concern forty years earlier when the Contagious Diseases Act was passed.[46]

In view of all the evidence to the contrary, it is not too fanciful to suppose that the alarm about physical and moral deterioration was itself a reflection of the rise in aims and expectations among the people as a whole and more especially among social commentators. As the standard of living of the working classes rose, which it undeniably did by the turn of the century, so any deviation from that standard became less acceptable. And as the ideals of morality and respectability became more pervasive, so any lapse from those ideals became more conspicuous and intolerable.

The idea of respectability was reinforced by the idea of the "gentleman," providing the working classes with a still more radical claim to moral equality. The term "gentleman" had always been ambiguous. Technically, a gentleman was someone who had heraldic or armorial status but was not of the nobility, ranking, in effect, just below the knight. Socially, it often connoted someone of independent means, not obliged to do anything so sordid as earn his living. In practice, however, it was often used, even in earlier centuries, as a distinction of character rather than of class. This was what Burke meant when he observed: "Somebody has said that a king may make a nobleman, but he cannot make a gentleman."[47] In fact, it was a king, James I, who is reputed to have said that. "I can make a lord," he told his old nurse when she begged him to make her son a gentleman, "but only God Almighty can make a gentleman."[48]

Just as Taine was impressed by the civility of the English common people, so he was impressed by the uniquely English phenomenon of the gentleman, a very different being from the French *gentilhomme*. Both were of the upper class, he said, but the *gentilhomme* evoked images "of elegance, style, tact, finesse; of exquisite politeness, delicate points of honour, of a chivalrous cast of mind, of prodigal liberality and brilliant valour"; whereas the English gentleman was a different species:

> A real "gentleman" is a truly noble man, a man worthy to command, a disinterested man of integrity, capable of exposing, even sacrificing himself for those he leads; not only a man of honour, but a conscientious man, in whom generous instincts have been confirmed by right thinking and who, acting rightly by nature, acts even more rightly from good principles.

Having initially defined the gentleman as a man of the upper class, Taine went on to say that not all of that class were gentlemen. "He is not a gentleman," someone had told him, speaking of a great nobleman in the diplomatic service. A gentleman might even be of the lower classes. Taine cited the novel *John Halifax, Gentleman,* in which a poor, abandoned boy ends by becoming the respected leader of his neighborhood. When he buys a house and acquires a carriage, his son exclaims, "At last, we are gentlemen!"—to which the father replies, "We have always been so, my son."[49]*

The Victorians took the idea of the gentleman seriously, and in much the sense of *John Halifax, Gentleman*. For every cynical reference to that idea—such as George Bernard Shaw's: "A gentleman of our days is one who has money enough to do what every fool would do if he could afford it: that is, consume without producing"[50]—there were numerous respectful ones. The gentleman was typically identified by his moral virtues: integrity, honesty, generosity, courage, graciousness, politeness, consideration for others. By "moralizing" the idea of the gentleman, the Victorians democratized it as well, extending it to the middle classes and even, on occasion, to the working classes.

As early as the 1820s a writer explained that the word "gentleman" did not "draw a line that would be invidious between high and low, rank and subordination, riches and

---

* Nothing in this novel is as authentically Victorian as the editor's account of the author, Mrs. Dinah Craik. (The modern reader may detect an ironic note in this, but the rest of the introduction suggests that it was meant in all seriousness.)

There is a tradition that she was engaged to a gentleman suited to her both in age and disposition; it was, however, considered advisable that before their marriage he should travel for two years, and at the end of that time they should be happily united. At the expiration of this period Miss Mulock went to the docks to welcome home the ship with its precious passenger; the lovers recognized each other, but the gentleman when leaving the ship in a state of pardonable excitement missed his footing, fell into the water, and before assistance could be rendered, was drowned. Miss Mulock consoled herself, however, as many a troubled one has done before, by a close and diligent application to literary work. . . . The total number of her separate works eventually reached fifty-two.[51]

poverty"; the distinction was "in the mind."[52] A few decades later, in *Self-Help,* Samuel Smiles wrote that the character of the true gentleman depended "not upon fashion or manners, but upon moral worth—not on personal possessions, but on personal qualities." The gentleman could be found in "all stages of society," so that even those who would not "bow to titular rank will yet do homage to the gentleman."[53] In the opening chapter of his last book, *Life and Labour,* Smiles gave examples of gentlemen who rose from the "sphere of labor":

Inigo Jones, the cloth-worker; Quentyn Matsys, the blacksmith; Josiah Wedgwood, the potter; James Watt, the mathematical instrument maker; John Hunter, the carpenter; Isaac Milner, the hand-loom weaver; Joseph Lancaster, the basket-maker; Robert Burns, the ploughman; and John Keats, the druggist.

In passing, Smiles distinguished between the "gentleman" and the "gent": "A gentleman will be merciful to his dog; the gent is not merciful even to his wife."[54]

Smiles may be a suspect witness; it was his mission, one might say, to glorify the work ethic and thus minimize the differences of class and rank. But other Victorians echoed him, and without any such motive. Thackeray, so contemptuous of snobbery, would have been delighted with Smiles's distinction between the gentleman and the gent, and would have endorsed his classless view of the gentleman. Satirical about so much else, he was not at all satirical about "the true gentleman."

What is it to be a gentleman? Is it to have lofty aims, to lead a pure life, to keep your honour virgin; to have the esteem of your fellow-citizens, and the love of your fireside; to bear good fortune meekly; to suffer evil with constancy; and through evil or good to maintain truth always? Show me the happy man whose life exhibits these qualities, and him we will salute as gentleman, whatever his rank may be; show me the prince who possesses them, and he may be sure of our love and loyalty.[55]

One prince notably failed to meet those qualifications—George IV, whose greatest distinction, Thackeray said, was the invention of a shoe buckle that covered almost the whole of his instep. Quoting from two journals published the same month (March 1784), Thackeray compared the account in one of the grand ball given by the prince in his lavishly renovated palace to celebrate (somewhat belatedly) his twenty-first birthday; and the account in the other of a ceremony in which a "great gentleman of English extraction" resigned as commander in chief of the army of the United States. "Which of these is the true gentleman," Thackeray asked, "yon fribble dancing in lace and spangles, or yonder hero who sheathes his sword after a life of spotless honour, a purity unreproached, a courage indomitable, and a consummate victory?"[56]

A Victorian could not have democratized the idea of the gentleman more dramatically than by denying that title to an English king and bestowing it upon an American commoner—except, perhaps, than by bestowing it upon a woman. The counterpart of "gentleman," Smiles pointed out, was "lady," which originally meant "bread-giver." The lady need not be "well-to-do, still less idle and finely clothed; for such are not the attributes of ladyhood"; on the contrary, "even the working-woman may exercise ladyhood with dignity."[57]

Anthony Trollope, who is sometimes accused of being excessively concerned with birth and rank, has one of his heroines ask herself, "What makes a gentleman? what makes a gentlewoman?" Her answer is: "Absolute, intrinsic, acknowledged, individual merit." She recognizes that that is the "spirit of democracy" speaking, but there is also in her a "spirit of aristocracy" which thinks that the title might be had by inheritance, "received as it were second-hand, or twenty-second-hand."[58] Another of Trollope's heroines is more single-minded. Madame Max Goesler is, and knows herself to be, a perfect gentleman (even "gentlewoman" or "lady" seems demeaning applied to her), although she is several times removed from any conventional claim to the title: she is a woman, a Jew, a foreigner, and of modest birth. She also happens to be rich (as the result of a former marriage), beautiful, and intelligent. But it is not these attributes that qualify her as a gentleman; it is her character, epitomized by the dramatic episode in which she rejects the duke's offer of marriage, out of respect for herself as much as for him.[59] (Madame Goesler presents a nice counterpoint to Augustus Melmotte in *The Way We Live Now*—another rich Jew, but one who is decidedly not a gentleman.)

By the end of the century, this idea of the gentleman was so pervasive that it appealed not only to moralists and novelists but to a hardheaded economist like Alfred Marshall, who took it upon himself to preach the gospel of the worker-gentleman. Marshall had no illusions about work; far too much of it, he knew, was backbreaking, mind-numbing, and degrading. But he was confident that technological progress would reduce and finally eliminate that kind of labor, releasing the "higher energies" and "higher nature" of workers.

The question is not whether all men will ultimately be equal—that they certainly will not—but whether progress may not go on steadily if slowly, till the of-

ficial distinction between working man and gentleman
has passed away; till, by occupation at least, every man
is a gentleman. I hold that it may and that it will.[60]

Not everyone so enlarged the idea of the gentleman as to
bring it within the compass of the working classes; more
often it was brought within the compass of the middle
classes. But that in itself was a considerable achievement,
serving as a bridge between the upper classes and the middle
classes—just as the idea of respectability served as a bridge
between the middle classes and the working classes.

If, as some historians maintain, Victorians succeeded in
"bourgeoisifying" their ethos, to that extent they also democratized it. In attributing to everyone the same virtues—
potentially at least, if not in actuality—they assumed a
common human nature and thus a moral (although not a
political or an economic) equality. Even the "gentlemanly"
virtues—honesty, integrity, courage, politeness—were not
above the capacity of the ordinary person. Still less were the
"respectable" virtues: hard work, sobriety, frugality, prudence. These were modest, mundane virtues, requiring no
special breeding, or status, or talent, or wisdom, or valor,
or grace—or even money. They were common virtues
within the reach of common people. They were, so to
speak, democratic virtues.*

They were also the virtues appropriate to a liberal society.
By putting a premium on ordinary virtues attainable by
ordinary people, the Victorian ethos located responsibility
within each individual. In an aristocratic age, only the ex-

---

* Smiles quotes Montaigne: "All moral philosophy is as applicable to a common and private life as to the most splendid. Every
man carries the entire form of the human condition within him."[61]

ceptional, privileged individual had been seen as a free moral agent, the master of his fate. In the evolving democracy that was Victorian England, all individuals were assumed to be free moral agents, hence their own masters. It is no accident that the Victorians put such a premium on the self—not only on self-help and self-interest but also on self-control, self-discipline, self-respect. A liberal society, they believed, required a moral citizenry.

The Victorians were not, however, utopians. Acutely aware of the frailties of human nature, they recognized the need for whatever inducements or sanctions—social, religious, legal, ultimately physical—might be required to encourage virtue and discourage vice. But they wanted to make those sanctions as painless and uncoercive as possible. The more effective the voluntary exercise of morality on the part of each individual, the more internalized that morality in the self (in the form of conscience, character, habit, or religion), the less need there would be for the external, punitive instruments of the state. It was the great mentor of the Victorians, Edmund Burke, who enunciated this principle:

> Men are qualified for civil liberty in exact proportion to their disposition to put moral chains upon their own appetites. . . . Society cannot exist unless a controlling power upon will and appetite be placed somewhere, and the less of it there is within, the more there must be without.[62]*

Just as law, in civilized society, is a surrogate for force, so morality is a surrogate for authority. And so too manners are a surrogate for morals. This was one of the functions of

---

* Today, among the disciples of Nietzsche or Foucault, it is precisely this self-induced morality, the internalized conscience, that is regarded as most coercive and tyrannical. This point of view would have been incomprehensible to virtually all Victorians.

respectability: to curb indecent language as well as indecent behavior, to preserve propriety as well as legality. Manners—Hobbes's "small morals"—were in a continuum with large morals. The Victorians might have cited Machiavelli (but would not have, because he was in ill repute): "For as good manners cannot subsist without good laws, so those laws cannot be put into execution without good manners."[63] But they did quote Burke:

> Manners are of more importance than laws. Upon them, in a great measure, the laws depend. The law touches us but here and there, and now and then. Manners are what vex or soothe, corrupt or purify, exalt or debase, barbarize or refine us, by a constant, steady, uniform, insensible operation, like that of the air we breathe in. They give their whole form and colour to our lives. According to their quality, they aid morals, they supply them, or they totally destroy them.[64]*

---

* Samuel Smiles had apparently imbibed the lessons of Burke so unconsciously that he echoed him without attribution:

> Morals and manners, which give colour to life, are of much greater importance than laws, which are but their manifestations. The law touches us here and there, but manners are about us everywhere, pervading society like the air we breathe.[65]

Household Gods and Goddesses

The bourgeoisie has torn away from the family its sentimental veil, and has reduced the family relation to a mere money relation. . . . The bourgeois sees in his wife a mere instrument of production. . . . Our bourgeois, not content with having the wives and daughters of their proletarians at their disposal, not to speak of common prostitutes, take the greatest pleasure in seducing each other's wives. Bourgeois marriage is in reality a system of wives in common. . . .[1]

Echoes of Marx can still be heard in radical-feminist charges that bourgeois marriage is a form of legalized prostitution and that wives are little more than instruments for the production of children. Yet Marx could not have been more wrong, especially in respect to England, the most bourgeois of nations. For there, and precisely among the bourgeoisie (the middle classes, as the English persisted in calling them), the family was not only revered but sentimentalized to a degree never known before or since. And it was precisely then, in the heyday of Victorianism, that the family, so far from being reduced to a "mere money relation" or "instrument of production," was elevated to a realm far removed from the arena of economic activity.

One might go so far as to say that Victorian England exhibited an inverse relationship between economics and the family. It was when the family ceased to be a significant economic unit (when farming was no longer a family activity and spinning no longer centered in the home) that the family became more of a domestic unit and the home the exclusive and private domain of the family. Not only were middle-class women kept out of the labor market; the men themselves retreated to the bosom of their family as if to escape from the harsh world of moneymaking and the cash nexus.[2] Domesticity, it has been said, was the "antithesis to the market—its necessary 'other,' " a haven from the "rationalistic, abstract and impersonal marketplace," where "organic relationships" could still flourish and everyone had a place in a hierarchical, patriarchal, deferential order.[3]

Yet well before the emergence of anything like the kind of rationalistic, abstract, impersonal marketplace depicted here (the model, presumably, of an industrial capitalist economy), the nuclear family had become the dominant form. Historians have traced it back to Elizabethan times and even to the medieval period.[4] It was the early-seventeenth-century jurist Sir Edward Coke who formulated the dictum "A man's house is his castle."[5] Coke meant this to be a universal principle grounded in Roman law, but it was soon identified with England particularly, as in the familiar adage: "An Englishman's home is his castle." There is no other national equivalent—no "Frenchman's home is his castle" or "American's home is his castle."

It was the French historian Elie Halévy, looking at England from the vantage point of his own country, who saw more clearly than any English historian the crucial influence of Wesleyanism in the history of England. He did not relate this specifically to the family, but he might have done so, for Wesleyanism and its offshoot Evangelicalism were powerful stimulants for those "family values" that were so much a part of "Victorian values." It was these religious movements and the "moral reformation" inspired by them, as much as industrialism or capitalism, that made the home a haven not only from the pressures of the marketplace but from the temptations of sin and corruption.[6]

The effects of that reformation survived long after the religious creed had become attenuated. As the influence of preachers and clerics waned, that of Queen Victoria grew. In a sense, she replaced them—as a "role model," we would say today. In expounding upon the "dignified" function of the monarchy, Walter Bagehot took the occasion to remark upon its "domestic" function as well:

We have come to regard the Crown as the head of our *morality*. The virtues of Queen Victoria and the virtues of George III have sunk deep into the popular heart. We have come to believe that it is natural to have a virtuous sovereign, and that the domestic virtues are as likely to be found on thrones as they are eminent when there.[7]

Benjamin Disraeli, the Queen's favorite statesman, was equally impressed by the moral example of the royal family:

England is a domestic country. Here the home is revered and the hearth is sacred. The nation is represented by a family—the Royal Family; and if that family is educated with a sense of responsibility and a sentiment of public duty, it is difficult to exaggerate the salutary influence they may exercise over a nation.[8]

*   *   *

The home was both a place of worship and an object of worship. The custom, among the middle classes especially, of assembling the family (including the servants) for prayers and Bible-reading was intended as much for purposes of moral edification—*pour encourager les autres,* the children and servants—as for religious observance. It also had an important, if unintended, civic effect: the hymns and prayers, biblical images and stories, were familiar to men, women, and children of all classes and regions, thus shaping and uniting an otherwise diverse culture. The religious texts were supplemented by secular ones—by novels, hortatory tales, and a plethora of journals whose titles testified to their familial function: *Household Words* (edited by Dickens), *The Home Circle, The Home Companion, Family Friend, Family Herald.* These were literally family papers, often read aloud by the father *en famille.*

Disraeli's dictum "Here the home is revered and the hearth is sacred" was echoed by John Ruskin: "Our God is a household God as well as a heavenly one. He has an altar in every man's dwelling." Again, repeating the image: Home is "a sacred place, a vestal temple, a temple of the hearth watched over by Household Gods."[9] The sanctification of family and home was so common that it found expression in the most unlikely places. The introduction to the 1851 census, not normally an occasion for sentimentality, explained why every Englishman wanted an entire house for his family: "It throws a sharp, well defined circle round his family and hearth—the shrine of his sorrows, joys and meditations."[10] The equally staid *City Press,* a journal for merchants and bankers, departed from its customary concerns to pay tribute to home and family: " 'Home' means comfort, rest, peace, love, holiness. There is sanctity in the word home, growing out of the sweetness of the affections it cherishes."[11] Religious metaphors—"God," "shrine," "holiness," "sacred," "sanctity"—were used so naturally and frequently in connection with family and home that G. K. Chesterton, who took a more severe view of religion, described the Victorians as the first generation that "asked its children to worship the hearth without the altar."[12]

The religious images were entirely fitting. Family and home constituted something like a civic religion, the natural, providential basis of the public as well as the private order. Edmund Burke had set the tone with his "little platoon" image: "To be attached to the subdivision, to love the little platoon we belong to in society, is the first principle, the germ as it were, of public affections. It is the first link in the series by which we proceed towards a love to our country and to mankind."[13] The family was that "little platoon": "We begin our public affections in our families. . . . Perhaps it is a sort of elemental training to those higher and more large regards, by which alone men come to be affected, as with their own concern, in the prosperity of a kingdom."[14]

Victorians of very different religious persuasions (or of none) agreed that family and home were the keystones of society and country.* Thus Lord Shaftesbury, the Evangelical reformer:

---

* The only notable dissidents were the Utopians, William Godwin and Robert Owen and their disciples. But Godwin's credibility was sorely damaged when, only a few years after publishing his great work, *Political Justice,* attacking marriage and the family (as well as all institutions created or sanctioned by government—constitutions, laws, courts, property, schools, religion)—and predicting the demise of sexuality itself, he had an affair with Mary Wollstonecraft, the celebrated feminist, and married her when she became pregnant. Nor was Owen as adamant as he professed to be in his opposition to the family and marriage. While his com-

There can be no security to society, no honour, no prosperity, no dignity at home, no nobleness of attitude towards foreign nations, unless the strength of the people rests upon the purity and firmness of the domestic system. Schools are but auxiliaries. At home the principles of subordination are first implanted and the man is trained to be a good citizen.[15]

Or Frederic Harrison, the Positivist:

Family is the first, the permanent, the elemental sphere of social life, of morality; and consequently, is the source of religion. . . . The Home is the primeval and eternal school where we learn to practise the balance of our instincts, to restrain appetite, to cultivate affection, to pass out of our lower selves—to *Live for Humanity*.[16]

Or James Anthony Froude, the historian and religious skeptic, who thought that Religion, God, and Heaven were "catchwords" for most people, but Home was not.

Home—yes, Home is the one perfectly pure earthly instinct which we have. We call heaven our home, as the best name we know to give it. . . . We talk much of the religious discipline of our schools, and moral training and mind developing . . . yet I question whether the home of childhood has not more to do

___

munity at New Lanark meant to substitute communal living for the private family, he did not propose to abolish marriage but wanted only to eliminate the religious oath and make divorce more available. (It should be noted that *Political Justice*, published in 1793, and the New Lanark community, started in 1800, were pre-Victorian. By the mid-nineteenth century, the influence of both Godwin and Owen was much diminished.)

with religion than all the teachers and the teaching, and the huge unfathomed folios.[17]

Or another historian, G. M. Young (who just qualified as a Victorian—a young man when the Queen died, he recalled seeing her twice and Gladstone once), who said that there were only two vital articles in the "common Victorian faith":

> What creed, what doctrine, what institution was there among them which was not at some time or other debated or assailed? I can think of two only: Representative Institutions and the Family. . . . The increasing secularism of English thought might have been expected to compel a more critical attitude to the family than in fact we find. Sexual ethic had attracted to itself so great a body of romantic sentiment: it was so closely associated, and even identified, with virtue in general, with the elevated, the praiseworthy, the respectable life, that the faintest note of dissidence might attract a disproportionate volume of suspicion and censure.[18]

If family and home were the repositories of both private and civic virtues, they were also the scene where men and women resided together yet existed in their "separate spheres." Men came home, Froude said, as a refuge from their worldly, workaday lives: "At home, when we come home, we lay aside our mask and drop our tools, and are no longer lawyers, sailors, soldiers, statesmen, clergymen, but only men."[19] Women—at least middle-class women—had no such problem. They did not have to come home; they were at home. And they had no masks to remove, because they were not "lawyers, sailors, soldiers, statesmen, clergymen," but only and always women. That was their entire identity and their sole profession. And the home was their domain, their natural, proper, separate sphere.

To the modern feminist (and to a few Victorian feminists, although they would not have used this language), the identification of women with a separate sphere epitomizes the "patriarchal" ethos that informs Victorian values in general and family values in particular. Whatever the nature of that sphere, however comfortable and congenial it might be for particular women or however exalted as an ideal, it is deemed oppressive and degrading, for it consigns women to a single role and a single place, thus depriving them of the essential human attributes of liberty and equality.

For most Victorians, the idea of a separate domestic sphere for all but the most remarkable women was as natural as the idea of the family itself. And, again for most Victorians (women as well as men), that separate sphere implied the natural inferiority of women and their incapacity for public life. For others, however, including some of the most eminent Victorians, that sphere was seen as separate but equal. And for some it was actually separate and superior. The Reverend Binney, a Congregationalist minister, started by saying that "women are not to be men, in character, ambition, pursuit or achievement"; then went on to explain that "they are to be *more;* they are to be the *makers* of men"; and ended with the startling assertion: "The Mother is the father of the child."[20] To the modern feminist, these distinctions—separate and inferior, separate and equal, separate and superior—are of no account, since any separation is regarded as odious; indeed, the ostensibly equal or superior status is seen as a hypocritical stratagem to ensure the segregation and subordination of women. But to the historian, trying to recover the Victorian ethos as Victorians saw it and experienced it, the nuances of that "separate sphere" are of some moment.

*   *   *

It is difficult to take seriously today such effusions as Coventry Patmore's "The Angel in the House," which catalogues the respective virtues of man and woman, with woman excelling at every point. "She succeeds with cloudless brow" where he agonizingly fails; and "she fails more graciously than he succeeds." She grows lovelier "the more she lives and knows," while he is "never young nor ripe." Her "facile wit" flies straight at the truth, which he "hunts down with pain." "Were she but half of what she is" and "he but twice himself," she is worthier than he; for love is her "special crown," as truth is his, and love is "substance," where truth is "form," and "truth without love were less than nought." In short, her "happy virtues . . . make an Eden in her breast," while his, "disjointed and at strife, . . . do not bring him rest."[21]

"The Angel in the House," most critics at the time (and even more today) agreed, was hardly a distinguished poem. But its message cannot be so easily dismissed, for it was enormously popular and reflected sentiments widely held in mid-Victorian England. Patmore, a friend and great admirer of Tennyson, so successfully modeled himself on his mentor that "Coventry Patmore" was thought by some to be a pseudonym of Alfred Tennyson. (It is interesting to note that after Tennyson's death, Patmore recommended a woman poet, Alice Meynell, to succeed him as poet laureate.)

Tennyson himself, as poet laureate, lent his considerable authority to a view of women that was more subtle and complicated than Patmore's, but finally not very different. Several years before "The Angel in the House," Tennyson's "The Princess" appeared. It describes the Princess's passionate desire to found a women's university and the Prince's effort, not to deter her, for he entirely approves of her goal, but to persuade her to be more temperate in pursuing it. A famous passage in the poem has been cited as if it represents Tennyson's own view of the proper roles of men and women.

> *Man is the hunter; woman is his game:*
> *The sleek and shining creatures of the chase,*
> *We hunt them for the beauty of their skins;*
> *They love us for it, and we ride them down.*
>
> . . . .
>
> *Man for the field and woman for the hearth:*
> *Man for the sword and for the needle she:*
> *Man with the head and woman with the heart:*
> *Man to command and woman to obey.*[22]

These words, however, are spoken not by the Prince but by his father, a cynical, coarse, and thoroughly unsympathetic figure.

The Prince, on the other hand, the hero of the poem, is so fulsome in his devotion to "the woman's cause" that the poem almost reads like a feminist tract. (Feminists were inspired by it to emulate the Princess and actually establish women's colleges.)

> *The woman's cause is man's: they rise or sink*
> *Together, dwarf'd or godlike, bond or free:*
>
> . . . .
>
> *We two will serve them both in aiding her—*
> *Will clear away the parasitic forms*
> *That seem to keep her up but drag her down—*
> *Will leave her space to burgeon out of all*
> *Within her—let her make herself her own*
> *To give or keep, to live and learn and be*
> *All that not harms distinctive womanhood.*

Tennyson (like most feminists at the time) did not deny the "distinctive womanhood" of women; he only—a very large only—sought to modify and mitigate it.

> *For woman is not undevelopt man,*
> *But diverse: could we make her as the man,*
> *Sweet Love were slain: his dearest bond is this,*
> *Not like to like, but like in difference.*
> *Yet in the long years liker must they grow;*
> *The man be more of woman, she of man:*
> *He gain in sweetness and in moral height,*
> *Nor lose the wrestling thews that throw the*
> *world;*
> *She mental breadth, nor fail in childward care,*
> *Nor lose the childlike in the larger mind . . .*[23]

What is notable about this compendium of virtues is the association of morality with women and intellect with men. For Victorians, who held the moral virtues in the very highest regard, this was tribute indeed. And it was for the sake of these moral virtues—the argument went—to protect women from the tainted atmosphere of man's world that they were placed in their separate sphere.

For Frederic Harrison, the moral superiority of women was a fundamental tenet of the Positivist credo, which assigned women the role of "Moral Providence" and located them at the very highest rung of the hierarchy. In his enthusiasm, he also credited them with being the "intellectual" genius of man's life, which gave women a place in the next rung of the hierarchy as well, that of "Intellectual Providence." Yet these considerable powers were to be exercised within the home, for only there could the "womanliness of woman" be ensured.

> Our true ideal of the emancipation of Woman is to enlarge in all things the spiritual, moral, affective influence of Woman; to withdraw her more and more from the exhaustion, the contamination, the vulgarity of mill-work and professional work; to make her more

and more the free, cherished mistress of the home, more and more the intellectual, moral, and spiritual genius of man's life.[24]

It was from a very different philosophical perspective that John Ruskin came to much the same position. In lectures delivered in 1865 and reprinted that year in his most popular book, *Sesame and Lilies,* Ruskin introduced the much quoted metaphors for men and women: the "Kings' Treasuries" and the "Queens' Gardens." Unlike Harrison's "Moral Providence," which was deemed superior to the "Intellectual Providence," Ruskin's metaphors suggest that the Queens' "Gardens" were of lesser importance than the Kings' "Treasuries"—an adornment, not a place of power. And unlike Tennyson, who saw the sexes as converging at least to some extent ("liker must they grow"), Ruskin had a more rigidly separatist view of their respective spheres: "Each has what the other has not; each completes the other, and is completed by the other: they are in nothing alike, and the happiness and perfection of both depends on each asking and receiving from the other what the other only can give."[25]

Like Tennyson and Harrison, Ruskin was a great advocate of women's education, insisting that a woman should study every subject a man did (with the exception of theology, which was too "dangerous" for the female sensibility). But she should study them all in a different fashion and for a different purpose—not frivolously or shallowly, but differently.

All such knowledge should be given her as may enable her to understand, and even to aid, the work of men: and yet it should be given, not as knowledge,—not as if it were, or could be, for her an object to know; but only to feel, and to judge. It is of no moment, as a matter of pride or perfectness in herself, whether she knows many languages or one; but is of the utmost, that she should be able to show kindness to a stranger, and to understand the sweetness of a stranger's tongue.[26]

And so with all other subjects: science should be studied not to master a particular discipline but to be trained in "habits of accurate thought" and to understand the "loveliness of natural laws"; or history, not to know the dates of events or names of celebrated persons but to "apprehend, with her fine instincts, the pathetic circumstances and dramatic relations, which the historian too often only eclipses by his reasoning."[27]

In the light of Ruskin's personal life—not only his much publicized impotency but also his mode of life and career—it is ironic to read his description of the "manly nature": "the doer, the creator, the discoverer, the defender"; "active, progressive, defensive"; displaying an "energy for adventure, for war, and for conquest." The woman's power, by contrast, is "for rule, not for battle"; her intellect "not for invention or creation but for sweet ordering, arrangement, and decision"; she "enters no contest, but infallibly adjudges the crown of contest."[28]* It is to guard her from the perils that beset man in the "open world," as well as to give him a haven from that world, that woman is confined to the home. "This is the true nature of home—it is the place of Peace; the shelter, not only from all injury, but from all ter-

---

* As late as 1889, two eminent scientists, Patrick Geddes and J. Arthur Thomson, in *The Evolution of Sex,* described the differences between the sexes: the man "katabolic"—active, energetic, variable; the woman "anabolic"—passive, sluggish, stable. These differences were said to be innate and immutable. "What was decided among the prehistoric Protozoa cannot be annulled by Act of Parliament."[29]

ror, doubt, and division."[30] (This too is ironic, for Ruskin's own home was anything but tranquil. Indeed, the whole of this essay is almost a reverse image of his own life.)

The superiority of women, Ruskin said, was attested by all great literature. Shakespeare, for example, "has no heroes . . . only heroines"; in every play the catastrophe is caused by "the folly or fault of a man," whereas redemption comes from "the wisdom and virtue of a woman"; his women are "infallibly faithful and wise counsellors,— incorruptibly just and pure examples—strong always to sanctify, even when they cannot save"; there is only one "weak woman" (Ophelia) and three "wicked women" (Lady Macbeth, Regan, and Goneril), the latter being "frightful exceptions to the ordinary laws of life."[31]

The view of woman as an exalted, almost divine being was so prevalent among Victorian writers that it acquired a name: "woman-worship." If Chesterton is right in saying that the Victorians worshipped "the hearth without the altar," one might also say that a good many of them professed to worship a Goddess rather than a God. The religious metaphor is apt, for it echoes a theme heard over and over again: in Patmore's eulogy of the "Angel" in the house; or Tennyson's description of the Prince's mother "dipt in Angel instincts . . . interpreter between the Gods and men"; or Charles Kingsley's portrayal of woman as "the natural and therefore divine guide, purifier, inspirer of the man";[32] or Beatrice Webb's reflections on "the holiness of motherhood."*[33]

---

* Beatrice Webb's identification of "womanhood" with "motherhood" is most interesting, because it comes from one of the most driven intellectuals of her time (to say nothing of her sex), who was not herself, to her great regret, a mother. Before her

It was against these woman-worshippers—"philogynists," he called them—that T. H. Huxley protested. In seeking to refute the antiquated views of the misogynists, he said, they became equally fanatical in insisting that woman was "the higher type of humanity"; that her intellect was "the clearer and the quicker, if not the stronger," than the male's and her moral sense "the purer and nobler"; and that man should "abdicate his usurped sovereignty over Nature in favour of the female line." One need not make such excessive claims, Huxley argued, in order to advocate the same education for girls as for boys. One need only believe that girls and boys had the same "senses, perceptions, feelings, reasoning powers, emotions," and that intellectually the average girl differed less from the average boy than one boy from another. For himself, neither philogynist nor misogynist, Huxley preferred to believe "that the ideal of womanhood lies neither in the fair saint nor in the fair sinner; that the female type of character is neither better nor worse than the male, but only weaker; that women are

---

marriage, Webb had suggested that the only way women could show their power was for "women with strong natures to remain celibate, so that the special force of womanhood—motherly feeling—may be forced into public work."[34] After her marriage she was dubious about how many women could fulfill themselves in that fashion. The highest mission of a woman, she then said, was to fulfill the "genius of motherhood." A woman should be encouraged to cultivate her mind, for without that she would be capable only of "the animal office of bearing children, not of rearing them." But no woman should be encouraged to forgo motherhood in favor of a purely intellectual life (as she herself had done, she explained, because of her late marriage and too many years of a "purely brainworking and sexless life"), because that would be to deny her very nature. In any case, no woman, however well trained, would ever attain that "fullness of intellectual life which distinguishes the really able man."[35]

meant neither to be men's guides nor their playthings, but their comrades, their fellows, and their equals, so far as Nature puts no bar to that equality."[36]

Most Victorians were neither "woman-worshippers" nor egalitarians. Many, if not most, took the separate-spheres idea to mean that women were inferior to men morally as well as intellectually—not angels in the house but servants in the house, not divine beings placed on a pedestal but lowly creatures capable of little more than menial tasks in the kitchen and dutiful submission in bed. This is the stereotype of the Victorian family, and there is a good deal of truth in it.*

But there was also a powerful countercurrent of thought that belied that view. This countercurrent played into the hands of the Victorian feminists, if only to break up the stereotype and make room for other ideas of the proper relations of men and women. The separate spheres (as the next chapter suggests) were never as separate in practice as in theory; in reality there were intermediate areas, a "social borderland," where they overlapped. But even in theory the separation was less firm, less inviolable, than some would have liked. However committed the woman-worshippers were to the notion that women could exercise their special and superior virtues only in the home, they unwittingly subverted their cause, for they opened the door to the claim that women so elevated could not and should not be confined to so restricted a sphere, that the angel in the house would not so easily be corrupted if she ventured outside the house, and that she might even have a duty to bestow upon all of society those gifts which were now the exclusive privilege of her family.

---

* Virginia Woolf described the angel in the house as an "intensely sympathetic," "immensely charming," "utterly unselfish" woman, who "sacrificed herself daily." "If there was chicken, she

*   *   *

If men and women were presumed to have distinctive attributes and virtues, it might be supposed that they were governed by different standards of behavior—a double standard, as the conventional view has it. Here too there is some truth, but only a partial truth, for if it describes a not uncommon practice, it does not at all describe the principle to which most people subscribed. That principle, the ideal of moral conduct, found its most dramatic expression in Tennyson's *Idylls of the King.*

This long poem, one of Tennyson's most admired and popular works, is a paean to chastity (in the familiar sense not of celibacy but of fidelity and modesty)—for men as much as women. It is curious to find that single standard ascribed not to the court of Queen Victoria, where it would have seemed perfectly natural, but to the court of King Arthur. One might have thought that the virtues associated with the king would be the traditionally masculine ones of the battlefield: heroism, courage, spirit, audacity, virility. The virtues celebrated in the *Idylls,* however, are those more often identified with women and domesticity: love, sweetness, gentleness, faithfulness, chastity. Yet it is the knights, not the ladies of the court, who are enjoined to cultivate these virtues, for these are "all that makes a man."

> To lead sweet lives in purest chastity,
> To love one maiden only, cleave to her,
> And worship her by years of noble deeds,

---

took the leg; if there was a draught she sat in it." She was also totally "pure," so pure as not to have a mind of her own. "Had I not killed her, she would have killed me," Woolf said. "Killing the Angel in the House was part of the occupation of a woman writer."[37]

Until they won her; for indeed I knew
Of no more subtle master under heaven
Than is the maiden passion for a maid,
Not only to keep down the base in man,
But teach high thought, and amiable words,
And courtliness, and the desire of fame
And love of truth, all that makes a man.[38]

The violation of this sexual code by Sir Lancelot and Queen Guinevere signals the fall from grace, the dissolution of the knightly ideal and of Camelot itself. Another knight, Sir Tristram, is emboldened to make a virtue out of their vice; what the lovers have done out of passion and weakness, he does arrogantly and willfully, thereby creating a new moral code, a code of immorality, so to speak. The knightly ideal of "high thought, and amiable words" is perverted into a coarse braggadocio and a gross libertinism. Tristram threatens to set up a rival court in the north, boasting that it will be full of knights who are adulterers and women who are whores. In the last tournament, the king—the "woman-worshipper," as he is mockingly called, who "fain had clipt free manhood from the world"—is mortally wounded, and Camelot is doomed. "The old order changeth, yielding place to new "[39]—a new order, it is implied, that has abandoned the old virtues and verities.

Tennyson's was not the only account of the Arthurian story. William Morris's "The Defence of Guenevere" was just that—a defence of illicit love. (The sequel, however, "King Arthur's Tomb," has Guenevere painfully aware of having sinned against Arthur and against society.) But it was Tennyson's tale that became the authorized Victorian version. And it was his Arthur whom Gladstone extolled as "a selfless man and stainless gentleman, . . . the great pillar of the moral order."[40]

*   *   *

One may question Tennyson's reliability as a witness to the manners and morals of his time; he was, after all, a poet, an incorrigibly romantic one, and Poet Laureate to boot. But one may be more trusting of foreigners who had no *parti pris* and who testified to the same ethos. Ralph Waldo Emerson visited England a few years before Victoria came to the throne, and again a decade into her reign. In *English Traits,* published in 1856, he reflected on the Englishman's passion for family and home: "Domesticity is the taproot which enables the English to branch wide and high. The motive and end of their trade and empire is to guard the independence and privacy of their homes." That passion, Emerson speculated, may have been produced by the vagaries of the climate, which keep the English indoors, but for whatever reason, the Englishman "dearly loves his house." He loves its furnishings, heirlooms, silver—and its inhabitants, tied together by some "invisible ligature." He especially loves the women of the house, who "inspire and refine" him. "Nothing can be more delicate without being fantastical, nothing more firm and based in nature and sentiment, than the courtship and mutual carriage of the sexes." William Cobbett, Emerson recalled, attributed the huge popularity of the then prime minister, Spencer Perceval, to the fact that he went to church every Sunday, "with a large quarto gilt prayer-book under one arm, his wife hanging on the other, and followed by a long brood of children."[41]

Hippolyte Taine, visiting England some years later, was no less impressed by the domesticity and sexual propriety of the English. In France too, he assured his readers, adultery was relatively rare, but it was not treated as solemnly as in England, where marriage was regarded with such profound respect that even in private conversation among men, adultery was regarded as a crime. He had been told that he could frequent every known salon in England over a period of many months without hearing of any case of adultery. Reminded of the French novels and comic papers where adultery was a subject of levity, he went through the bound volumes of *Punch* and found not a single cartoon on infidelity; instead they were full of scenes of conjugal bliss.[42]*

Taine was especially, and agreeably, surprised by the fidelity of women. To account for that curious fact, he contrasted the lives of middle-class English women with those of their French counterparts. Having enjoyed more freedom as children, English women were used to exercising self-control; brought up in the company of young men, they were less given to illusions and romantic dreams; being better educated, they thought for themselves and were sensible; living in the country for a good part of the year, they were removed from temptation; having many children and a large staff to supervise, they were fully occupied; reading the same books as men, engaged in philanthropic work, traveling, physically active, they had little time or energy for "unwholesome ideas." (Taine might have added, as did other observers, that arranged marriages were rare in England, so that couples were united by sentiment and love as well as practical considerations.)

The most provocative of Taine's observations concerned

---

* Every now and then one finds a surprising lapse of reverence, even on the part of the most proper Victorian. Samuel Smiles quoted Coleridge (who was echoing Montaigne): "The most happy marriage I can imagine or picture to myself would be the union of a deaf man to a blind woman"—to which Smiles added: "It would probably have been well if Coleridge's wife had been deaf as well as blind," an allusion to his incessant monologues. Smiles's lists of unmarried geniuses, in philosophy, science, art, poetry, history, and politics, may also have given his readers pause.[43]

the different sources of morality in the two countries, the French deriving from the idea of honor, the English from the idea of duty. Whereas the first could be arbitrary, the second was so strict that it allowed of little compromise. This stern notion of duty meant that the English woman lacked the flexibility and dexterity to cope with intrigue: "Ambiguity is repugnant to her clear-cut character."[44] Although Taine did not make the point (because he was concerned only with explaining the character of English women), it is obvious that the emphasis upon duty rather than honor is even more telling in the case of men. Traditionally, honor is the virtue associated with men and duty with women. To define morality entirely in terms of duty is to deprive men of the latitude inherent in the idea of honor, thus constraining them by a far more exacting principle of conduct and subjecting them to the same, single, rigorous standard as women.

Taine did not mention a book published in 1857, two years before his first visit to England, which might have suggested to him other differences between the French and the English, as well as quite another view of English marital and sexual relations. This was Dr. Acton's *The Functions and Disorders of the Reproductive Organs*. It is this book that has perpetuated one of the most enduring of the myths about the Victorian woman—or rather, about the two types of Victorian woman: "the womanly woman and her negation, the whorely whore: the pure and the impure."[45] The image of the first, the respectable woman, finds support in the frequently cited quotation from Acton's book:

The majority of women (happily for them) are not very much troubled with sexual feeling of any kind. . . . As a general rule, a modest woman seldom desires any sexual gratification for herself. She submits to her husband, but only to please him; and, but for the desire of maternity, would far rather be relieved from his attentions.[46]

This passage appears in one of the two brief sections dealing with women, in both of which it is assumed that most men have mistresses as well as wives and that mistresses have sexual feelings whereas wives do not. If, "happily for them," wives do not have such feelings, it is also a happy circumstance for their husbands, who do not have to worry about satisfying both wife and mistress: "He need not fear that his wife will require the excitement, or in any respect imitate the ways of a courtezan." Similarly, young unmarried men accustomed to the "loose women" of the street would be pleased to know that they need not dread or avoid marriage, suspecting that their "marital duties" might be "beyond their exhausted strength." Their worries, Acton assures them, are groundless. "The best mothers, wives, and managers of households, know little or nothing of sexual indulgences. Love of home, children, and domestic duties, are the only passions they feel."[47]

When Acton was rediscovered a century later, he was pronounced a "truly representative Victorian," and his book was said to represent "the official views of sexuality held by Victorian society."[48] According to one historian, he exposed the sexual repression that was at the heart of the Victorian age, a time when "hypocritical prudery" combined with "sexual asceticism" to produce a "concept of women as sexless, domesticated, child-bearing machines."[49] For another, he confirmed the view of women as "either sexless ministering angels or sensuously oversexed temptresses of the devil."[50]

There are good reasons, however, to distrust Acton's book. Mistresses were not a commonplace of Victorian life—certainly not among the middle or working classes—so that most men need not have worried about overtaxing their sexual capacities. Nor were prostitutes as plentiful as some contemporaries thought.[51] Nor were the concepts of the "sexless" wife and the "oversexed" mistress or prostitute nearly as pervasive as Acton made it appear.[52] The memoirs and letters of some contemporary women, including eminently respectable ones, testify to a recognition of a strong sexual desire on their part; since this was not a subject that was readily discussed, even in private communications, one may assume that there were a larger number of such women than has been supposed. There were also other doctors who had a more modern conception of female sexuality. One was England's first woman doctor, Elizabeth Blackwell, who believed female sexuality to be as strong as that of males. Another was James Paget, a distinguished teacher and surgeon, the author of classic medical works who was far more influential than Acton (he was consulting surgeon to Queen Victoria) and who had much more moderate views on the subject of sexuality.[53]

In addition to medical books, there were marital and sex manuals, which in themselves belie the image of a thoroughly repressed and inhibited society. If some books were counseling women that it was their duty to "suffer and be still,"[54] others were assuring them that they could be no less dutiful, and respectable, while enjoying sex. One popular book, by a Dr. Solomon, *Guide to Health, or Advice to Both Sexes,* first appeared in 1782 and was reprinted well into the 1870s, most of the editions running to thirty thousand copies or more. It was perfectly natural, Dr. Solomon told his readers, for both sexes to experience the "exstacy" of intercourse. He warned them only against "over-indulgence," which on the part of the man could lead to "lassitude, weakness, numbness, a feeble gait, headache, convulsions of all the senses, dimness of sight and dullness of hearing, an idiot

look, a consumption of the lungs and back, and effemi-
nacy." Women were even more vulnerable than men, because the nature of their blood made them excitable and
insatiable and therefore prone to exhaustion and a degeneration of their sexual organs. Dr. Solomon obligingly produced remedies for those of both sexes who wanted to
indulge their passions without ill effects: for men a "Cordial
Balm of Gilead" and for women a "Special Cordial Balm of
Gilead," obtainable, he noted, in market towns throughout
Britain at the cost of 10s. 6d. a bottle.[55]

In the absence of any Victorian equivalent to the Kinsey
Report (which itself is notoriously unreliable), it is hard to
speak confidently about Victorian sexuality—even about
ideas of sexuality, let alone practices. Yet there is enough
evidence to suggest that the conventional view of sexual
repression is much exaggerated; the many happy marriages,
for example, surely testify to satisfactory sexual relations. It
is also significant that whereas Evangelical writings in the
early part of the century tended to be puritanical about sex,
the later ones stressed the importance of conjugal sex for a
happy and healthy marriage.

If we are in a "revisionist" phase in respect to the sexual life
of the Victorians, we may be entering such a phase in regard
to another aspect of Victorian society: the domestic life of
the working classes. One of the stereotypes about Victorian
England is that the family values eulogized by poets and
writers applied preeminently to the middle classes, less to
the upper classes, and least of all to the working classes.

There may have been some justification for this view
(although not as much as is commonly supposed) in regard
to early-Victorian England, but not to the later period. At
the extremes of the social spectrum—aristocratic rakes and
artistic bohemians at the one end, "roughs" at the other—

the ethos was often violated; and throughout the century there were individuals who flouted it. The mistresses living in grand seclusion in St. John's Wood and the prostitutes lurking in the streets are evidence of that. But what is remarkable about Victorian England (and the late-Victorian period especially) is that in this class-conscious society, there was a common ethos that most people, including a majority of the working classes, subscribed to even if they did not always abide by it.[56]

If there was any divergence among the classes, it occurred toward the end of the century and was the reverse of the stereotype. While the middle classes were becoming somewhat less home-centered (going out to restaurants or clubs and engaging in social activities outside the home) and more permissive in regard to their children (indulging them with toys and allowing them greater liberties), the working classes were becoming more home-centered (discouraging socializing in the streets, for example) and stricter about their children's manners and conduct.

It is still more remarkable that the working-class focus upon home and family came at a time of great social and economic dislocation: of urbanization and industrialization, geographical and occupational mobility, expanding educational opportunities, a growing consumer economy, a rising standard of living, and a heightened social consciousness. In this world, contrary to Marx's assertions about the "practical absence of the family among the proletarians" ("all family ties among the proletarians are torn asunder, and their children transformed into simple articles of commerce and instruments of labor"),[57] the working-class family was more stable than ever.

Only a decade ago, Asa Briggs, the most sensitive and authoritative commentator on Victorian England, wrote: "Family values within the working-class home are still largely hidden from the historian's view."[58] The following year, a book appeared that casts much light on just this subject. Elizabeth Roberts's *A Woman's Place* is an oral history based upon extensive interviews with working-class women (and some men) in three Lancashire towns covering the period 1890 to 1940. Although her work deals largely with the early part of this century, it illuminates the late-Victorian period as well because the participants were asked to recall their mothers' lives and compare them with their own. Its credibility comes not only from these firsthand sources but also from the author herself, a feminist who has sedulously refrained from imposing upon her subjects her own assumptions and who has been willing to rebut those assumptions when they were not borne out by her material.

Among the myths finally laid to rest by this book is the idea of an indigenous working-class culture with values radically different from those of the middle class. The working-class family is now shown as the repository of the conventional Victorian values: respectability, hard work, self-help, obedience, cleanliness, orderliness. These values were shared by the parents and consciously inculcated in the children. Children were expected to have "a clear idea of morality, or to behave on command in a moral way, without necessarily understanding the reason for their actions."[59] They were brought up to believe that work not only was necessary for the survival of the family but also had an "intrinsic *moral* value," those who did not work being regarded as idlers or "good-for-nothings."[60] They were taught, from the earliest age, the habits of cleanliness: to wash their hands and face, keep their shoes clean, and take regular (usually weekly) baths. They were responsible for household chores: caring for the younger children, cleaning, cooking, sewing, shopping, running errands. They followed a regimen of fixed mealtimes, playtimes, and bedtimes. And they were expected to observe the rules about table manners, language, and conduct.

All these habits were reinforced by school, which taught obedience, punctuality, and cleanliness (nails, hands, shoes, and handkerchiefs were inspected daily) as naturally and authoritatively as they taught reading and writing. Boys and girls had the same curriculum (except for handicrafts) and were governed by the same rules. There was little or no truancy, teachers were held in respect, even awe, and disobedience was punished with a smack of the ruler or the strap.[61] For the most part, corporal punishment (in school, as at home) was relatively mild and accepted as just by children and parents; when it was excessive, the parent often complained to the teacher or headmaster.

The conventions governing sex varied somewhat in different parts of the country and even in adjoining villages. In Roberts's Lancashire towns, premarital sex was condemned and great pains were taken to prevent it. A young couple "walking out" would be accompanied by a younger sibling and were expected to return to the girl's home in the early evening. "We used to go into the parlour when Reg and I were courting," one woman recalled, "and about half past nine they used to give Reg a cup of tea and m'dad would get the alarm clock off the mantelpiece and wind it, he was ready for bed and that was a good hint for Reg to go."[62] The rigor of these rules is all the more remarkable—and perhaps all the more necessary—in view of the length of the courtships; they often went on for years, partly because the family was dependent upon the child's wages and partly because the young man could not afford to get married. There was no double standard; boys as much as girls were expected to "behave themselves." Among Catholics, "keeping out of trouble" was taken more seriously than marrying out of the faith.

There were, of course, out-of-wedlock pregnancies, but these were almost always followed by marriage, so that there were relatively few illegitimate births. In the few cases where marriage did not occur, the child was accommodated in the family or, more rarely, put out for adoption. One woman recalled her mother, poor and illiterate, as "one of those good girls who never went out and she had to stay at home and look after ten children [her siblings]." She did, apparently, go out when she was thirty-six, with a man who neglected to tell her that he was married. When she found out that she was pregnant, she tried to commit suicide. But she did have the child, who later remembered her home, with her mother, grandmother, and aunt, as a happy and loving one. "I have been blessed that way. It's never weighed upon me that I am what you would call illegitimate at all. It's what you are that counts." Other stories ended less happily, a few in suicide, more in disgrace, although not in ostracism. "They wouldn't shun her or anything, but she would know they had been talking about her. It was quite a thing."[63]* In one notably "rough" family, a man was not ashamed of having fathered an illegitimate child, but he was proud of keeping up his child-support payments.

What is most remarkable about these accounts of childhood and youth is that the memories were overwhelmingly agreeable. Rarely is there a complaint about overdiscipline, overwork, cruelty, or repression, although all of these, of course, existed. The main regret of the women is that they were kept in ignorance not only of sexual intercourse but of

* This is confirmed by a study based on the records of the Foundling Hospital, which admitted only illegitimate children. The mothers reported that they had not been excluded from their families or neighborhoods. "If great efforts were sometimes made to move a girl out of the family home for confinement, it was not to hide her shame from the neighbors but for health reasons: to remove her from a cramped and overcrowded dwelling."[64]

such "unseemly" subjects as menstruation. Making all allowances for memories recollected in tranquillity, the reader, like the author, is impressed by the strong sense of a way of life that was regarded as natural, right, and, for the most part, happy. Indeed, many of the respondents spoke nostalgically of that earlier time when life was more rigorous and restrictive but also, they thought in retrospect, more orderly and satisfactory.

Even more striking is the contentment expressed by the women with their roles as wives and mothers—not mere acquiescence but a sense of satisfaction and fulfillment. Although herself a feminist, Roberts acknowledges that her book is not an "obviously feminist history," for it confutes some of the main theories of such a history.

> As a feminist, in the face of the empirical evidence, I have been forced to conclude that it is not sufficient to indict the injustices of the past, nor allow one's concern for women's causes of today to obstruct the understanding of women's roles and status yesterday. Consequently, some feminists may be disturbed to find that the book does not seek to investigate patriarchy or male oppression of women.[65]

The book does not deal with patriarchy or male oppression, Roberts explains, because contrary to her own expectation, her research did not bear that out. Most of the women she interviewed did not feel that they or their mothers had been exploited by men, at least not by their own men. A few had been maltreated by their husbands, but apparently only a very few, to judge by the case studies. If there was any sense of exploitation, it was that they—men as well as women—were exploited by employers who happened to be men. The patriarchal model is doubly unfortunate, Roberts finds, for by focusing upon the negative aspects of women's lives, it distorts the true picture of their marriages and lives.[66]*

It also distorts the true picture of the men's lives. One respondent was asked what kind of man he thought of as a "real gentleman." His answer, according to Roberts, reflected the widely held working-class ideal of marriage:

> I think it was more of the moral line as to how you were as a parent, such as he's a good man is Mr. X, gives his wife his pay packet and she'd perhaps give him his pocket money. He's very good to his children, works round the house and looks after his wife and very kind to you if you're ill. . . . The man who was considered not good would be a man that would be drinking his pay. When he got his pay go in the pub and drink it before he went home, and when he got back home there was nothing left for the wife to look after the children. He was considered a bad sort of man, not a nice man to know. . . . A man was estimated in that light. The height of anyone's life was how they looked after their family and again, from the woman's point of view, whether she had debts, whether she run into debt or whether she'd make do and mend or do without rather than get into debt. That was the main goal of people, if they could live their life without getting into debt and meet their requirements they were all quite happy. They thought that was wonderful.[67]

Marriage, Roberts observes, was regarded as a "life-long working partnership," with husband and wife having clearly defined roles. Even where the wife worked, the man

---

* Another historian, Joan Perkin, makes a similar point. "What is astonishing to modern feminists is that many women in the past who left any record of their feelings not only regarded marriage as their inevitable role in life, but actually welcomed it as an emotionally satisfying, and, indeed, emancipating experience."[68]

was regarded as the basic wage earner and the woman as the household manager responsible for the rearing of the children.* It was because of his role as wage earner, and because his work generally involved hard physical labor, that the husband was fed first at the dinner table and received the choicest food. This was regarded, by wife and children alike, as natural and proper. When times were bad and food was scarce, it was the mother who deprived herself so that her family could be fed; this too was regarded as natural and proper—a sign not of inferiority or submissiveness but of duty and love.

If the patriarchal model distorts the marriage relationship, Roberts says, it also fails to do justice to the real "power and achievements" of the women.[69] She quotes the Victorian social worker Helen Bosanquet: "In reference to the outside world, man has power & woman 'influence.' Within the home woman has the active power and man 'influence.' "[70] This was even more true of the working classes than of the middle classes, where women shared power, in a sense, with maids and nannies, sent their sons off to boarding schools and turned their daughters over to governesses, and where their husbands took care of the family finances. (The wife kept the household accounts, but these were checked by the husband, and the bills were paid by him.)

In the working-class family, the women were far more

---

* Roberts reminds us how large a part of women's lives was spent in child rearing. In 1900, a woman of twenty could expect to live another forty-six years and would spend about one-third of that time bearing and rearing children. This compares with the average woman of twenty in 1960 who could expect to live another fifty-five years and would spend only 7 percent of that time in childbearing and maternal care.[71]

dominant. There, in their separate sphere, they constituted something very like a matriarchy. (A two-generational matriarchy, since most of the women lived very near their mothers and had the closest relations with them; in families where the women worked, their mothers, particularly if they were widowed, often lived with them.) The woman's power was exercised in the form of "moral force," but it went well beyond moral example or suasion—and also well beyond the rearing of the children. In the working-class household, the woman was not only the household manager but also the keeper of the household finances. In every family but one in Roberts's sample, the woman had complete control over the family income. (The one exception was of a teetotaling father and a nonteetotaling mother, who was prevented from drinking in excess by his control of the money.) The husband generally handed over his entire pay packet to his wife, who then gave him pocket money; in this respect he was treated like the working child who gave his mother his earnings and was given an allowance in turn. In some families, the father's pocket money came out of overtime pay, so that there were times when he had no spending money; in others, he retained enough money for an occasional drunken spree.*

The stereotype of the tyrannical, abusive paterfamilias applied to a small minority of Roberts's sample; it was the exception, not the rule, and an exception much frowned upon by neighbors and relatives. That minority, to be sure, inflicted untold misery upon their families. The misery was usually suffered in silence, but when a wife brought an official complaint, the court generally found in her favor, granting her a judicial separation and a maintenance allow-

---

* In London, another historian finds, it was common for the husband to give his wife what he regarded as sufficient for the family's needs, retaining the rest for himself.[72]

ance and sentencing the husband to several months at hard labor.

An abusive husband was seen as a genuine grievance, but the domestic role of the woman was not. None of Roberts's respondents expressed any dissatisfaction with their mode of life or craved to break out of their separate sphere, which was why they were largely indifferent to such feminist issues as the suffrage and greater employment opportunities. Many would have liked to work less hard at home, but none sought the freedom to work outside the home. On the contrary, they would much have preferred not to have to do so. When they did have jobs, as was often the case, it was by necessity, not choice. No one reported having been told as a girl that "a woman's place is in the home"; those with working mothers knew otherwise. But they were aware that whatever other work a woman did, the center of her life was her home and family.

A "woman's place" in working-class society, Roberts concludes, was defined by a clearly understood although rarely articulated set of mores:

> These produced women who were disciplined, inhibited, conforming and who placed perceived familial and social needs before those of the individual. Women did not seek self-fulfilment at the expense of the family because they saw little distinction between their own good and that of their families. There was a very low level of self-awareness. Women's considerable powers were all exercised, firmly, in the perceived interests of their families—that is how they saw their "place."[73]

One can hear the rhetoric of modern feminism in that conclusion—"self-fulfilment," "self-awareness"—but also the historian's awareness that this was not the language or sentiments of the women of that time and place. Roberts's book is all the more impressive because it resists the familiar ideological distortions: attributing to these working-class women a latent sense of oppression and repression, an internalized discipline that was a self-imposed subjugation, a "false consciousness" about their real interests and powers. A woman reader comes away from the book not only with an understanding of the values and experiences of women very different from her own, but with a genuine respect for those women.[74]

Roberts's findings are borne out by other historians and contemporary memoirs, so that we can now appreciate the gratifications, as well as the hardships, of working-class lives.[75] It was not only middle-class moralists like Samuel Smiles who assured hardworking mothers that the home was "the most influential school of civilization" and that "one good mother" was "worth a hundred schoolmasters."[76] Working-class memoirs are full of tributes to the mother: "My mother, a model housewife, kept everything tidy, and did her best to protect me"—to protect him, that is, from becoming a "rough" and thereby losing all claim to respectability and the opportunity for a decent life for himself and his children.[77] Another laborer apologized for his poor hand and spelling:

> My mother was a big strong Woman, and not cast down with a little thing, but strugled through with a family of seven Sons and tow daughters, with a man that did not seem to take very little interest in home Matters, We were all under controle of the Mother who held a Masterly hand.[78]

It is also now possible to put to rest some of the stereotypes that have distorted our view of the Victorian working classes. Their family values—most notably, the idea of the separate spheres—may not be ours; but neither were they as oppressively patriarchal as they have been made out to be. Nor was working-class life the unrelieved, joyless toil one might think it. Family life was much enhanced by the general rise in the standard of living and social conditions in the course of the century; the five-and-a-half-day workweek that became the norm in mid-Victorian times (*"la semaine anglaise,"* as it was enviously known on the Continent), the August bank holiday officially instituted in 1871, the paid summer holidays common by the end of the century, cheap excursion rates on trains, Cook's bus tours (to the Great Exhibition of 1851, for example, when Londoners were pleasantly surprised by the good behavior of the "trippers"). All of these had the effect, if not the intention, of enhancing a family-centered culture. So did such other amenities, common in the latter part of the century, as family allotments for gardening, private privies for working-class houses, a parlor reserved for solemn family occasions, or a piano (to be found in many working-class homes, even in the country, by the end of the century).

Victorian poets and preachers surely overromanticized the family, but they did not overemphasize it. "Family values" were indeed at the heart of Victorian culture and society.

Feminism, Victorian Style

A classic text on Victorian England is entitled *The Age of Reform*.[1] "Reform" is not usually included in the canon of "Victorian values," but it surely deserves a place of honor there, for it was as much a part of the ethos as family, work, thrift, self-reliance, or respectability. And "reformer" was as much a profession, and a respectable one, as doctor, lawyer, writer, or politician. It is in this estimable company that the newest species of reformer was to be found—the "feminists," as they came to be known.

The words "feminist" and "feminism" first appeared toward the end of the century and did not come into general usage until the Edwardian age, when they were applied to the militant "suffragettes" of that time—a very different breed (as the new name suggests) from the Victorian "suffragists."[2] Yet the term "feminist" aptly describes those Victorian women who took up one or another "woman's cause." Like the other reformers, the feminists belonged to no one party: Josephine Butler and Millicent Fawcett were Liberals, Emily Davies and Frances Cobbe Conservatives (although, of course, they could not actually vote for either party). Like the others, they were a heterogeneous group; indeed, to speak of them as a group is a misnomer, since some feminists were as passionately devoted to one cause as they were opposed to another. And like the others, they exercised an influence disproportionate to their numbers.[3] They did not always prevail (any more than the other reformers did), but even when they failed, they succeeded in admitting to the realm of public discourse subjects once regarded as too controversial or unseemly to be discussed in public.

It is one of the many ironies in this story that the most influential of the feminists should have been a man. John Stuart Mill was not the first to propose that women be granted the franchise; the Chartists, among others, had done so earlier. But he was the first eminently respectable thinker to take up the cause and the first to provide a serious, sustained rationale for it. "The Subjection of Women," published in 1869, is still the classic text on the subject, although it is now more often revered than emulated.*

Mill's argument for the franchise is simple: Women should be given the vote on the same grounds as men, because the principles of liberty and equality apply to them as much as to men. They should be enfranchised not as

---

* An earlier essay, "Enfranchisement of Women," published in 1851 under Mill's name, was written, he later claimed, by his wife; it is more likely that they coauthored it.[4] In spite of the many years separating the two essays, they are so similar, in substance and even wording, that one can quote from them alternately without distorting Mill's argument. One suspects that he had the earlier one in front of him as he wrote the later, lengthier one.

women per se but as individuals, as persons who cannot legitimately be confined to any "proper sphere" by virtue of their sex but should be free to participate in public life as and when they like. It is significant that when Mill was in Parliament, he did not introduce a bill for the enfranchisement of women. Instead he moved an amendment to the Reform Bill of 1867, simply proposing to replace the word "man" with "person."*

Much of Mill's argument is by now so familiar that it seems banal. Yet at the time it was radical enough, and even now parts of it are startling. "What is wanted for women," Mill declared, "is equal rights, equal admission to all social privileges; not a position apart, a sort of sentimental priesthood."[5]† If the first part of this statement was directed against those who denied the equality of women, the second part was directed against those who asserted not their inferiority but their superiority—the "woman-worshippers" of the time. It may seem curious that Mill should have ex-

---

* The expression "male person" first appeared in the Reform Act of 1832, with the deliberate purpose of excluding women. Before that, the franchise had varied from locality to locality, with no specification as to sex; in some areas women actually had the vote. The act of 1832 was the first attempt not only to broaden the suffrage but to make it uniform, thus converting it into an exclusively male prerogative. It was for this reason that suffragists condemned the three reform acts of the century as regressive.

† "Sentimental priesthood" is clearly a reference to Comte's "moral providence." By the time this essay was written, Mill had become disaffected with Comte, not only because of the illiberal implications of what by then had emerged as a full-fledged theocracy, but also because of other of Comte's eccentric views—his insistence, for example, that the sanctity of marriage prohibited both divorce and the remarriage of a widow. For the Mills, who were married after the death of Harriet Taylor's husband, this prohibition was particularly objectionable.

pended so much energy attacking those who might have been considered his allies. Yet it was essential to his argument that he do so, for they violated the principles of liberty and equality as surely as those who deemed women to be inferior. The "cant" about the moral superiority of women, Mill protested, was nothing more than an excuse to keep them in a position of inferiority. "We are perpetually told that women are better than men, by those who are totally opposed to treating them as if they were as good."[6]

Mill's objections to the woman-worshippers went beyond the suspicion that in elevating women to that exalted moral sphere, they were relegating them to the old separate sphere. He also disputed the idea that women were morally superior. There was a time, he conceded, when women did exercise a favorable moral influence by stimulating those chivalric sentiments that infused an element of morality into a society otherwise dominated by the idea of prowess. But that time had long since passed. Moral life now had a different source: not chivalry but justice. And in this respect, women had a deleterious effect upon men. In the conflict between interest and principle, between private concerns and public justice, women were inclined to favor the former. And when they extended themselves beyond the home and entered the public realm, their influence was "at least as often mischievous as useful." It was especially mischievous in the area of philanthropy, where women were especially active, for here their education—"an education of the sentiments rather than of the understanding"—proved most unfortunate, encouraging a shortsighted benevolence and discouraging the sterner virtues of "self-respect, self-help, and self-control."[7]

In their present condition, then, women were inferior to men in "mental ability" and even more in moral quality. "Public spirit, sense of duty towards the public good, is of all virtues . . . the most rarely to be found among them."

They even lacked what in men was often a partial substitute for public spirit, "a sense of personal honour connected with any public duty."[8] A woman, concerned only with family and home, "neither knows nor cares which is the right side in politics, but she knows what will bring in money or invitations, give her husband a title, her son a place, or her daughter a good marriage."[9] The effect was to drag down her husband to her level, for even the most virtuous of men might not be able to resist her appeals to the comfort and social standing of the family. "Whoever has a wife and children," Mill pronounced, "has given hostages to Mrs. Grundy."[10]*

This judgment was even more damning because, as Mill went on to say, domestic life had become more important than ever in the lives of men, so that the influence of women was both greater and more pernicious.

> Formerly, their [men's] pleasures and chosen occupa-
> tions were among men, and in men's company: their
> wives had but a fragment of their lives. At the present
> time, the progress of civilization, and the turn of opin-
> ion against the rough amusements and convivial ex-
> cesses which formerly occupied most men in their

---

* This recalls Francis Bacon's dictum: "He that hath wife and children hath given hostages to fortune; for they are impediments to great enterprises, either of virtue or mischief."[11]

It should be noted that Mill exempted his own wife from these strictures, representing her as the embodiment of all moral and spiritual as well as intellectual virtues. She was a paragon of "speculative intellect" and "practical capacity"; she had "the perfection of a poetic and artistic nature"; she was "the most unselfish and high-minded of characters"; she had the soul and eloquence of a "great orator" and the discernment and sagacity of the most "eminent among the rulers of mankind"; she combined "the most genuine modesty" with the "loftiest pride. . . ."[12]

hours of relaxation—together with (it must be said) the improved tone of modern feeling as to the reciprocity of duty which binds the husband towards the wife— have thrown the man very much more upon home and its inmates, for his personal and social pleasures: while the kind and degree of improvement which has been made in women's education, has made them in some degree capable of being his companions in ideas and mental tastes, while leaving them, in most cases, still hopelessly inferior to him.

The result, Mill unhappily concluded, is that "young men of the greatest promise generally cease to improve as soon as they marry, and, not improving, inevitably degenerate."[3]

The strategy behind Mill's argument was to implicate men in the cause of women's equality by giving them a stake in that cause, making it as much in their own interest as in that of women to give women all the rights and privileges they themselves enjoyed, for only then would women become their equals morally and intellectually. But the argument had the equivocal, and surely unintended, effect of painting so disagreeable a portrait of women as they actually were that his readers might well have been wary of admitting them to all those rights and privileges until they had attained a state of moral and intellectual equality. That moral and intellectual state, however, Mill believed, could not be attained by formal education alone; it required the kind of practical education that came with active participation in the public realm. It was a "catch-22" situation: moral and intellectual equality were dependent upon political equality; but political equality was perilous without moral and intellectual equality.

Contemporaries were aware of this dilemma and responded to it in different ways. George Gissing explained that it was precisely because he had so little respect for women's intellectual capacity that he supported both their enfranchisement and their education:

> My demand for female "equality" simply means that I am convinced there will be no social peace until women are intellectually trained very much as men are. More than half the misery of life is due to the ignorance and childishness of women. . . . I am driven frantic by the crass imbecility of the typical woman. That type must disappear, or at all events become altogether subordinate.[14]

Charles Kingsley, on the other hand, supported women's education but not the suffrage, on the ground that so many women were "sedentary, luxurious, full of petty vanity, gossip, and intrigue, without work, without purpose, except that of getting married to any one who will ask them," that unless they were educated they were fated "to bring up sons and daughters as sordid and unwholesome as their mothers." But until they were so educated, they could not be trusted with the suffrage.[15]

The modern reader may find other ambiguities and paradoxes in Mill's argument. For one thing, it suggests that there was already, in mid-Victorian England, a considerable measure of equality in the domestic sphere at least, and that women were more influential, less passive and submissive, than is generally supposed. The problem, as Mill saw it, was not that women were ignored and powerless but that they were all too much heeded—and to ill effect.*

---

* Victorian novels, journals, and comic papers—*Punch,* most conspicuously—are full of domineering wives and henpecked husbands. Samuel Butler's *The Way of All Flesh,* famous for its portrait of a particularly tyrannical paterfamilias, opens with a

A more serious objection, for some modern feminists, is the liberal, individualistic nature of his argument. Mill proposed to admit women to full rights in the public sphere as individuals ("persons") rather than as a class (or, as we would now say, "gender"); it was as individuals that they were to have the same freedom that individual men had. His argument derived more from the idea of liberty than of equality—the liberty of women to compete among themselves as well as among men, the freedom of opportunity to cultivate their individual interests and talents without hindrance or prejudice.

For many feminists today, it is equality rather than liberty that is the primary goal—and not the equality of opportunity for individuals but the equality of results for the group as a whole, the test of that equality being the numbers of women in various occupations and positions. For some feminists, it is not even equality that is the goal but power; here too the focus is upon women as a group rather than as individuals. It was to forestall just this view that Mill adamantly opposed the phrase common at the time, "the woman's question"; the issue, as he formulated it, was the rights of "women," in the plural. If he disliked the singular form "woman," implying a homogeneity and collectivity that he denied, he would have disliked even more the idea of a "sisterhood" with a shared "consciousness" and a commitment to "womanpower."*

---

sketch of a "not unhappily" married couple in which the woman is indisputably the master of the house. Mr. Bumble, in *Oliver Twist,* told that he is guilty of his wife's crime because the law assumes that she acted under his direction, utters the memorable words: "The law is a ass—a idiot." If that is the law, the law must be a bachelor, and all Mr. Bumble can wish for him is "that his eye may be opened by experience—by experience."[16]

* "Sisterhood" was generally used at this time in an invidious sense, as in the expression "shrieking sisterhood."

A more recent criticism on the part of some feminists is that Mill displayed not only a conventional political bias but also a conventional masculine, indeed patriarchal, one. Because he had the typical "male tendency to think only in terms of general principles," he did not see that women could contribute to political life on the basis of their uniquely feminine experiences. Although he ostensibly opposed the idea of a separate sphere for women, it is said, he retained the traditional view of the "masculine nature of public life" and of the "patriarchal division of male and female sexual spheres."[17]

The suffrage campaign itself, fueled by the debates over the Reform Acts of 1867 and 1884 that enfranchised most men, was full of anomalies—again, from a modern point of view. One might expect that women's suffrage would have had the support of all good "progressives"—socialists, radicals, liberals, trade unionists. But some of the leading socialists and radicals opposed it: H. M. Hyndman, the leader of the Social Democratic Federation; Belfort Bax, the editor of its journal; the eugenicist and Marxist Karl Pearson (who altered the spelling of his first name to conform to that of his idol); the Comtean socialists Frederic Harrison and E. S. Beesly; John Ruskin, the art critic who was also a critic of capitalism; and many of the Fabian socialists, including the Webbs.

Some prominent Liberals also came out against the suffrage: John Morley, John Bright (who had first been persuaded by Mill to support it but then had second thoughts), James Bryce, William Harcourt, Lord Rosebery, Lord Asquith, and, most notably, Gladstone himself. (Robert Lowe, on the other hand, who vigorously opposed the extension of the suffrage to the working classes, supported the enfranchisement of women who met the same property qualifications as men.) Some of the Liberals objected to it for pragmatic reasons, because they suspected, probably rightly, that most women would vote for the Conservatives. Lord Acton, who on other occasions bitterly criticized those who abandoned principle in favor of opportunism, advised Gladstone that "there is no higher law deciding the question [of women's suffrage] and that it falls within the computations of expediency"—in which case, since women would be likely to vote Tory, Gladstone need not sacrifice "the great interest of party." If it could be proved otherwise, Acton conceded, if women would vote Liberal or at least divide equally, "the balance is, very slightly, in favour of giving them the votes."[18]

Trade union leaders had their own reasons to be wary of the women's suffrage movement. They were suspicious of the middle-class women who led it. They were loath to support a cause that might distract from their own concerns. They were still less sympathetic than middle-class men to the social as well as political emancipation of women—to anything that might violate the proper sphere of women. And they had better cause than middle-class men to fear a change that would take women out of that proper sphere and into the workplace, where they would compete with men and depress their wages. A corollary of the feminist demand for "the right to vote" was "the right to work," and this was anathema to most trade unionists. Henry Broadhurst, addressing the Trades Union Congress in 1877, explained that men had the future of their country to consider: "It was their duty as men and husbands to use their utmost efforts to bring about a condition of things, where their wives would be in their proper sphere at home, instead of being dragged into competition for livelihood against the great and strong men of the world."[19]

The feminists, for their part, were equally antagonistic to the trade unionists. They suspected that working-class men, even more than middle-class men, were hostile to any kind of emancipation for women. Moreover, some of them, like Millicent Fawcett, objected to the factory acts that the trade unions had fought so hard for, because they opposed any special restrictions placed on women's labor, even those meant to benefit women. One of the early women's organizations, the Women's Protective and Provident League, campaigned against the extension of those acts. By the end of the century, most feminists had reversed themselves on this issue and welcomed protective legislation for women. But they did not retreat from their determination to break out of the confines of "woman's work" and enter the larger workplace, thus placing themselves at odds with the trade unionists.

A more painful anomaly, for the Victorian as much as the modern feminist, was the opposition to the suffrage of many distinguished Victorian women, including the most eminent of them all, George Eliot. Knowing of her interest in higher education for women (she was an early champion and sponsor of Girton College) and perhaps assuming that her own defiance of the marriage convention made her a natural ally in their cause, some feminists called upon Eliot to support Mill's suffrage amendment. They were dismayed by her refusal, on the grounds, as she explained to John Morley, that because woman has "the worse share in existence," that was all the more reason for "a sublimer resignation in woman and a more regenerating tenderness in man."[20] A petition in favor of the suffrage was signed by fifteen hundred women, but not by Eliot or by such other women writers as Charlotte Brontë, Mrs. Gaskell, Elizabeth Barrett Browning, Christina Rossetti, Charlotte Yonge, and Margaret Oliphant.

Florence Nightingale's name was also conspicuously absent. When Mill personally approached her to join a committee for the suffrage, she refused, explaining that she was not opposed to woman suffrage but neither did she think it of much importance; there were far worse evils to be addressed, such as the laws denying a woman the control of her own property. She feared that if women received the suffrage before these other reforms were made, the reforms themselves would be impeded because they would then be the subject of political partisanship. When Mill objected on moral grounds to the "indirect influence" that was the only means available to women at present, Nightingale replied that such influence could be actually greater than political power. She herself, she assured him, had never felt the want of a vote; indeed, she had more power than she would have had as an elector in a borough returning two members to Parliament. Nightingale did finally join the committee the following year, but she never played an active role in the movement.[21]

As late as 1889, there was still much resistance among women to the suffrage. That year, an "infamous" petition, as one historian calls it,[22] appeared in *Nineteenth Century,* opposing yet another women's franchise amendment. Organized by the novelist Mrs. Humphry Ward, it was signed by over a hundred women, including Christina Rossetti, Eliza Lynn Linton, and Beatrice Potter (later Mrs. Webb), and by others who were eminent by virtue of their husbands (many of them Liberals and Radicals): Lady Randolph Churchill, Mrs. T. H. Green, Mrs. J. R. Green, Mrs. Leslie Stephen, Mrs. T. H. Huxley, Mrs. Walter Bagehot, Mrs. Herbert Asquith, Mrs. Matthew Arnold, Mrs. George Goschen, Mrs. Frederic Harrison, Mrs. Edward Beesly, Mrs. Arnold Toynbee, and Mrs. Henry Buckle. A later, supplementary list added some two thousand names. Frederic Harrison, who helped organize it, was especially proud of the 128 titled women among them. More noteworthy were the dozen students from each of two new women's colleges, Girton College in Cambridge and Lady Margaret Hall in Oxford.

A counterpetition published in the *Fortnightly Review* featured an equally lengthy and eminent roster of women. In her opening statement, Millicent Fawcett commented on the anomaly that women who organized so effectively to oppose the suffrage should deem it inappropriate for women to participate in politics. Women, she said, were already part of the political "machinery," and they were as fit to exercise the vote as the men who were recently enfranchised. The argument that women were different from men was a reason to favor the suffrage, since it was precisely that difference that should be represented in the political process. And it should be represented not only to correct the inequities that still existed but for the more important reason that the franchise would elevate "the character of women, and consequently the whole national character."[23]

Fawcett could not resist pointing out that the names in the antisuffrage petition were notable mainly because of "the distinguished men who have fought the battle of life for them," and that "hardly one has stood alone in the world to 'journey her stage and earn her wage.'"[24] Her own list, however, opened with the names of titled women and consisted of a great many others, identified only as the wives of well-known or not-so-well-known men. And the opposing list did include women who were notable in their own right and even dependent on their own earnings. Throughout the suffrage campaign, such women—writers, philanthropists, social workers, educators—appeared in both camps.

The case of Beatrice Webb is especially interesting, because she was both a socialist and an intellectual. She signed the antisuffrage petition shortly before she joined the Fabian

Society and saw no reason to change her mind afterward. Professing to speak for all "collectivists," she explained that while she did not want to preserve "the old regimen of economic and personal dependence," neither did she want to jeopardize the special virtues of women as mothers and wives.

> Most of us distrust the reform as much as we dislike the evil. We do not believe that the cry for equal opportunities, a fair field and no favour, will bring woman to her goal. If women are to compete with men, to struggle to become wealth producers and energetic citizens, to vie with men in acquisition of riches, power or learning, then I believe they will harden and narrow themselves, degrade the standard of life of the men they try to supplant, and fail to stimulate and inspire their brother workers to a higher level of effort. And above all, to succeed in the struggle, they must forgo motherhood, even if, in training themselves for the prize fight, they do not incapacitate themselves for childbearing. And what shall we gain? Surely it is enough to have half the human race straining every nerve to outrun their fellows in the race for subsistence or power? Surely we need some human beings who will watch and pray, who will observe and inspire, and, above all, who will guard and love all who are weak, unfit or distressed? Is there not a special service of woman, as there is a special service of man?

Socialists, she argued, had an additional reason for not getting involved in this issue. Before trying to attack individualism—"or, as we prefer to call it, anarchy"—in the stronghold of the home and family, they had to replace it by "deliberate collective rule" in factories, mines, and the economy as a whole. The "woman's question" had better be left to the next generation. But even then it would be of no great consequence, for the controversy that now appears so important, she predicted, "will seem barren and useless to our great-grandchildren."[25]

Beatrice Webb was apparently expressing the dominant view among the Fabians, for while they occasionally made token references to "universal suffrage," they remained conspicuously aloof from the women's suffrage movement. When it was suggested that they publish a tract on this subject, as they did on so many others, they could not agree on an acceptable formulation, and the tract never appeared. It was not until 1906, when the suffrage movement was at its height, that the executive committee of the Fabian Society first refused and then grudgingly agreed (at "pistol-point," as one observer put it) to amend its charter to include women's suffrage.[26]

Reflecting upon this issue much later, Webb attributed her own "anti-feminism" to a nature that was "conservative by temperament, and anti-democratic through social environment." Like Florence Nightingale, she felt she had never suffered the disabilities associated with her sex; being a woman was an asset to her as a social investigator and spared her the need to earn a living. She noted that when the suffrage was finally granted after the First World War, she had not bothered to mention it in her diary. She had assumed political democracy to be a necessary part of government, but had never exerted herself to get it. "It has no glamour for me—I have been, for instance, wholly indifferent to my own political disfranchisement."[27]

Beatrice Webb's reasoning—the peculiar combination of the traditional "womanly" argument and the socialist one— may have been unusual; she was a most unusual woman. But one or another part of that argument was reflected in the views of other talented, strong-minded, professional women. The housing reformer Octavia Hill was so adamantly opposed not only to the suffrage but to any political role for women that she would not lend her name to an antisuffrage statement lest this too be seen as a political act.[28] As late as 1910, she wrote to *The Times* protesting against the suffrage: "I believe men and women help one another because they are different, have different gifts and different spheres, one is the complement of the other: and it is because they have different powers and qualities that they become one in marriage and one also in friendship and in fellow work."[29]

For every Beatrice Webb, Octavia Hill, or Mrs. Humphry Ward opposing the suffrage, there was a Harriet Martineau, Josephine Butler (the social reformer), or Emily Davies (the founder of Girton College) favoring it. And for all the arguments against it, there were as plentiful and cogent arguments for it. If the antisuffragists figure more prominently here, it is because they remind us that not all women—not even all well-educated, socially conscious, and professionally active women—were of a mind on this subject. It takes no great act of imagination to reconstruct the case for the suffrage, which now seems so obvious and natural as to require no explanation or defense. What does require imagination is understanding the reasoning of those opposed to it, particularly women who were already active in public affairs and who had in their own lives transgressed the boundaries of the "separate sphere."

The feminists lost the battle over the vote—they were not to gain that until after the war. But the campaign itself was a minor triumph, for it brought women on both sides of the issue into the political arena and thus into the public sphere. It is generally thought that the Victorian period was regressive for women, confining them more than ever to their separate sphere. Yet much of the evidence for this theory actually tells against it. The opposition to the suffrage, among women as well as men, was a response to the first serious, concerted movement *for* the suffrage. Similarly, the romanticization and idealization of women, intended to confine them to their exalted sphere, had the unintended effect of justifying their claim to a larger sphere. "The literature of separate spheres," Linda Colley writes of the pre-Victorian period, "was more didactic than descriptive."[30] This is all the more true of the Victorian period, when many women became more assertive and many men became not more repressive but more defensive and permissive.

The separate sphere became less separate, less restrictive, as women pushed against its limits, expanding that sphere sometimes unwittingly. Although most middle-class women did not normally work for pay—it was almost a requirement of middle-class status that they not do so—a large number did do serious, regular, *un*paid work outside the home. One historian describes this as a "social borderland," a "moving frontier" between the private and public spheres, where women, at least to some extent, "subverted" the dominant "masculinist and bourgeois" values.[31] It is a suggestive idea but perhaps misleading, for those dominant values were the values of the working classes as well as of the bourgeoisie, and of most women as well as men. And the image of a "borderland" may give the mistaken impression that the women were working in a peripheral, marginal area outside the mainstream of Victorian life.

The main activities open to women in that borderland—philanthropy, social work, social reform, education, local government—were not minor but major concerns of the Victorians.* Nor can they be regarded simply as an exten-

---

* A pre-Victorian example of the "social borderland" was the antislavery movement. Ladies' associations played an important

sion of the private sphere, with women performing on a larger scale those "nurturing" functions that were their traditional tasks in the home; men were also engaged in these occupations, without in any way diminishing their masculinity or their professional status. Nor did the conspicuous presence of women, in high positions as well as lesser ones, detract from the respectability of these occupations. These were not Lady Bountifuls carrying bread baskets to the poor. They were women who prided themselves on being highly professional in the way they conducted themselves and discharged their duties—this in spite of their being unpaid volunteers. Florence Nightingale, Emily Davies, Octavia Hill, Helen Bosanquet, Josephine Butler, and scores of others were among those "governing and guiding women," as Beatrice Webb called them (she herself was the archetype),[32] who presided over important enterprises, lectured and wrote about social issues, conducted campaigns for one or another reform, served on local boards, and testified before government commissions.

The social borderland was a major expansion of the separate sphere, all the more effective because many of these "governing and guiding women" had no political or ideological agenda. Indeed, many of them were not feminists, and some of them were actually antifeminists. Yet they went about their work, as Beatrice Webb said, with "the dignity of habitual authority."[33] And that authority, as well as the importance of their work, did as much as any feminist

---

part in that campaign, organizing the boycott of slave-grown sugar, writing and distributing literature, getting signatures on petitions, and raising funds. William Wilberforce, the guiding force of the movement, was grateful for their help but disconcerted by their activism. "Private exertions" were appropriate for ladies, but for them "to meet, to publish, to go from house to house stirring up petitions—these appear to me proceedings unsuited to the female character as delineated in Scripture."[34]

campaign or reform to alter the perceptions of Victorians about the proper sphere of women.

Beyond the social borderland was a sphere where women worked, not out of conviction and principle, but out of necessity. It was for these women that the "right to work" was more important than the right to vote—or rather not the right to work but the opportunity to work in fields from which women were traditionally excluded. Throughout most of the century, one-quarter or more of English women of working age worked outside the home or at home for money. Most of these were working-class women, the largest category consisting of servants; in 1891, the peak year for domestic service, 16 percent of the labor force, and about 12 percent of the total female population, were servants.[35]* But there was a minority from the middle classes as well, mostly unmarried women employed as governesses, teachers, dressmakers, nurses, and clerks. The most publicized grievances concerned governesses, who were often well bred but ill educated and ill equipped, and who found themselves in badly paid, precarious, and abject positions. Writers were rarely included in the category of women workers, perhaps because many of them were not only self-supporting but enjoyed the fame and status that came with professional success.†

---

* Some absolute numbers put this in perspective. In 1891, over 2 million people, in a total population of 29 million, were resident servants. In 1961, there were 103,000 in a population of 46 million.
† It is not true, as is often said, that women writers were obliged to adopt masculine names in order to be taken seriously.[36] The Brontë sisters and George Eliot did so, but their reputations and popularity suffered not at all when their identities became known. Olive Schreiner's first book was originally published under a pseudonym, but she had made no secret of her authorship (George

What made the question of women's work particularly urgent at this time was not the agitation of feminists but the hard facts of demography. With the emigration from England and Wales of some five million people, mainly men, since 1830, the proportion of females to males steadily increased, until by 1891 there were almost a million more women than men in a total population of twenty-nine million.[37] These "surplus" or "redundant" women, as they were called, together with the normal complement of widows, were a powerful argument for the opening up of trades and careers to women. (They were also an argument for the suffrage, since they were unmarried and therefore "unrepresented" by husbands.)

It was less for reasons of equality than out of economic necessity that the issue of work arose. There was very little of the kind of romanticization of the working woman that only a male poet like Arthur Hugh Clough could display:

> *Oh, if our high-born girls knew only the grace, the*
> *   attraction,*
> *Labour, and labour alone can add to the beauty of*
> *   women.*[38]

Meredith, the reader for the publisher who recommended it, knew her personally), and she shifted to her real name for a later edition issued within the year. Some little-known novelists adopted male pseudonyms, with no apparent advantage to their careers. Most women writers, however, wrote under their real names from the beginning: Mary Shelley, Elizabeth Browning, Frances Trollope, Mary Russell Mitford, Harriet Martineau, Maria Edgeworth, Eliza Cook, Elizabeth Gaskell, Charlotte Yonge, Margaret Oliphant, Mrs. Humphry Ward, Mary Kingsley, Christina Rossetti, Beatrice Webb, Mary Somerville, and many whose names mean little today but who were among the best-selling authors of their time. Throughout the nineteenth century, more novels were published by women writers (under their own names) than by men.

More often, the romantic argument was invoked to discredit the idea of women's work. Visiting the United States just before the Civil War, Anthony Trollope was impressed, and dismayed, by the good-looking, intelligent, educated, but "unwomanly" women who were demanding the right to work. "Humanity and chivalry have succeeded after a long struggle in teaching the man to work for the woman; and now the woman rebels against such teaching,—not because she likes the work, but because she desires the influence which attends it." Or perhaps, he suspected, it was not she who desired it but her "philanthropical philosophical friends" who desired it for her.[39]

The women who took up the cause of work had a more practical, less "philanthropical" or "philosophical" view of it:

It is work we ask, room to work, encouragement to work, an open field with a fair day's wages for a fair day's work; it is injustice we feel, the injustice of men, who arrogate to themselves all profitable employments and professions, however unsuited to the vigorous manhood they boast, and thus, usurping women's work, drive women to the lowest depths of penury and suffering.[40]

The work they sought was not only in the professions but in much more mundane jobs. By the end of the century, as a result of technological and economic innovations as much as of the efforts of feminists, there was a vast increase in employment opportunities for women—as typists, bookkeepers, postal workers, photographers, clerks, waitresses.

For middle-class as well as working-class women, improved opportunities for work and public careers came with improved education. This was one of the "women's causes" that were as popular among men as among women, and among those who opposed the suffrage (Harrison, Ruskin, Eliot) as well as those who favored it.

While Tennyson's hero was urging the Princess to proceed cautiously in her plans for a women's college, such plans were well under way in the real world. The first "colleges" for women (actually secondary schools) were founded in London in the late 1840s and 1850s, and university-level colleges soon followed. Girton and Newnham colleges (as they were later named) opened in Cambridge in 1869 and 1870, and Somerville and Lady Margaret Hall in Oxford ten years later; London University admitted women in 1878. The latter came too late to benefit the two prominent women doctors, Elizabeth Blackwell and Elizabeth Garrett Anderson, who had to receive their medical training abroad. By 1901, twelve universities and colleges gave women degrees (although Cambridge and Oxford started to do so only in the 1920s, and even then without full university status).

As with all the women's issues, this too had its anomalies. There was the example of Alfred Marshall, a thoroughly humane and enlightened man, who argued eloquently for the potentiality of workers as "gentlemen," who invited trade unionists to dine with him at Cambridge and address his students, and whose wife was a woman of great intellectual distinction—a graduate of the first class of Newnham College, a lecturer there in economics, a collaborator with her husband on a primer on economics, and a true intellectual companion during a long and happy marriage. Yet Marshall was one of the strongest opponents of university education for women, and not for any pragmatic or social reasons (others argued that the presence of women would distract the men, or make women less feminine, or interfere with the natural functions of womanhood), but on the grounds of the natural mental inferiority of women. Workers, he evidently believed, could be gentlemen, but women could not be graduates.

The case for women's education was complicated by a bitter controversy among the educators themselves. The establishment of the women's colleges at Cambridge happened to coincide with a movement for the reform of the curriculum. Among the reformers were some, like Henry Sidgwick, who were firmly committed to women's education and as firmly committed to the modernization of the curriculum, putting less emphasis on Latin and Greek and more on the sciences and modern languages. Emily Davies, the founder of Girton College, was more single-minded in her purpose. Determined that the women of Girton conform to the highest, most rigorous standards, she opposed any change of the curriculum that might raise the suspicion that their education was in the least different from or inferior to the traditional one. Although the proposed changes would apply to men as well as women, the public might assume that they were instituted at this time to accommodate the women by lowering the requirements.*

Because Davies was so adamant on this subject, she found herself in opposition to some of her most prominent supporters, women as well as men, and to other educators who would have been her natural allies. Just as the "woman's movement" was not all of a piece, so reform movements were not all of a piece. What seemed a reform from the point of view of an educator was not necessarily a reform from the point of view of a women's educator.

---

* For the same reason, Davies insisted that the women observe the strictest, most conventional norms of propriety regarding dress and demeanor. So too she tried to dissociate the cause of women's education from that of the suffrage (which she privately favored) and, still more, from the "new women" seeking sexual or marital liberation (of which she heartily disapproved).[41]

*   *   *

One issue that might have provoked much controversy but did not do so was divorce. It is curious that John Stuart Mill did not discuss divorce in his essays on women, although the first, written in 1851, was actually prompted by the editor of the *Westminster Review* who asked him to write on that subject. (A Divorce Commission had just been appointed by Parliament.) Mill declined to do that essay but agreed to write another that would put the issue in the larger context of the legal and social status of women. Later he expressed somewhat conflicting views about divorce. In 1855, he went much further than the proponents of reform, arguing that although any "relaxation of the irrevocability of marriage" would be an improvement, what was ultimately desired was "entire freedom on both sides to dissolve this like any other partnership"; the only thing requiring legal regulation was the maintenance of the children in those cases where the parents could not arrange that amicably.[42] In *On Liberty,* published in 1859, he qualified that position, suggesting that people should be legally free to end a marriage but that their "moral freedom" was not so unlimited, since they had moral obligations beyond their legal ones.[43] Later still, at the time of the writing of "The Subjection of Women," he explained that he chose to avoid the discussion of divorce, not only because he did not want to prejudice his argument for the suffrage by associating it with divorce, but also because the subject was better deferred until women had a voice in determining such issues. All he would then commit himself to was "the general principle of relief from the contract in extreme cases."[44]

The Divorce Act of 1857 owed nothing to Mill; certainly it fell far short of his original proposal (but was perhaps more in keeping with his later views). Before 1857, appeals for divorce came before the ecclesiastical courts or, on rare occasions, could be obtained by a special act of Parliament.

The 1857 act removed divorce from the jurisdiction of the church and made it a civil action, thus more accessible to the less wealthy. It has generally been assumed that the act was utilized only by the middle and upper classes and largely by men, but recent scholarship has shown that in the first ten years, about 30 percent of divorce petitions came from the working classes and slightly more than half from women, the women being as successful as the men in their suits.[45]* The conditions imposed upon women, however, were more onerous. While a man seeking a divorce had merely to prove adultery on the part of his wife, a wife had to prove not only adultery but some "aggravated enormity," such as incest, bigamy, rape, sodomy, bestiality, cruelty, or desertion without cause. Moreover, the husband, whatever the charges against him, was almost invariably given custody over the children. Subsequent amendments to the act retained much of this double standard (it was not entirely abandoned until after the First World War) but relaxed the laws of custody and made the process of divorce cheaper and easier.

The double standard was justified as a matter of prudence, to make it more difficult for a child conceived in adultery to become the heir to the family estate or title. It was not that men and women were being held to different standards of sexual morality; rather that immorality on the part of women had different consequences and therefore had to be treated differently. This was in accord with the separate-spheres doctrine, which assigned separate roles to men and women but did not place them under separate moral codes. Morality was assumed to be universal and indivisible, men as much as women being bound by the

---

* Novelists of the time knew what scholars had painfully to discover. In Hardy's *Jude the Obscure,* divorces were obtained, at no great expense or difficulty, by two quite indigent couples.

precepts of chastity and fidelity. Although that single standard did not always prevail in practice—men violated it more often and with greater impunity—the principle was clear. And when the principle itself was violated, as in the case of the divorce act, it required some special and urgent justification, such as the legitimacy of the bloodline. In the course of the debate in the House of Lords, one peer was indiscreet enough to suggest that the law should not be too harsh on a husband who was "a little profligate." His remark was reported with indignation in the press, and he was sharply rebuked by *The Times*.[46]

The Divorce Act of 1857 also introduced the first reform of the property laws affecting women. Before then a woman owned no property in her own right, not even her earnings. Although her husband could not dispose of the property she brought to the marriage, he could burden it with debt or expend its entire income. The 1857 act was the first of several laws that, by the end of the century, gave women full contractual and testamentary control over their own property and earnings.

One historian describes the question of the property laws as "not one of property but of power—of 'sexual politics,' to use a twentieth century phrase."[47] To the Victorian jurist A. V. Dicey, the issue was simply one of equity. Long before the reforms, he pointed out, Chancery, through the device of trusts, had "habituated English gentlemen" to the idea that a married woman of wealth ought to control her own property. The reforms were only a tardy recognition of arrangements the gentry had had for generations. "The rules of equity," Dicey observed, "framed for the daughters of the rich, have at last been extended to the daughters of the poor." This was yet another application of the principle that "in England the law for the great men has a tendency to become the law for all men"[48]—and for all women as well.

*   *   *

As the separate spheres became less rigid, so too did the sexual taboos. One of the curious episodes in Victorian England, which now seems peculiarly un-Victorian because it was so blatantly sexual, was the agitation over the Contagious Diseases Acts of 1864–69.* Responding to the evidence of a high rate of venereal diseases among soldiers and sailors, Parliament provided that in specified garrison towns, women suspected of being prostitutes were to be examined periodically and hospitalized if infected. The initial opposition to the act came from those who objected to any kind of government regulation, and especially to the regulation of prostitution, which seemed to imply its legalization. Florence Nightingale denounced the act as "morally disgusting, unworkable, and unsuccessful in results."[49]

When the measure was extended to civilian areas, it provoked more widespread opposition. The campaign against it was led by Josephine Butler, who had earlier been involved in the movements for women's education and the reform of the property laws. She was joined by women who had been active in other causes such as the abolition of slavery—hence the name they now gave themselves, New Abolitionists. Conspicuously absent were some of the leading suffragists, who did not want their cause tainted by this

---

* Another was the Deceased Wife's Sister Bill of 1866, which would have lifted the prohibition against marriage with a deceased wife's sister. The bill inspired a passionate controversy, one of its defenders hailing it as "a great sexual insurrection of our Anglo-Teutonic race," and Matthew Arnold denouncing it as a violation of the sacredness of marriage, a regression into "darkness and anarchy," reminiscent of that archphilistine Henry VIII, who combined "the craving for forbidden fruit and the craving for legality."[50]

less savory one. Mill, for example, opposed the acts and testified to that effect before a Parliamentary commission, but insisted that the suffrage movement remain aloof from this one.

Although the opposition included men as well as women, and Butler herself said that this was not a women's issue, the arguments soon took on a distinctly feminist tone. The acts were said to humiliate innocent women and stigmatize as professionals those who were only "casual" prostitutes. They were also accused of perpetuating a double standard, punishing "the sex who are the victims of vice" and leaving unpunished "the sex who are the main causes both of the vice and its dreaded consequences."[51]

One of the oddities in this debate was the similarity of the claims made on both sides, each professing to further the interests of the weakest members of the weaker sex. Dr. Acton, better known for his theories about male and female sexuality, was influential in securing the passage of the initial act. In the book urging that measure, he did not condone prostitution, any more than Butler did. Like her, he directed his harshest criticism against the "respectable" classes who patronized the prostitutes. But since prostitution was inevitable, he reasoned, society should not ignore or try to repress it but recognize and regulate it, and should do so in such a way as to protect the prostitutes as well as their clients. At the risk of weakening his case for regulation, he assured his readers that prostitutes were not doomed to the "harlot's progress" of degradation, disease, and a wretched death. Most were "casuals," who eventually returned to a normal, respectable life. The typical prostitute, he maintained, was healthier and stronger than either her working sister, ravaged by toil in factory or shop, or her married sister, worn down by virtuous but arduous labor in the care of her family.[52]

After almost two decades of agitation, the acts were first

suspended and then repealed—a notable success for the women reformers and some small compensation for their failure on the suffrage.[53] Even more notable is the willingness of so many proper middle-class women to become publicly involved in so "indelicate" a matter. It was this seeming impropriety, as much as the substance of the issue, that exercised most of the critics of the movement. The *Saturday Review* was appalled at the "free and unembarrassed kind of talk" it generated, not only between men and women but among unmarried girls; the *Review* could only charitably suppose that those women and girls did not understand what they were talking about. The candor of such talk was itself an argument against repeal. "The instinct of mankind which has always held the purity of the maiden, and her comparative ignorance of the grosser things of life, as a sacred and lovely thing, is more to be trusted than the defiant daring of a small sect who would have nothing sacred, nothing veiled, nothing hidden."[54] A typical letter by a doctor to the editor of his local paper protested against one of Butler's speeches as the "height of indecency." "No men, whoever they may be, admire women who openly show that they know as much on disgusting subjects as they do themselves, much less so those who are so indelicate as to discuss them in public."[55]

Some of the women who participated in the movement had to overcome their own instinctive revulsion. The wife of the bishop of Salisbury, asked to organize a meeting, admitted that she had been reluctant to do so, "sensitive in the highest degree to the hatefulness of women knowing enough of the subject to be able to carry out organized help, and keenly distressed to think that in order to lessen the terrible evil an association would have to be formed involving talk about it." She did, however, call the meeting and later thanked God for permitting her to do the great work that "*only* pure minded women could do."[56]

Butler sympathized with these qualms. Insisting that the acts violated the respect due to "womanhood," she was as eloquent in deploring prostitution as in denouncing the laws. Prostitution was an evil "which threatens the purity and stability of our homes, which stabs at the very heart of pure affection, which degrades all womanhood through foul associations of thought and feeling, and which murders chivalry and generosity towards women in the hearts of our sons and brothers." It was for these reasons, out of reverence for "the sacredness of the maternal function of a woman," that the rights of all women should be respected, "the most virtuous and the most vicious equally."[57]

It is unclear how many people were actually affected by the acts or by their repeal. For obvious reasons, estimates of the number of prostitutes varied enormously. In the 1850s, Henry Mayhew gave the number in London alone as 80,000, while police records put it at a tenth of that, with about 28,000 in all of England and Wales. By 1868, when the acts were extended, the official figures were under 6,000 in London and over 24,000 in the country as a whole. About this time, the *Westminster Review* came up with the figure of 368,000 for the country, which would have made prostitution a major female occupation. It was generally agreed that the proportion of prostitutes to the population fell in the course of the century; many estimates had the absolute numbers remaining constant or even declining, while the population increased.[58]

Just as one indelicate subject was put to rest, another was raised. At the same time that the Contagious Diseases Acts were being repealed, a pamphlet appeared that focused attention on a still more scandalous, and salacious, issue. *The Bitter Cry of Outcast London,* issued in 1883 by the London Congregational Union, was the sensation of the season.

Claiming to be a realistic account of the lives of the "abject poor," it described, in graphic detail, the miserable houses, crowded slums, and unsanitary conditions that were conducive to drink, depravity, and the "vilest practices." After hinting at evils too shocking to be named, it did finally name the most shocking of these: incest. The pamphlet was provocative enough to attract attention without this fillip, but the single mention of that word—almost as proscribed in speech as in practice—undoubtedly contributed to its phenomenal success.[59] It also contributed to the partial lifting of this verbal taboo. Three years later, in a poem that has distinct echoes of *The Bitter Cry,* even Tennyson was emboldened to utter the dread word:

> *There the smouldering fire of fever creeps across the rotted*
> *   floor,*
> *And the crowded couch of incest in the warrens of the*
> *   poor.*[60]

What was permissible for the Poet Laureate, however, was not so for a woman writer—at least not in a respectable journal. In 1888, Beatrice Webb (then Potter) wrote an article for *Nineteenth Century,* "The Pages of a Workgirl's Diary." This was reproduced verbatim from her own diary, she later explained, "sufficiently expurgated to be 'suited to a female pen.' "[61] One of the expurgated sentences referred to the prevalence of incest in one-room flats. Webb had no more evidence for this than did Tennyson or *The Bitter Cry;* she simply assumed that incest was a natural consequence of the overcrowded living conditions of the very poor.

The new sexual candor was promoted by the "new journalism," a word coined by Matthew Arnold to describe the sensationalist reporting associated with W. T. Stead, the editor of the *Pall Mall Gazette.* Stead, who took over the editorship of the paper at the very time that *The Bitter Cry* appeared, published a series of articles quoting liberally from that pamphlet (especially its more lurid passages), as well as editorials, letters, and similar accounts from other sources. Two years later, he launched another sensationalist series on the "white slave market." "The Maiden Tribute of Modern Babylon" graphically described the selling of young girls into prostitution and their treatment in brothels and on the streets. While some critics accused him (justly, as it turned out) of vastly exaggerating the problem, he was defended by men of such unexceptionable respectability as Lord Shaftesbury. In one issue Stead printed samples of the favorable letters he had received, under the headings: "Peers," "Bishops," "Members of Parliament," "The Clergy of all Denominations," and "Public Men." The ordinary public showed its appreciation by swamping the offices of the *Gazette* to get copies of the paper when they were sold out on the streets. It is interesting that there was no serious attempt to stop the publication of the articles or to prosecute the publisher.

This popular support was all the more remarkable because Stead made no secret of his own sympathies. He professed his "respect and admiration for the extraordinarily good behavior of English girls who pursue this dreadful calling." It was not the prostitutes but their persecutors who were the villains. "The publicans and harlots are nearer the Kingdom of heaven than the scribes and pharisees who are always trying to qualify for a passport to bliss hereafter by driving their unfortunate sisters here to the very hell of police despotism."[62] Like Josephine Butler, who successfully combated another form of "police despotism," Stead had the satisfaction of achieving a frequently proposed but long deferred reform: the passage of an act raising the age of consent in sexual relations to sixteen.

Perhaps the more important result of this campaign was the spawning of the "social purity movement," exemplified by the National Vigilance Association for the Repression of Criminal Vice and Immorality. The organization was dedicated to the rescue of prostitutes, the protection of young girls, and the promotion of sexual morality. Enjoying wide support in the various women's movements and endorsed by such prominent feminists as Josephine Butler, Millicent Fawcett, and Frances Cobbe, the association is an embarrassment to some historians. Among its other activities were a vigorous campaign against the publication and distribution of immoral books, including works by Rabelais, Balzac, and Zola; opposition to the dissemination of birth-control information; pressure to prevent prostitutes from plying their trade on the streets (Butler had some reservations about this aspect of its program and later resigned from the organization); and protests against philandering politicians like Charles Parnell and Charles Dilke.

Today the National Vigilance Association may seem retrograde, a throwback to puritanical censoriousness and censorship. To most Victorian feminists, however, believing both in sexual equality and in moral reformation, it was admirable and progressive. Even a later generation of suffragettes was well disposed to it, as is evident from the popular slogan: "Votes for Women, Chastity for Men."

Of all the women's issues, birth control had the least public support among feminists and perhaps the most popular (if unarticulated) support among ordinary women. Although the term itself did not come into use until shortly before the First World War, and then primarily in the United States, contraceptive techniques and devices had long been known and had been widely disseminated. From at least the time of Malthus, clergymen (like Malthus himself) had condemned "artificial" and "unnatural" modes of contraception, in contrast to "natural" modes based on "moral restraint." It is ironic that in the 1820s, Malthus unwittingly inspired the first campaign in England for artificial birth control by those who saw it as the only practical means of limiting the growth of population, which, according to Malthus himself, was threatening to overwhelm the civilized world. (The young John Stuart Mill was among those who were then arrested for distributing "obscene" literature about contraception.)

The most highly publicized event in the birth-control movement was the trial in 1877 of Charles Bradlaugh and Annie Besant, charged with inciting Her Majesty's subjects to "indecent, obscene, unnatural and immoral practices" by selling "a certain indecent, lewd, filthy, bawdy, and obscene book."[63] Although they were found guilty, the charges were dismissed on a technicality. The trial is notable not only for the public attention it aroused but also because it was the first such prosecution in England, which is perhaps why it received so much attention. That it was the first is all the more remarkable because the offending book, written by an American doctor, Charles Knowlton, and innocuously entitled *The Fruits of Philosophy*, had been published in England almost half a century earlier, had been repeatedly reprinted, and had sold hundreds of thousands of copies by the time of the trial; the latest edition alone sold over 165,000 copies. (Perhaps this edition was chosen for prosecution because it contained illustrations that even a modern historian describes as "definitely pornographic.")[64] And this was only one of several books on the subject. Another more formidable one (six hundred pages) by an English doctor, George Drysdale, appeared in 1854 and went through twenty-nine printings and 77,000 copies by the early 1890s. The various pamphlets had even larger sales, starting with *Every Woman's Book* by Richard Carlile in 1828, which sold 10,000 copies within five months of publication and continued to be sold, along with numerous other tracts and manuals, well into the century.

While some of the press waxed indignant about this literature—"no poison," said the *Evening Standard,* "moral or material, was ever offered to mankind so evil as this philosophy"[65]—the demand for it continued to grow. The misnamed Malthusian League published and distributed vast numbers of pamphlets recommending birth control, women's magazines advertised contraceptive devices, and Bradlaugh and Besant lectured to packed audiences. Besant proceeded to write a booklet of her own, which sold over 175,000 copies in little more than ten years; she withdrew it in 1889 not as a result of legal action but because of her conversion to theosophy. She did, however, lose custody of her daughter (she had been separated from her husband for some years), on the grounds that the writing and publishing of these works were such "violations of morality, decency, and womanly propriety" that a child associated with her might well "grow up to be the writer and publisher of such works."[66]

One of the paradoxes of this situation was that although the birth control movement continued to flourish and various contraceptive devices were generally available by the 1870s (condoms cost as little as a halfpenny), this "artificial" mode was not the decisive factor in the limitation of families in the latter part of the nineteenth century. According to J. A. Banks and Olive Banks, who have made the most careful study of the subject, "moral restraint" before marriage—the deliberate delay of marriage until a man could afford to raise a family in desirable circumstances—was more important in limiting the size of the family than birth control after marriage. The main cause of the decline of the size of the family was the desire of the middle classes to attain or retain a standard of gentility that made large families inadvisable.[67]

Another paradox, as a modern might see it, was the indifference and even hostility of many feminists to the birth control movement. The leading feminist journals ignored the Bradlaugh-Besant trial, partly out of prudence—they did not want their own cause to be compromised by an even more controversial one—but also because many feminists had principled objections to birth control itself and even more to the literature propounding it. Millicent Fawcett, one of the staunchest suffragists, refused to testify on Bradlaugh's behalf, agreeing with the prosecution that the book was indecent. And Dr. Elizabeth Blackwell, known for her advanced views on women's sexuality and the need for sex education, said that she was opposed to all such "artifices to indulge a husband's sensuality while counteracting Nature"; they were not only bound to fail but also "eminently noxious to the *woman*." It was a "grave national danger," she warned, to teach men to "repudiate fatherhood" and women to "despise motherhood and shrink from the trouble involved in the bearing and nurturing of children."[68]

As if to confirm Blackwell's fears, when Annie Besant defended birth control in the progressive Men's and Women's Club, all the men but one agreed with her, while the women were split. Even those women who said they favored it preferred "self-control and long periods of abstinence." Birth control might be a necessary evil, one woman explained, but it made a woman more than ever a vehicle of man's pleasure, since there would be no other restraint on him, such as an undesirable offspring. Others protested that it degraded women and "vulgarized the emotions."[69]

One is reminded once again that Victorian feminists were not all of a kind and did not all subscribe to the same "progressive" causes. If there was one common denominator among them, it was the belief that liberation—whether by means of the suffrage, or work, or education, or property and divorce reforms, or birth control—should not be purchased at the expense of "womanliness" and the "domestic virtues." Fawcett spoke for many of her generation when she said that those virtues included "purity" as well as "propriety" and that anything that loosened the bonds of marriage and family meant the "immeasurable degradation of women."[70]

It was this concern for the feminine virtues—purity, propriety, womanliness—that distinguished the Victorian suffragists from many (although not all) of the Edwardian suffragettes. And it was the concern for the domestic virtues—family, marriage, children—that even more sharply distinguished the Victorian feminists from the "new women" of the *fin de siècle*.[71] The Victorian feminists were not rebels; they were reformers. And they were *Victorian* reformers, committed to those values, including family values, that were so deeply ingrained in Victorian culture and society.

"The Mischievous Ambiguity
of the Word *Poor*"

In 1833, Alexis de Tocqueville visited England and recorded his impressions in a "Memoir on Pauperism," published two years later. It opened with a typically Tocquevillean paradox.

> When one crosses the various countries of Europe, one is struck by a very extraordinary and apparently inexplicable sight. The countries appearing to be the most impoverished are those which in reality account for the fewest indigents, and among the people most admired for their opulence, one part of the population is obliged to rely on the gifts of the other in order to live.[1]

The most opulent country, of course, was England, the "Eden of modern civilization." Yet it was there that Tocqueville discovered, with "indescribable astonishment," that "one-sixth of the inhabitants of this flourishing kingdom live at the expense of public charity"—this compared with Portugal, where the people were visibly in a state of abject poverty, yet the number of paupers was insignificant, one in twenty-five according to one account, one in ninety-eight according to another. The explanation was simple: A country where the majority is well fed, clothed, and housed feels it a great misfortune that some should lack those goods and tries to "cure evils which are not even recognized elsewhere," thus giving relief to larger numbers of people, who are then deemed paupers.[2]

Tocqueville sympathized with the impulse behind this benevolence. He found it a moving sight to contemplate a society "continually examining itself, probing its wounds, and undertaking to cure them." Unfortunately, those good intentions had "fatal consequences." By guaranteeing to all the means of subsistence as a legal right, England had relieved the poor in more than the obvious sense—relieved them of the pains of acute poverty, but relieved them too of the obligation to work and to maintain themselves. The establishment of relief as a matter of right, so far from elevating the recipient of relief, degraded him, for it was a public acknowledgment of dependency and inferiority. "What is the achievement of this right if not a notarized manifestation of misery, of weakness, of misconduct on the part of its recipient?" Public relief (unlike private charity, Tocqueville thought) not only demeaned the pauper; it exacerbated the relations of the classes, depressed the economy, and ultimately, when the sources of relief were depleted, might provoke a "violent revolution."[3]

Tocqueville's visit prompting these dour reflections came on the eve of one of the most important, certainly the most debated, social reforms of the century—the Poor Law Amendment Act of 1834. The New Poor Law, as it was called, did not amend the crucial aspect of the old poor law that Tocqueville objected to: the legal right to relief. What it did do (or tried to do, with varying success) was to circumscribe a right that was of too long duration to be annulled.

The historicity of that right played a prominent part in the debate. William Cobbett traced it back to the English Reformation, when the monasteries were destroyed and the state assumed the obligation, previously discharged by the church, of giving alms to the poor; or further back, to the Norman Conquest, when the king (as Cobbett thought) became the sole proprietor of the land, holding it in trust for the nation and securing every person in his right to life, including the right to relief; or further back still, to the Bible, which had established a "legal provision" for the poor in the form of the tithe. In any case, he claimed, relief was part of an inalienable "social compact" and thus of the very foundation of government.[4]

Most historians take a more mundane view of poor relief, finding its genesis in the Elizabethan poor laws, which established the principle of a legal, compulsory, secular, national (although locally administered) provision for relief. Although the practical implementation of these laws varied enormously from time to time and region to region, the principle itself was rarely disputed until late in the eighteenth century—not, however, as one might think, by Adam Smith, who is generally identified with the doctrine of laissez-faire. Smith had no objection to the poor laws themselves; his only objection was to the settlement laws, which made relief a condition of "settlement" in a particular locality, thus preventing the laborer from seeking employment and residence elsewhere. It was Malthus, toward the end of the century, who launched the first serious assault upon the poor laws, inspired partly by his "law of population," which posited a vast discrepancy between the growth of population and the availability of food supply, and partly by the enormous expansion of relief that had taken place in recent years.

The poor laws had been designed for the unemployed and the unemployable, providing "outdoor" relief in the form of the dole (or food, clothing, medical help, or whatever else the parish might think fit) and "indoor" relief in the workhouse or poorhouse. In the last decades of the eighteenth century, because of the economic dislocations resulting from the industrial revolution and the French Revolution, the number of people receiving relief in one form or another had greatly increased, and the cost of relief (the "poor rates," as they were called) had risen commensurately. This situation was exacerbated in 1795, when a particularly bad harvest prompted the justices of the peace of Berkshire to propose yet another form of public assistance, which significantly altered both the terms of relief and the nature of the recipients of relief. The "Speenhamland system," as it became known (after the town where the justices had met), provided that "every poor and industrious man" whose earnings fell below a given standard, determined by the price of bread and the size of his family, should receive an allowance from the parish to bring his income up to that subsistence level. This provision, of "rates in aid of wages," was soon adopted by other counties in the depressed rural areas of the south, with the result that a considerable number of agricultural laborers were being subsidized, entirely or in part, by the parish.[5]

Many contemporaries, including the prime minister, William Pitt, defended this policy as humane and just.*

---

* Inspired by Speenhamland, Pitt introduced a bill in Parliament the following year that expanded poor relief further by including not only rates in aid of wages but also family allowances, sums of

Others, like Edmund Burke, thought it a social and economic disaster, undermining individual exertion, encouraging dependency upon the parish, and transforming laborers
into paupers—"pauperizing the poor," as was said. In the
following years, this expanded system of poor relief was
criticized for setting in motion a series of other economic
evils: depressed wages for the independent laborer (since the
parish undertook to supplement his wages), reduced pro-
ductivity (pauper labor being less efficient than independent
labor), higher food prices (as a result of the decline of pro-
ductivity), lower real wages for the industrial worker (because of the rise of food prices), an increase of population
(relief encouraging the poor to marry earlier and have more
children), a further decline of wages (because of the increase
of the labor force), and so on, in a continuing cycle of
impoverishment, pauperization, and economic depression.[6]

It was at this time, in 1798, that Malthus wrote his famous *Essay on Population*, which added to all these dire
predictions yet another, about the effect of the "law of population" in aggravating the conditions of the poor and of the
economy in general. The law of population could not be
annulled, but the poor laws could, and this was what he
advised. Since these laws tended to "create the poor which
they maintain," by encouraging them to marry and have
children they could not support, the only solution was to
abolish the laws entirely.[7] In the second, much revised and
expanded, edition of his book, published five years later,
Malthus modified this by proposing a brief period of transition. A law should be passed declaring any child born

---

money for the purchase of a cow or some other worthy purpose,
wastelands to be reclaimed and reserved for the poor, and other
means of assistance. In committee, still other forms of relief were
proposed, until the multiplicity of provisions and administrative
agents exposed the bill to ridicule and it was finally withdrawn.

within a year or two ineligible for relief, thus giving the people due notice that they would no longer receive relief as a matter of right.[8]

In spite of the enormous influence of Malthus's book and the growing concern about the problem of pauperism, nothing was done for a generation or more, while the poor rates continued to rise. Having more than doubled in the last quarter of the eighteenth century, from a not insignificant £1.5 million (in a population of 7.5 million) to £4 million (in a population of 9 million), they doubled again between 1800 and 1817, peaking at almost £8 million (in a population of 11 million). Perhaps provoked by the "Swing riots" in 1830 (a kind of rural Luddism directed against the new threshing machines and taking the form of rick and barn burning), a royal commission on the poor laws was appointed in 1832. Its report, issued two years later, was the theoretical basis of the New Poor Law of 1834 and is as important a social document as the Beveridge Report a century later, which established the rationale for the welfare state.

The first principle enunciated by the report has been insufficiently attended to by historians, perhaps because many see the New Poor Law as nothing but a regressive or reactionary measure.[9] Yet it was of vital importance, for it reaffirmed not only the institution of poor relief but the right to relief. Rejecting Malthus's proposal, the commission recommended that the poor laws be amended rather than repealed—but amended in such a way as might eliminate the evils associated with relief.

This was the purpose of the second principle: the definition of those coming within the province of the laws. Protesting against "the mischievous ambiguity of the word *poor*," the report made it clear that the poor laws were intended not for the "poor," as that word was commonly understood—the "laboring classes," who, however poor, were self-sustaining—but for the "indigent," or "paupers," who were unable to support themselves. (The Poor Law, the report implied, was misnamed; it should more properly have been called a "Pauper Law.") Paupers fell into two categories: the "impotent"—the sick, the aged, and widows with small children—and the "able-bodied." For the first, there would be no essential change; they would continue to receive outdoor relief in whatever form was convenient. The "able-bodied" were the problem, and it was for them that the reform was particularly intended. They too would receive relief (anything else would be "repugnant to the common sentiments of mankind"),[10] but only of such a kind and degree as to encourage them to remove themselves from the state of pauperism, and, more important, to discourage independent laborers from lapsing into that state.

The distinction between "poor" and "pauper" inspired the third principle: "less eligibility." The condition of able-bodied paupers should be less "eligible"—desirable, agreeable, favorable—than that of the "lowest class" of "independent" (self-supporting) laborers. A corollary of this was the "workhouse principle": relief should be given to the able-bodied pauper and his family within the workhouse, for it was only there that the requirement of less eligibility could be fulfilled. It was this provision that made the New Poor Law infamous for many contemporaries and most historians. Yet the workhouse itself was no innovation; it was as old as the poor law itself. ("Poorhouse" and "workhouse" had been used interchangeably, some of the inmates being obliged to work on such tasks as breaking stones, grinding corn, or picking oakum.) What was new was the function assigned to the workhouse: to distinguish between the able-bodied pauper and the independent poor—literally to segregate the two—and to ensure that the conditions within the workhouse be less eligible than those outside. Confinement to the workhouse, being a loss of liberty and of status, was itself a primary attribute of less eligibility. It was even suggested that conditions within the workhouse might actually be better than those outside in terms of food and physical comfort, since the workhouse itself was sufficient deprivation.

The workhouse principle served as a "self-acting test" for the able-bodied applicant for relief. It would require no magistrate, no government official, no "means test" ("merit test," as it was called at the time), to determine the neediness of the applicant; if he was willing to receive relief on condition of entering the house, that would be evidence enough of his need. "When that principle has been introduced, the able-bodied claimant should be entitled to immediate relief on the terms prescribed, wherever he might happen to be; and should be received without objection or inquiry; the fact of his compliance with the prescribed discipline constituting his title to a sufficient though simple diet."[11] (The sick and infirm, as well as widows and children, might choose to enter the house if they could not maintain themselves outside; for them the work provision would be waived.)

The law that was passed was less rigorous than the recommendations of the royal commission, and the application of the laws was laxer still.[12] Instead of having the power to "disallow" outdoor relief, the poor law commissioners were merely authorized to "regulate" such relief, a concession that permitted many parishes to continue outdoor relief even for the able-bodied. And where the report would have compelled the "unions" of parishes to raise rates for the building of workhouses, the government placed so low a ceiling on the compulsory levy as to make it difficult for many unions to construct workhouses.

*   *   *

The New Poor Law represented a powerful symbolic statement and was resented more for what it said than for what
it actually did. While the advocates of the law argued for it
on humanitarian grounds, claiming that the distinction between pauper and poor elevated the poor even as it stigmatized the pauper, opponents condemned it as derogatory to
both; indeed, they objected to the distinction itself. The
proprietor of *The Times,* John Walter, insisted that the parish had an obligation to provide its needy with work that
would neither "degrade the party receiving it, nor change
his domestic habits."[13] *The Times* itself led the attack against
the law, fulminating against the poor law commissioners,
the "Three Tyrants of Somerset House," who would subvert the British constitution and "bully, tyrannize over, and
trample" upon the poor. The workhouse was nothing other
than a jail; "Why not at once have the boldness to declare
poverty 'penal'?"[14] Disraeli echoed this theme: "I consider
that this Act has disgraced the country more than any other
upon record. Both a moral crime and a political blunder, it
announces to the world that in England poverty is a
crime."[15]

Others opposed the new law because it enlarged the role
of the government and created an obtrusive centralized bureaucracy, or because it was a radical change in the English
constitution (the arch-Tory Lord Eldon was as violently
opposed to the New Poor Law as he had been to the Reform
Act of 1832). But the main objection was to the workhouses—"Bastilles," as they were called. The picture of the
workhouse in Dickens's *Oliver Twist,* which appeared in
1837, probably did more than any other single source to fix
the image of that institution, for contemporaries as well as
historians. The opening scenes are unforgettable, starting
with Oliver's birth in the workhouse, where his first cry
signaled to the inmates "the fact of a new burden having
been imposed upon the parish," to his rolling about the

floor with twenty or thirty other "juvenile offenders against the poor laws . . . without the inconvenience of too much food or too much clothing," culminating in the famous "More" scene and the dictum that "all poor people should have the alternative . . . of being starved by a gradual process in the house, or by a quick one out of it."[16]

The Times reprinted the more colorful parts of this chapter, following them with ostensibly factual reports about conditions in real workhouses, thus confounding fiction and fact. The poor law commissioners proved that some of the *Times*'s most sensational accounts—of women stripped and beaten, of men sloshed with water in an icy courtyard, and of a boy forced to eat a mouse—were totally false. Although the rebuttals were duly reported in the paper, the stories continued to be circulated and believed. The commissioners also insisted—and in many cases were able to demonstrate—that conditions in the workhouses were generally better than they had been before the new law. But here too the reality could not prevail against the Dickensian image. John Walter, having visited some workhouses, was said to have been "much disappointed" to find in them a reasonable degree of "order, regularity, and *comfort*"; but "no facts," he was quoted as saying, would persuade him to alter his opinion.[17]

The facts, it is now evident, were more in keeping with the reformers' claims than with those of the critics.[18] If the workhouses were not the "pauper palaces" that some thought them, they were, for the most part, better than they had been earlier in the century. It became a complaint among the working classes that paupers in the workhouse were fed better than they were, and in some cases this was true. It was also true that the able-bodied pauper often worked fewer hours and less strenuously than the independent laborer. The greatest grievances of the paupers were not the material and physical discomforts of the house. The objections were of a quite different order: the separation of the family within the house, the segregation from the community, the loss of liberty, and, above all, the stigma attached to the house. It was in these respects that the workhouse embodied the principle of less eligibility.

When Hippolyte Taine, in the 1850s, visited a workhouse outside of Manchester, he was agreeably surprised. Built at a cost of £70,000 and designed to accommodate 1,900, it had only 350 inmates at the time. His description is so idyllic that one might suspect it of being a "Potemkin village" workhouse: spacious, surrounded by gardens, clean and bright, with separate rooms for "lunatics" and "female idiots," classrooms for the children, a chapel, and a diet that included meat once a week. Taine was astonished: "Beside the rows of hovels in which the poor live, this place is a palace." More astonishing still was the fact that there was not a single able-bodied man in that workhouse and would not be until wintertime. "I am told that they will stick to their 'home' and their liberty at any price and cannot bear to be shut up and become subject to discipline. 'They prefer to be free and to starve.' . . . The workhouse is looked upon as a prison and the poor make it a point of honour never to enter one."[19]

If the able-bodied managed to stay out of the workhouse, it was not only because they preferred their liberty at all costs but because there were alternative means of relief. The workhouse principle was more often breached than observed, with many able-bodied paupers continuing to receive outdoor relief. In 1846, the Poor Law Commission officially decreed that the workhouse test should apply only to rural areas. But even there it was frequently ignored. In rural Norfolk, from 1840 to the end of the century, 75 percent or more of the able-bodied paupers received outdoor relief; in the 1870s, the proportion was over 86 percent.[20] In urban regions, the numbers on outdoor relief were even greater: in West Riding in 1855, only 4 percent of the able-bodied received relief in workhouses; in Bradford between 1858 and 1871, fewer than 15 percent did, and in all but two of those years there were no able-bodied men in the workhouses.[21] Throughout most of the century and in most parts of the country, the inmates were predominantly the aged and sick, the workhouses serving, in effect, as poor-houses. There were occasional attempts to reverse this tendency, such as the Goschen Circular of 1869, instructing local officials to observe the workhouse principle, but these had only limited and sporadic effects.

As one historian has observed, "the dictates of humanity happily coincided with those of economy."[22] Many of the poor law guardians, living in the areas they supervised and having a paternalistic regard for "their" poor, disliked the workhouse as much as the paupers did. They also disliked the idea of paying higher rates, first to build houses that they regarded as disagreeable and unnecessary, and then to maintain the paupers in them. In the 1850s, the annual cost for each workhouse inmate in Lancashire and West Riding was £5 10s.; for each outdoor pauper, £3 11s.[23] In the country as a whole, the Local Government Board estimated in 1871, a family in the workhouse cost 10s. a week, while outdoor relief cost 4s.[24]

However inconsistently the New Poor Law was carried out, it had a shock effect that was very real. The number of paupers decreased substantially after the passage of the law, although it is difficult to say by how much exactly.* The

---

* The historian Geoffrey Best has complained of "the idiocy of the official statistics," which counted the number of paupers, in and out of the workhouses, on two days every year, without any suggestion that those days were at all typical. Nor do the figures tell us how long the paupers were on relief; a "casual" might be

decline in the cost of relief is better documented. The average annual poor rate in the five years before 1834 was £6.7 million; in the five years after, £4.5 million—this in spite of a population increase of about a million.[25] A more dramatic contrast is the peak year of 1817, when the poor rates were almost £8 million in a population of 11 million, and 1871, when the rates were almost exactly the same for double the population.[26] During the latter half of the century, the rates were stable in relation to the population, except in London, where they rose significantly.[27]

While the decrease in the number of paupers and in the poor rates was most striking in the years after the passage of the law, it is not clear how much of the decline in the later decades can be attributed to the law and how much to the improvement of the economy. In the 1830s and 1840s the prohibition of rates in aid of wages hastened the migration of agricultural laborers, thus eliminating much of the rural underemployment that had made relief necessary and restoring agricultural wages to their economic level. By mid-century, the economy in general was also improving, and with it the conditions of the poor. Between 1850 and 1885, real wages rose by almost 50 percent, and by the end of the century, by another 40 percent. (Even taking unemployment into account, the figures are 40 percent from 1850 to 1885, and another 40 percent to 1900.)[28]* And wages ac-

---

in the workhouse overnight, while another person might be on the dole for months. Both the official statistics and those compiled by Best show a considerable decrease of pauperism after the passage of the act.[29]

* It is against the background of these statistics that one must consider the much publicized finding by Charles Booth, in the late 1880s, of 30 percent of the population of London in poverty. His "poverty" was clearly not that of the early- or mid-Victorian periods. A better basis for comparison would be his class of the

counted for only part of the rise in the standard of living. Public education, sanitary and health reforms, hospitals and clinics, free municipal facilities (baths, libraries, parks), workingmen's clubs, cheap transportation—these cannot be quantified but must surely enter into the equation. In addition, there were the temporary measures adopted in periods of emergency: rates in aid of wages during the Lancashire cotton depression at the time of the American Civil War, or public works projects in the depression of 1886.

Far more important than public relief were the private charities. In London in 1870, £1.5 million was spent on relief and something between £5.5 and £7 million on charities (this in a population of around 3 million.)[30] It is deceptive to consider poor relief in isolation from charity, for they complemented and supplemented each other. As often as not, the poor law guardians were also prominent in one or another philanthropic cause. Even the early opponents of poor relief, like Burke and Malthus, were in favor of private charity. And those who were later most aggressive in urging the rigorous enforcement of the New Poor Law were also the most active and enthusiastic philanthropists.

It is often said that the New Poor Law was little more than an attempt to reduce the poor rates, of which the middle classes bore the heaviest burden. It was that, to be sure, but it was also motivated by a genuine conviction that poor relief, unlike charity, had a demoralizing effect upon the poor and a deleterious effect on the economy. If it were only a matter of money, the same middle classes would not have contributed, voluntarily and generously, to the multitude of

---

"very poor," which included not only paupers but those who were employed irregularly and at low wages. The whole of this class constituted 7.5 percent of the population. The proportion of paupers in the entire country at this time was 2–3 percent.[31]

societies and committees that were constantly raising money for one or another worthy cause.

With a rise in the standard of living and the decline of pauperism toward the end of the century, it is not surprising that there was little pressure for another reform of the poor law, although the temper of the time would have tolerated a more liberal system of relief.* Public attention and social policy were then directed to a quite different concern. "The problem of poverty is changing its character," Alfred Marshall informed a royal commission in 1893. "While the problem of 1834 was the problem of pauperism, the problem of 1893 is the problem of poverty." With a three- to fivefold increase in the purchasing power of the ordinary laborer, he explained, the old kind of destitution was now drastically reduced.[32] (Earlier, in a debate with the socialist Henry George, he had said that the "lowest stratum" of the working classes was less than half the size, in proportion to the population, than it had been earlier in the century.)[33]

A Poor Law Commission appointed in 1905 issued not one but two reports in 1909, provoking an interesting debate, but resulting in no action at all. The reforms of the late-Victorian and Edwardian periods dealt with issues that affected the laboring poor rather than paupers: housing, schooling, school meals, workmen's compensation, labor exchanges, unemployment and health insurance. The Old Age Pensions Act of 1908 was the only measure that had a significant impact on potential pauperism, since the aged were a large proportion of those receiving relief. Yet the act

---

* By the end of the century, the central government was relaxing the provisions of the law, permitting paupers to receive relief even if they had savings in the form of annuities, benefits from friendly societies, or other private resources.

itself excluded paupers as well as those who "habitually failed to work." The National Insurance Act of 1911, covering unemployment and health, also effectually left out paupers; since it was a contributory scheme, those who did not work did not receive benefits. Except for minor amendments, the New Poor Law remained in force until the National Assistance Act of 1948 pronounced it officially dead. "The existing Poor Law," it decreed, "shall cease to have effect."[34]*

The Dickensian image of the poor law, which associated relief with the workhouse and the workhouse with naked, starving children, drunken matrons, and sadistic overseers, was far from the reality even in the early part of the century, still less later. But the reality was disagreeable enough. The poor law reformers were, for the most part, Benthamites, and they had all the failings of that species: they were excessively rationalistic, utilitarian, single-minded. It was with good intentions, for example, that they tried to abolish the "mixed" workhouses, where young and old, sick and able, were "indiscriminately" forced to live together in the closest quarters. But it was folly to apply this principle so mechanically as to insist upon the separation of families in the workhouse. Certainly it was in violation of those "family values" that the Victorians held in such high esteem, which is why so many Englishmen—and not only the poor—objected to the law.†

---

* The announcement of its death was premature, for the poor law was shortly revived under the name National Assistance Act, which provided for "supplementary benefits," a euphemism for poor relief.

† The reformers were always uncomfortable with this provision of the law, but they saw no easy way of remedying it while also

It cannot be said too often: by the standards of the present day, the New Poor Law was grudging and harsh. But it was not the simple punitive measure it is so often described as being. A truly punitive policy would have denied to the able-bodied any relief at all. Instead the intention was to provide minimal relief for the able-bodied pauper without encouraging him to prolong his dependency—and, more important, without tempting the laborer, the working poor, to lapse into a condition of dependency. In this respect, the law was at least partially successful. If the reformers did not achieve all they had hoped, it was because they were frustrated not only by an older, more traditional humanitarianism that resisted their innovations, but also by the social realities of the time.

As relief and charity had a symbiotic relationship, so did pauperism and poverty. The Poor Law Report of 1834 tried resolutely to eliminate "the mischievous ambiguity of the word *poor*." But the obdurate fact remained: poor and pauper existed in a continuum—a constantly shifting continuum, in which a workingman might find himself, for a shorter or longer period, having to resort to relief or charity. The word "poor" was ambiguous because the reality was. The reformers, of course, knew this; they themselves continually used "poor" where they meant "pauper." But for the sake of the poor as much as for society and the economy, they sought to remove that ambiguity.

At a time when poverty and pauperism coexisted so closely, when there was such a narrow margin separating

---

ensuring the separation of the sexes and the young from the old. In 1847, an act was passed permitting workhouses to exempt married couples over the age of sixty, provided they had separate sleeping accommodations. In 1876, this exemption was extended to those cases where the husband or wife was infirm or sick. (In fact, most of the workhouses did end up "mixed.")

the two, reformers thought it reasonable to try to prevent the poor from lapsing into pauperism by making that prospect repugnant. This was the rationale of less-eligibility and of the stigma of pauperism. Today the very word "stigma" has become odious, whether applied to dependency, illegitimacy, addiction, or anything else. Yet stigmas are the corollaries of values. If work, independence, responsibility, respectability are valued, then their converse must be devalued, seen as disreputable. The Victorians, taking values seriously, also took seriously the need for social sanctions that would stigmatize and censure violations of those values.

"Gain All You Can.... Give All You Can"

———◆———

"Gain all you can. . . . Save all you can. . . . Give all you can."[1] For John Wesley, this trinity was one of the central tenets of Methodism. Max Weber cited it as the essence of the "Puritan ethic."[2] More recently, Margaret Thatcher recommended it as the guiding precept of conservativism.[3] It may also be taken as the perfect expression of the apparent paradox behind the Victorian ethos: the fact that the most individualistic of countries was also the most philanthropic-minded.

One of the many myths about Victorianism is that it was ruthlessly materialistic, acquisitive, and self-centered. The myth starts with the image of the hardheaded, hard-nosed Victorian employer who regarded his workers as instruments of production rather than as human beings, and who exploited them under the cloak of principle, invoking the natural, even divine, laws of political economy. The sole function of government in this laissez-faire system is said to have been the preservation of law and order, which in practice meant keeping the potentially lawless and disorderly lower classes in a state of docility and subjugation. Those who professed a concern for the poor are dismissed as eccentric do-gooders, condescending Lady Bountifuls, or officious philanthropists who pretended to help the poor for their own self-serving motives.

Part of this myth is easily disproved. Neither in principle nor in practice was political economy as rigidly laissez-faireist as this picture suggests. The first of the factory acts limiting the hours of work for children was passed in 1833; within a decade it was followed by laws limiting the hours of women, and somewhat later, the hours of men. In the course of the century, Parliament enacted scores of other reforms concerning health, sanitation, housing, education, transportation, even holidays, while the municipalities assumed responsibility for the water supply, sewage, public baths, street lighting, street cleaning, libraries, parks. All of these reforms coincided with a period of rapid economic growth, so that by the last quarter of the century the standard of living of the working classes had risen considerably, thus belying the Marxist theory of "immiseration": the idea that capitalism inevitably results in the growing misery and poverty of the proletariat.

Even more notable than the improvement in the conditions of the working classes was the enormous surge of social consciousness and philanthropic activity on the part of the middle and upper classes. This is not to say that there had been no such consciousness and activity in the previous century. When John Wesley preached "Gain all you can. . . . Save all you can. . . . Give all you can," he gave practical effect to those principles by taking up collections for the poor, setting up loan funds and work projects, and instructing his followers to pay "visitations" to the sick and to prisoners in jail. It is not surprising to find Methodists and Evangelicals prominent in the founding of orphanages, schools, hospitals, friendly societies, and charitable enterprises of every kind. By the late eighteenth century, the principle of "philanthropy" (still carrying with it its original meaning of "love of mankind") had given rise to full-time philanthropists like John Howard, who agitated for the reform of the prison system, and Jonas Hanway, who devised the "boarding out" system to remove infants from the poorhouses. Hannah More, preferring moral reformation to philanthropy, characterized this period, not altogether in praise, as the "Age of Benevolence."[4] A London magistrate, deploring the corruption of "virtue" into "good affections," complained: "We live in an age when humanity is in fashion."[5]

That magistrate would have had more to complain of in the nineteenth century, when the fashion for humanity expressed itself in a score of legislative and administrative reforms as well as a renewed burst of philanthropies and social activities. So far from supplanting private, voluntary efforts, as many people had feared, the government seemed to inspire them to greater exertions. For Hippolyte Taine, this was yet another of the peculiarities of the English. Citing an article in the *Edinburgh Review* in 1861, he noted that of the £13 million spent on public education in the preceding twenty-one years, only £4 million was contributed by the state; the rest came from private subscriptions. (Even after the institution of compulsory, publicly supported education in 1870, church-endowed and private schools continued to play a large part in the educational system.) And education was only one of the causes that drew upon private funds.

> There are swarms of societies engaged in good works: societies for saving the life of drowning persons, for the conversion of the Jews, for the propagation of the Bible, for the advancement of science, for the protection of animals, for the suppression of vice, for the abolition of tithes, for helping working people to own

their own houses, for building good houses for the working-class, for setting up a basic fund to provide the workers with savings banks, for emigration, for the propagation of economic and social knowledge, for Sabbath-day observance, against drunkenness, for founding schools to train girls as schoolteachers, etc., etc.

What was even more remarkable, Taine observed, was that an Englishman regarded this kind of "public business" as "*his* business," feeling obligated to contribute to the "common good" and bringing to it the same conscientious attention as a Frenchman brought to his private business affairs.[6]

Two decades later, Taine would have had still more societies to add to his roster and more reason for astonishment. The 1880s saw a veritable explosion of social concerns and activities. In 1884, the journal of the leading philanthropic association, the Charity Organisation Society, reported: "Books on the poor, poverty, social questions, slums and the like subjects, rush fast and furious from the press. The titles of some of them sound like sentimental novels."[7] That same year, Beatrice Webb wrote in her diary: "Social questions are the vital questions of today: they take the place of religion."[8]

There was, in fact, a religious, almost revivalist tone in this accession of social consciousness. Beatrice Webb has left a memorable description of what she called the "Time-Spirit" of this period. The spirit was a compound of two elements: the first, a religious dedication to the service of others, inspired not by orthodox religion or a belief in God but by a secular religion, the "Religion of Humanity"; the second, the faith in science, the idea that the welfare of society could best be promoted by scientific, rational, organized means.[9]

To one degree or another, these elements manifested themselves in the multitude of philanthropic enterprises, reform movements, humanitarian societies, research projects, publications, and journalistic exposés that flourished in the last quarter of the century. Some were overtly religious, such as the Salvation Army and the Christian Social Union. But many more exhibited the kind of sublimated, secularized "religion" described by Beatrice Webb. In this respect, the time-spirit of late-Victorian England was in notable contrast to that of earlier periods. Most of the reformers earlier in the century, such as the Evangelicals who led the movement for the abolition of the slave trade, had been inspired by a firm religious creed; they were reformers, one might say, because they were devout Christians. Many of the later reformers were less devout, but no less ardent in pursuing worthy causes. Just as they redoubled their moral zeal to compensate for their loss of religious faith, so they redoubled their humanitarian zeal as well. Humanitarianism became, in effect, a surrogate religion. This quasi-religious spirit was evident even in socialist organizations like the Fabian Society, which was professedly secular, or the Social Democratic Federation, which was ostensibly Marxist.

The scientific aspect of the time-spirit also took many forms. For socialists (in the Fabian Society, Social Democratic Federation, and Socialist League), science meant the rational, planned organization of the economy and society. For social workers (in the Charity Organisation Society), it meant the rational, planned organization of charity and relief. For settlement-house workers (in Toynbee Hall), it meant the education and edification of the working classes. For social researchers (like Charles Booth or Seebohm Rowntree), it meant the systematic investigation and analysis of the different classes of the poor, their material and moral conditions, their problems and prospects of improvement.

It was this combination of religiosity and rationality that informed the social consciousness of the late Victorians. Critics at the time complained that the Religion of Humanity had the effect of diluting and distorting religion, replacing the old stern Puritanism with "a vapid philanthropic sentiment . . . a creed of maudlin benevolence."[10] The new philanthropy, however, was neither vapid nor maudlin. The God of Humanity proved to be as stern a taskmaster as the God of Christianity. The Charity Organisation Society instructed its social workers that "scientific" charity should not be "indiscriminate" or "promiscuous," distributed without regard to need or worth, lest it contribute to the very evil it was designed to remedy, the pauperization and demoralization of the poor. True humanitarianism was said to be an exercise in doing good, not feeling good—doing good to others, even if it meant curbing one's own spontaneous, benevolent impulses.

The dispensers of charity, no less than the recipients, were held to high standards. They were expected to give generously of their time and resources and to have a sustained personal involvement in their work. This was not "checkbook philanthropy," satisfied merely by the contribution of money (although such contributions were expected, in small amounts as well as large, since the organizations were entirely dependent on private funds). Nor was it the kind of "telescopic" philanthropy satirized by Dickens in the character of Mrs. Jellyby, in *Bleak House,* who was so preoccupied with the natives of Borrioboola-Gha that she neglected her own children. Nor was it professional philanthropy in the current sense, where everyone from the director of the charity to fund-raisers, social workers, and clerks is a salaried employee, paid to do a job quite like any other.

Victorian philanthropists, social workers ("visitors," as they were called), settlement house "residents," even researchers, were personally involved in the day-to-day lives of the poor with whom they were concerned. And while they brought to their work a spirit of professionalism, seeking to dispense charity or conduct their inquiries "scientifically," they also brought to it the dedication of unpaid, voluntary workers giving a good deal of their time, their energy, and their money to the welfare of those less fortunate than themselves.

Charles Booth's survey of London, the voluminous *Life and Labour of the People in London,* which today would have been financed by a government agency or a tax-exempt foundation and would have employed a full complement of project directors, supervisors, interviewers, writers, consultants, and accountants, was entirely organized and supported by Booth himself. The research was conducted by him personally with the help of a few assistants, and the seventeen volumes were written by him and his aides—all of this while he was actively engaged in his shipping business. It was a remarkable enterprise, not only for the massive amount of data and analysis that it produced, but for the massive contribution of time, effort, money, and personal dedication that it represented. Booth was the epitome of Webb's time-spirit, the very model of a Victorian philanthropist. A Unitarian turned Positivist, he undertook this vast project not only out of scientific interest and intellectual curiosity, nor simply as a means of developing well-informed social policies, but as his personal contribution to the public welfare, a way of discharging what he called, in a moving testament of faith, his "great debt to Humanity."[11]

*   *   *

Toynbee Hall exemplified the same time-spirit. The proto-
type of the settlement house, Toynbee Hall was founded in
the East End of London in 1884 by the Reverend Samuel
Barnett, vicar of St. Jude's. It was dedicated to the memory
of Arnold Toynbee, the historian and social philosopher,
who had died the previous year at the tragically young age
of thirty. Toynbee himself had no part in the planning or
even the conception of Toynbee Hall, nor, for that matter,
much experience in social work; the only time he lived in
the East End was as a student at Oxford, when he spent a
fortnight's vacation doing volunteer work for the Charity
Organisation Society. Yet Toynbee Hall was a fitting me-
morial to him, for it was inspired by his philosophy and,
even more, his passion.

Shortly before his death, Toynbee delivered a lecture that
culminated with a passionate *mea culpa* addressed to the
working classes:

> We—the middle classes, I mean, not merely the very
> rich—we have neglected you; instead of justice we have
> offered you charity, and instead of sympathy, we have
> offered you hard and unreal advice; but I think we are
> changing. If you would only believe it and trust us, I
> think that many of us would spend our lives in your
> service. You have—I say it clearly and advisedly—you
> have to forgive us, for we have wronged you; we have
> sinned against you grievously—not knowing always;
> but still we have sinned, and let us confess it; but if you
> will forgive us—nay, whether you will forgive us or
> not—we will serve you, we will devote our lives to
> your service, and we cannot do more.

This passage is often quoted as if it were the peroration
and summation of the lecture. It was followed, however, by
a request for a *quid pro quo* from the working classes:

We will ask you to remember this—that we work for you in the hope and trust that if you get material civilisation, if you get a better life, you will really lead a better life. If, that is, you get material civilisation, remember that it is not an end in itself. Remember that man, like trees and plants, has his roots in the earth; but like the trees and plants, he must grow upwards towards the heavens. If you will only keep to the love of your fellow men and to great ideals, then we shall find our happiness in helping you, but if you do not, then our reparation will be in vain.[12]

Today these sentiments are likely to offend or embarrass us. We may find them mawkish, condescending, at the very least unpersuasive and unrealistic. To try to understand them as contemporaries did is to come to terms with a culture and ethos very different from ours—and to come to terms also with attitudes and assumptions on our own part that may inhibit such an understanding.

Social service, as Toynbee understood it, was the dedication to the common good, and that commitment was as binding on the working classes as on the middle classes. It was the faith that united them in a common cause, a common "citizenship." There is a nice coincidence in the founding of Toynbee Hall in 1884 and the passage that year of the Reform Act enfranchising most of the working classes. If the suffrage was the formal manifestation of citizenship, Toynbee Hall was the hope of its existential realization.

For Toynbee, as for his mentor, the philosopher T. H. Green, citizenship was not only the right to vote (although they did not belittle that right). It was also the right and the obligation of each citizen to cultivate his "best self" and to pursue the "common good." This idea of citizenship was related to what Green called "positive freedom." In contrast to John Stuart Mill, Green insisted that freedom is not the right of every individual to "do as he likes so long as he does not prevent another from doing so." The individual—or "citizen," as Green preferred—is a "grown man" in civil society who wants more from freedom than the right to get drunk. He wants, and deserves, the freedom to realize his best self. "When we speak of freedom as something to be so highly prized, we mean a positive power or capacity of doing or enjoying something worth doing or enjoying, and that, too, something that we do or enjoy in common with others."[13] Every person, not just the superior person, has the capacity to realize his best self and, in community with everyone else, to realize the common good. This is the freedom enjoyed by the citizen, and only by the citizen.

"Positive freedom," however, does not mean the intrusion of a "paternal government." If the state has the duty as well as the right to promote morality, it has to do so in such a way as to strengthen the "moral disposition" of the individual rather than subject him to a new form of "moral tutelage."

> The true ground of objection to "paternal government" is not that it violates the "laissez-faire" principle and conceives that its office is to make people good, to promote morality, but that it rests on a misconception of morality. The real function of government being to maintain conditions of life in which morality shall be possible, and morality consisting in the disinterested performance of self-imposed duties, "paternal government" does its best to make it impossible by narrowing the room for the self-imposition of duties and for the play of disinterested motives.[14]

* * *

It was this philosophy that Toynbee adopted from Green and that the Reverend Barnett sought to realize in Toynbee Hall. Toynbee Hall was to be civil society "writ small," a microcosm of the larger community, a social laboratory that might achieve on a small scale what could not be realized on a large scale. On this model of civil society, Barnett, himself a minister of the Church of England, insisted that Toynbee Hall be nonsectarian (which made it especially attractive to the Jews of Whitechapel; by the turn of the century, one-quarter of the students in the university extension courses were Jewish). He also insisted that it was not a "mission" in any sense. The residents were not missionaries bringing the faith to the heathen; nor were they almoners bringing them money or food. They were "settlers" who came to live among the poor—"to learn," Barnett said, "as much as to teach, to receive as much as to give."[15]

In Toynbee Hall, the focus of citizenship was the community—or rather the relationship between two communities, the hall and the neighborhood around it. The young men who came down from the university to reside in Toynbee Hall and work in the East End aspired to be citizens in the higher sense of the word, fulfilling their own best selves by helping those less privileged than themselves to fulfill their best selves, thus realizing the common good. This explains much about Toynbee Hall that might otherwise be thought eccentric.

It explains, for example, why Toynbee Hall resembled a civic and educational institution more than a charitable one. Instead of dispensing relief, it dispensed learning, culture, and social amenities. The calendar of educational activities in a typical month included classes on arithmetic, writing, drawing, citizenship, chemistry, nursing, and music (one class was on "18th Century Music—works by Handel, Bach, Scarlatti, etc."); afternoon classes for girls on dressmaking, writing and composition, geography, bookkeeping, needlework, hygiene, reading and recitation, French, singing, cooking, and swimming; and evening sessions on legal and social issues. In addition, there was a university-extension curriculum that many a college today might well envy, with courses on geology, physiology, botany, and chemistry, Hebrew, Greek, and Latin, European and English history, and a wide range of literary subjects: *Pilgrim's Progress,* Walter Scott, Browning, the Elizabethan dramatists Dekker and Lyly, Shakespeare (this particular month featured *Hamlet* and *The Taming of the Shrew*), Dante, Goethe, French literature (Diderot, Molière, and *Hamlet* in French translation).

All this was taking place in Whitechapel, the poorest section of London. It is not surprising that most of the students attending the university-extension courses were, as the economics teacher reported, the "best sort" of workers, "steady, thrifty, interested in the improvement of their order"; or that the Latin and Greek students were mainly clerks and small tradesmen (one was a foreman at the docks).[16] The "Popular Lectures" on Saturday night attracted a larger audience to hear such notables as Charles Booth (who used Toynbee Hall as a source of information for his survey); Leslie Stephen, the prolific author and editor of the *Dictionary of National Biography;* the Greek scholar Arthur Sidgwick and his brother Henry Sidgwick, the philosopher; the novelist Mrs. Humphry Ward; the jurist A. V. Dicey; the Liberal Party leaders Herbert Asquith and Richard Haldane; the socialist Tom Mann; and, before notoriety overcame him, Oscar Wilde.

And then there were all the other activities sponsored by Toynbee Hall: social clubs (a Shakespeare Society, an Elizabethan Society, a Smoker's Club, where political passions were supposed to be tempered by tobacco, a Travellers' Club, which arranged trips abroad mainly for local schoolteachers), flower shows, concerts, art exhibits (when the paintings and photographs outgrew Toynbee Hall, the Whitechapel Art Palace was erected), a library open to the public (and utilized by over 13,000 people each year), and—Barnett's personal favorite—the Children's Country Holiday Fund, which in one year sent more than 17,000 children to the country. The hall also served as a civic center, a meeting place for the county council and school board, social workers and investigators, trade unions, strike committees, and tenant representatives.

In addition, and not least, Toynbee Hall was a residence—home to fifteen or so young men, who lived in it for periods ranging from three months to several years. It has been said that the hall served the interests of the residents better than those of the outside community. But this is to misunderstand one of its essential purposes. From the beginning, the residential function was given as much weight as the communal function, both being essential to the idea of citizenship. The young men were to live among the poor so that they would become better acquainted with them, move more easily among them, understand and sympathize with them, and serve them in whatever way they could. But they were not to live the life of the poor or lose themselves in the service of the poor. They were not to be latter-day Saint Francises. On the contrary, they were to show the poor the possibility of a more elevated and cultivated life, a life that the poor would not be able to emulate but that would, by its example, enrich and enlarge them.

Toynbee Hall was not simply a settlement house; it was a "university settlement," in appearance as well as reality. The residents were university men, and it was deliberately constructed (except for its red-brick facade) to resemble a college hall, complete with quadrangle and mullioned windows. It contained suites and bed-sitters for the residents, much like those in an Oxford college, a classroom that could accommodate three hundred, a "conversation" room, a drawing room, and a dining room *cum* library decorated with the crests of Oxford and Cambridge colleges. In this collegial setting—"civilised" but without "undue luxury or display," the architect described it—the residents lived.[17] And here the workers in the neighborhood came to attend classes and meetings, mingling with university men and community leaders, and experiencing, at least briefly, a mode of life very different from their own. (The two other settlements founded soon afterward were named Balliol House and Wadham House.)

The residents not only volunteered their services; they paid for the privilege of doing so. And it was regarded as a privilege. Applicants were judged and approved by a committee of the house, were admitted on probation, and had to be confirmed after three months. The residents were bound by rules reminiscent of boarding schools more than colleges. They dined at specified hours, had a fixed bedtime, and were assigned particular duties. Some worked in the East End, while others pursued careers elsewhere in the city, as teachers, civil servants, lawyers, or whatever. But all were expected to devote their spare time to communal affairs.

When William Beveridge (author of the Beveridge Report) was sub-warden of Toynbee Hall in 1904, he delivered a paper entitled "The Influence of University Settlements," which was devoted entirely to their influence upon the residents. The paper, he admitted, was a "foolish leg-pull." But it was serious in suggesting that the "essence" of the settlement house lay in the "individual lives of the residents, as they are affected by the special experience of living in that particular place."[18] Jane Addams, who founded Hull House in Chicago on the model of Toynbee Hall, made no secret of her belief that service in the settlement house was "more for the people who do it than for the other class." Her first reason for establishing Hull House, she confessed, was to give purpose and meaning to her own life; her second was the desire to help the poor.[19]

This dual motive, to serve others while fulfilling a personal moral need, was reflected in most of the philanthropic enterprises of the time. When Beatrice Webb started work as a visitor for the Charity Organisation Society, she weighed the relative importance of the "moral facts" and "economic facts" involved in charity, "the relationship of giver and receiver," and "the moral effect on the person who receives." She concluded that it was "distinctly *advantageous to us* to go amongst the poor," not only to have a better understanding of their lives and problems but because "contact with them develops on the whole our finer qualities, disgusting us with our false and worldly application of men and things and educating in us a thoughtful benevolence." In some instances, she recognized, benevolence might take the form of "pharisaical self congratulation." But the real philanthropist would not be guilty of this, for he would be too aware of the "mixed result" of his work (if indeed it had any result) "to feel much pride over it."[20]

Today such statements are often taken as evidence of the elitist, authoritarian, self-serving nature of philanthropy in general and of the settlement house in particular—an institution satisfying the interests of the residents rather than of the workers and designed to imbue the workers with the alien values of a middle-class culture and ethic. But they can as well be taken as evidence of a self-sacrificing, even self-abasing spirit, a belief that the "privileged," no less than the poor, had spiritual needs, that they had to "give" (as Wesley said) as much as the poor had to receive, and that what they had to give was of themselves. Even a Fabian socialist like Walter Besant paid tribute to the principle of the "new philanthropy," as he called it: "Not money, but yourselves."[21]

The settlement house also reflected the democratic assumption that the poor were able and willing to receive what was given them by way of educational and cultural enrichment, and that they could do so because they shared common values and aspirations, and thus a common citizenship. This was what Jane Addams meant when she said that it was important to hold all men to "one democratic standard."[22] And it was what T. H. Green meant when he insisted that man by nature—not by class, birth, or wealth, but by simple human nature—was a rational, moral being capable of realizing his best self and pursuing the common good.

This was also what contemporaries meant when they spoke of the settlement house as a bridge between the classes, the "two nations," in Disraeli's famous metaphor. That bridge was intended not to abolish classes but to connect them, to create the common bond of citizenship that would mitigate not only class distinctions but also individual distinctions of wealth, occupation, status, and talent— distinctions that were natural and inevitable but that should not be allowed to obscure the common claim to citizenship. The settlement house was not an experiment in egalitarianism; it was an experiment in democracy.

Nor was it an experiment in socialism or even in a social welfare state. It is often said that the great achievement of Toynbee Hall (and of the other settlement houses modeled upon it) was the recruitment and training of a professional corps of social administrators, who then assumed important positions in the burgeoning social service agencies of the government. To some extent this was true. William Beveridge, who first outlined the program for the welfare state, and Clement Attlee, the Labour prime minister who put it into effect, are only the better known names among a host of civil servants and members of Parliament who served their apprenticeship, as it were, in Toynbee Hall. But the creation or implementation of a welfare state was not the intention of the founders of Toynbee Hall; nor was it the practical function of the hall in its early years. Although neither Toynbee nor Barnett had any objection to social legislation in principle—they both advocated specific measures of reform—they were wary of anything resembling "continental socialism" (as Toynbee referred to Marxism) or "paternalistic socialism."[23] In any case, they believed that social legislation and government administration were no substitute for the kind of private, voluntary educational and cultural institution represented by Toynbee Hall.

Two criticisms are commonly made of Toynbee Hall in particular and of Victorian philanthropy in general. The older, more familiar one is that even at the time, such philanthropy was obsolete and irrelevant. The social and economic problems of late-Victorian England, it is said, could not be solved by private, voluntary efforts but required substantial legislative and administrative action by the state or radical structural changes in the economy. Philanthropy was not only inadequate but counterproductive, since it distracted attention from real remedies for all too real problems. From the beginning, the argument goes, and certainly by the end of the nineteenth century, industrialism and urbanism had created social evils that were beyond the scope of individuals. Poverty, unemployment, bad housing, overcrowded slums, unsanitary conditions, were the result neither of a failure of character on the part of workers nor of a lack of goodwill on the part of employers and landlords. Therefore they could not be solved or even alleviated by well-disciplined workers, well-intentioned employers, or well-wishing philanthropists.

More recently, criticism has taken another turn. The

gravamen of the charge now is that philanthropy is all too often a self-serving exercise on the part of philanthropists at the expense of those whom they are ostensibly helping. Philanthropy stands condemned, not only as ineffectual, but as hypocritical and self-aggrandizing. In place of "the love of mankind," philanthropy is now identified with the love of self. It is seen as an occasion for social climbing, for joining committees and attending charity balls in the company of the rich and the famous. Or as an opportunity to cultivate business and professional associations. Or as a way of enhancing one's self-esteem and self-approbation by basking in the esteem and approbation of others. Or as a method of exercising power over those in no position to challenge it. Or as a means (a relatively painless means) of atoning for a sense of guilt, perhaps for riches unethically acquired. Or as a passport to heaven, a record of good works and virtues to offset bad works and vices. Or (the most recent addition to this bill of indictment) as a form of "voyeurism"; Charles Booth is said to have taken up social research as an "urban male spectator and flaneur," whose "masquerade" as one of the people implicitly "articulated a questioning of his own class/gender position."[24]

This kind of criticism is often advanced as a corollary to the "social control" thesis. Just as Victorian values are interpreted as an instrument for the pacification of the working class, so Victorian philanthropy is described as a device for the subjugation of the even more vulnerable class of the poor. By discriminating between the "undeserving" and the "deserving" poor, the dispensers of charity managed to keep the former in a condition of servility in the workhouse while forcing the latter into the labor market on terms set by the employers. Thus profits were enhanced, the status quo was maintained, discontent was suppressed, and revolution was averted.

The difficulty with the "social control" thesis is that it can be neither proved nor refuted, since any empirical fact can be interpreted in accord with it. If some philanthropists and reformers advocated a system of free, compulsory education, it can be said that they did so only because educated workers were more efficient and therefore more profitable than uneducated ones; and if others opposed such a system (ostensibly out of a distrust of any kind of state-controlled education), it was to keep the poor in a state of ignorance and submission. By this mode of reasoning, any philanthropic enterprise, regardless of its nature, purpose, or effect, can be demeaned and discredited.

The other familiar argument, that philanthropy was no solution to the problem of poverty, would have been conceded by the Victorians, who never made any such claim, if only because they did not believe that poverty was a "problem" that could be "solved." At best they thought it could be alleviated, and this only for some individuals or groups, in certain circumstances, and in particular respects. The entire purpose of Charles Booth's study was to break down the category of "poor" into distinctive "classes," analyzing each of them in terms not only of income but also of the regularity of their work and earnings, their living and working conditions, their habits and moral qualities. The effect was to distinguish the various problems that went under the umbrella term "poverty," and thus the specific remedies— not "solutions"—appropriate to those specific problems.

This "disaggregation," as we would now say, was typical of Victorian reformers and philanthropists, who were perfectly aware of the special and limited nature of their enterprises. The Charity Organisation Society, which tried to coordinate the activities of the many philanthropic groups, made a great point of differentiating between the function of private charity and that of public relief. Where the poor law was directed to the relief of the indigent, charity should be reserved for those who were needy but not actually destitute, who were generally employed and might even have some resources, such as savings or small possessions, but who had temporary problems that, unless alleviated, might lead to pauperism. Relief, in short, was meant for paupers; charity for the poor. And neither relief nor charity would solve the problem of poverty; at most they would alleviate it.

Nor did Octavia Hill have any illusions about solving the housing problem when she embarked upon her projects. She hoped that the principles she established for her houses—that tenants pay their rent promptly, that "rent collectors" (in effect, social workers) respect the privacy of the tenants and assist them unobtrusively, and that the houses include such "amenities" as ornaments and gardens as well as essential utilities—would be applied on a larger scale by private owners and institutions. But she also knew the limitations of her financial resources, the relatively few families she could accommodate, and, more important, the particular kinds of workers she wanted to accommodate. She made it clear that her houses were not meant for the artisans who could afford the "model dwellings" erected by the Peabody Trust and other building societies, or for the vagrants who found refuge in the "common lodging houses," but rather for the "unskilled laborers" who constituted the bulk of the "industrious, thrifty working people."[25]

Latter-day critics, who fault the Victorians for not solving the problems of poverty or housing, use such words as "vague" and "illogical," "ambivalent" and "ambiguous," "transitional" and "halfway house" to describe the ideas of these philanthropists, reformers, and thinkers.[26] The implication is that Victorian England can be understood only as a prelude to the welfare state (or, as some historians would prefer, to socialism); anything short of that is regarded as naive and futile. If most Victorians objected to a large extension of state control, if they preferred small measures of reform to large ones and local laws and regulations to national ones, if they persisted in expending their energy and resources on private, voluntary efforts, it could only be, so it is supposed, because of a failure of imagination, a weakness of will, or a commitment to an outmoded ideology or vested interest.

This reading of the past in terms of the present—the "Whig interpretation of history," as it has been called—is no more satisfactory for the nineteenth century than for any other period of history. It does not begin to appreciate the quality of mind that Victorian philanthropists brought to their problems. There are very few criticisms currently made of them that they did not anticipate and try to address. And criticisms not only of their programs and institutions but of themselves personally, their motives and behavior. Reading their books and memoirs, one is struck by how sensitive they were to the imputations of condescension and complacency. This is not to say that they were innocent of those vices. But many of them, including the more prominent ones, were at least as self-conscious and self-critical as their counterparts today.

The Charity Organisation Society has often (and with some justice) been charged by historians with callousness, officiousness, and intrusiveness. Yet its annual report, only a year after its founding, admonished its "visitors" to behave to the poor as they would to their friends: "Well-to-do strangers should no more knock at the door of a working man without some distinct object or introduction than they should at the door of one in their own rank of life."[27] Helen Bosanquet, a member of the council of the society (who is generally regarded as one of the sternest and most dogmatic of Victorians), reminded her colleagues that "inquisitiveness into another person's affairs, and especially intrusion into their home unbidden, is a great offence against social etiquette."[28]

If "social etiquette" was of some importance, it was because these philanthropists and social workers were personally involved with their clients. To use an un-Victorian metaphor, they put their money where their mouths were—and, more than their money, their careers and lives. At no other time did so many people of talent and distinction give so much of themselves to good works. To some historians this too is seen as a flaw. Just as private institutions are thought inferior to public ones, so voluntary, unpaid social workers are denigrated as amateurs in contrast to paid professionals. The Victorians took quite the opposite view, regarding public relief as less responsive to the specific needs of the poor, and paid social workers as less dedicated and public-spirited.

If Victorian philanthropists did not believe that there were comprehensive solutions to most social problems, they did believe that some problems could be alleviated and that it was the duty of the more fortunate to do what they could to relieve the conditions of the less fortunate. This was the moral imperative that made philanthropy so important a part of Victorian life. But there was another moral imperative: that every proposal for alleviation should produce moral as well as material benefits—at the very least that it not have a deleterious moral effect. This was the common denominator that linked together public relief and private charity, settlement houses and housing projects, socialist organizations and temperance societies. Whatever was done for the poor was meant to enable them to do more for themselves, to become more self-reliant and more responsible—to bring out, as T. H. Green said, their better selves. "Charity," wrote the secretary of the Charity Organisation Society, "is a social regenerator. We have to use Charity to create the power of self-help."[29]

Charity and self-help: today they appear to be contradictory. For the Victorians they were opposite sides of the same coin. Samuel Smiles did not invent the expression "self-help," but he did make it a key word in the Victorian vocabulary.* Published in 1859 (that *annus mirabilis* that is more notable for the appearance of *On Liberty* and *Origin of Species*), *Self-Help* was an enormous popular success. Four editions appeared in the first year alone; by the time of Smiles's death, in 1904, it had been reprinted over fifty times and had sold a quarter of a million copies in English. It was translated into virtually every language, including Japanese, Arabic, Turkish, Albanian, and several of the native languages of India—although the title itself was, in most languages, untranslatable. (In Japan it appeared as *European Decision of Character Book.*)

In English at least, the title almost certainly contributed to its success. It helped focus and personalize the subject as

---

* Carlyle used "self-help" in *Sartor Resartus* (1833–34) and again in *Heroes, Hero Worship and the Heroic in History* (1841). It is curious that Smiles, who was so lavish in quotation, did not cite the passage from Carlyle in which he explains Professor Teufelsdröckh's success: "Thus from poverty does the strong educe nobler wealth; thus in the destitution of the wild desert does our young Ishmael acquire for himself the highest of all possessions, that of Self-help."[30] Smiles did, however, quote other passages from Carlyle. And he repeatedly used Carlyle himself as an exemplar of that essential attribute of self-help, perseverance, as manifested in the episode of the accidental burning by a "literary neighbor" of the manuscript of Carlyle's book on the French Revolution, which he then entirely rewrote. (That neighbor was, of course, John Stuart Mill.)[31]

a more abstract word, like "individualism," would not have done. Yet Smiles regretted using it. In the preface to a new edition in 1866, he said that the title was unfortunate, since it led some to suppose that the book was a "eulogy of selfishness," whereas exactly the opposite was his intention. His examples of men of distinction were meant to demonstrate that "the duty of helping one's self in the highest sense involves the helping of one's neighbours." And the reader was urged to remember that success can be achieved only by "application and diligence," "patience and perseverance," and that, above all, "he must seek elevation of character, without which capacity is worthless and worldly success is naught."[32]

This was not, as one might suspect, an afterthought on Smiles's part. "Duty" and "elevation of character" had been central to his theme from the beginning. Indeed, they had figured in the talk to a group of workingmen fifteen years earlier that was the genesis of his book. Happiness, he told them, depended mainly upon themselves—"upon their own diligent self-culture, self-discipline, and self-control—and above all, on that honest and upright performance of individual duty which is the glory of manly character."[33] *Self-Help* itself is full of homilies about character, duty, and virtue. But it is not the sermons that are memorable. It is the life stories of people—patriots, missionaries, martyrs, reformers, inventors, philanthropists—who used their talents not only for their own advantage but for the sake of others. And not only in the Adam Smith sense, in which self-interest is necessarily conducive to the general interest, but in a more conscious, positive sense. One of Smiles's books, *Duty,* was devoted entirely to that virtue. It might have been a devotee of the Religion of Humanity, rather than the famous exponent of Self-Help, who gave his blessing to philanthropy:

Sympathy, when allowed to take a wider range, assumes the larger form of public philanthropy. It influences man in the endeavour to elevate his fellow-creatures from a state of poverty and distress, to improve the condition of the masses of the people, to diffuse the results of civilisation far and wide among mankind, and to unite in the bonds of peace and brotherhood the parted families of the human race. And it is every man's duty, whose lot has been favoured in comparison with others, who enjoys advantages of wealth, or knowledge, or social influence, of which others are deprived, to devote at least a certain portion of his time and money to the promotion of the general well-being.[34]

In the age of Carlyle and Mill, Eliot and Arnold, Smiles hardly ranks among the notable moralists. But he was a moralist of sorts—Everyman's Carlyle, one might say. Certainly he was not the unregenerate materialist and philistine that he has been made out to be. He did emphasize the common virtues—thrift, industry, diligence, perseverance—that he believed to be within the capacity of all men; but he included among these other virtues—courage, inventiveness, "elevation of character"—that are perhaps not quite so common. And while he made common sense more important than genius "in the pursuit of even the highest branches of human inquiry," it was for the sake of those "highest branches" that common sense was so valuable.[35] In view of his repeated insistence upon the importance of intelligence, education, cultivation, and knowledge (and knowledge, he emphasized, for its own sake), the charge of "anti-intellectualism" seems misguided.[36] Moreover, the books themselves belie that charge; they are full of the most varied and often recondite references to people, books, and events, ranging over all times and places, with quotations in

Latin, German, and French, and showing a familiarity with major and minor writers that would surely be the envy of most scholars today.*

Nor is it fair to say that Smiles sought to "reconcile men to the station to which it had pleased God to call them, by insisting upon their duty of discovering for themselves what that station was."[37] All of his books, and most notably *Self-Help,* are a refutation of just that notion. His message is not that men discover for themselves the station to which God has been pleased to call them; it is that they make for themselves, by their own efforts and aspirations, their own station. (Smiles himself, the son of lower-middle-class shopkeepers, had defied whatever station society might' have assigned to him by becoming first a doctor and then an enormously successful author.)

The Victorians were avowedly, unashamedly, incorrigibly moralists. They were moralists on their own behalf—they engaged in philanthropic enterprises in part to satisfy their own moral needs. And they were moralists on behalf of the poor, whom they sought not only to assist materially but also to elevate morally, spiritually, culturally, intellectually—and whom, moreover, they believed capable and desirous of such elevation. Just as it is demeaning to the working classes to suggest that work, thrift, prudence, so-

---

* The first dozen pages of a typical chapter of *Self-Help* contain references to or quotations from Burns, Shakespeare, Bulwer-Lytton, Henry Taylor, the New Testament, John Sterling, John Russell, Samuel Drew (the "philosophical shoemaker"), Socrates, Cobden, Bright, Montaigne, Swift, Francis Horner, Bacon, Goldsmith, Fichte, Johnson, Locke, the duke of Wellington, and Washington. And these appear not in a string of names but in the context of particular stories or quotations.[38]

briety, self-help, were middle-class values imposed upon them from above, so it is demeaning to the philanthropists to suggest that they promoted these values solely for their own ulterior motives. In any case, whatever their motives (and there were surely self-serving, self-aggrandizing, self-satisfied individuals among them), the values they commended to the poor were those that they cherished for themselves and for their own families. It was no small achievement that people of very different political and philosophical persuasions, engaged in very different philanthropic enterprises, should have agreed on this: that the poor had the will to aspire to these same values and the ability to realize them.

VI

The Jew as Victorian

———•◆•———

"Victorian values," historians have observed, were not peculiarly or uniquely Victorian. They were Christian—Protestant, Puritan, Methodist; or perhaps not religious at all but rather secular—bourgeois, middle-class, capitalist. They were also, some Victorians discovered to their astonishment, Jewish. About a century before Margaret Thatcher revived talk of Victorian values, Beatrice Webb wrote an essay about the Jewish community in the East End of London, which, as she described it, perfectly epitomized those values. "For instance is no proof," an old saying has it. But in history, "for instance" is sometimes as close to proof as one can get. And the instance of this Jewish community, seen through the eyes of a Victorian, tells us a good deal about the Victorian sense of Victorian values.

That Mrs. Thatcher's values correspond so closely to these Victorian Jewish values comes as no surprise to those commentators who have remarked upon the large number of Jews in her constituency, Finchley, and, more significantly, in her cabinets. Harold Macmillan is reported as saying, of her first cabinet: "There are more old Estonians than old Etonians in this government."[1] Others have noted that she was the first prime minister to befriend and ennoble the Chief Rabbi of Great Britain, who is himself a great advocate of Jewish *cum* Victorian values. She has a special affinity with Jews, it is said, not only because she approves of their creed of "self-help" but also because they are outside the conventional economic and social establishments and therefore receptive to her ideas of individuality and entrepreneurship. Her biographer explains: "As a moral code for upward mobility of the kind the MP for Finchley never ceased to preach, Judaism embodied many useful precepts and could produce many shining exemplars."[2] A reviewer of that biography puts it more coarsely: "Mrs. Thatcher instinctively warms to the Jewish *nouveaux riches* of North London and seems to see Judaism as an exemplary religion of capitalism."[3]

If Mrs. Thatcher would have found much to admire in Mrs. Webb's account of the Jewish community, she would have found little to admire in the author of that essay. Beatrice Webb was not only a socialist; she was a "social engineer" *par excellence,* with all the disagreeable traits of that species—she was officious, presumptuous, humorless, ruthless. Early in his career, Winston Churchill, rejecting an offer to head the Local Government Board, explained that he did not want to be "shut up in a soup-kitchen" with Mrs. Webb[4]—a sentiment shared by many others. Yet she produced some memorable works, including several volumes of a diary that is an invaluable source for the "time-spirit" of late-Victorian England.

It was earlier in her life, before she became Mrs. Webb— that is, before she married Sidney Webb, joined the Fabian Society, and started to hector people like Churchill—that she wrote about the Jews. She was Beatrice Potter then, serving her "apprenticeship," as she put it, in the craft of social research by assisting Charles Booth in his mammoth work, *Life and Labour of the People of London*. The first volume, published in 1889, contains the essay on the Jewish community by Beatrice Webb. (She will be referred to here by that familiar name, although she was not yet married.)

Some historians have accused Beatrice Webb of being anti-Semitic.[5] There is no good evidence of this, although she and her husband were certainly, later in life, vigorously anti-Zionist, as were so many other socialists. (There were also a good many Victorian socialists—like H. M. Hyndman, leader of the Social Democratic Federation—who were clearly anti-Semitic.)[6] Other historians have claimed that she was, or believed herself to be, one-quarter Jewish. There are cryptic remarks in her autobiography that lend themselves to such speculations. She described herself and her sisters as "unmistakably Potters, the descendants of the tall dark woman of Jewish type who read Hebrew and loved music."[7] (This may have been an allusion to her grandmother, who took upon herself the mission of leading the Jews back to Jerusalem and got as far as Paris before being rescued by her family, only to spend her last years in a lunatic asylum.) Her own talents, she believed, were a "tireless intellectual curiosity together with a double dose of will-power"; the latter, inherited from her father, was a "racial characteristic" of the Jews whom she knew in East London.[8]

Whether the Potters were part Jewish or whether she believed them to be so, Beatrice Webb, in this early period of her life, at any rate, was anything but anti-Semitic. Certainly her essay was not that. Written at a time when the Jews of the East End were generally identified, as either workers or employers, with the much reviled "sweatshops," and when there were vociferous demands to limit

or prohibit the immigration of Jews into England and even
to expel those who were already there, the essay sounds
positively philo-Semitic.

If there are expressions in it that today seem disparaging,
it is because the reader is unfamiliar with Victorian rhetoric
or with Webb's own attitudes. At one point she commended
"the skill, the tenacity, and above all, the admirable temper
with which our Hebrew fellow-countrymen have insinuated themselves into the life of the nation, without for-
saking the faith of their forefathers or sacrificing as a
community the purity of their race."[9] But there is nothing
suspect in the word "race"; to Webb, as to most Victorians,
"race" was an ethnic rather than a biological term, and
"purity of race" was a worthy ideal. Nor was the word
"insinuated" meant to be pejorative; the Fabians commonly
used that word to describe their own political strategy.
Webb herself once boasted, "I could insinuate myself into
smoking-rooms, business offices, private and public con-
ferences, without rousing suspicion."[10] Similarly, her description of the Polish Jew who "suffers oppression and
bears ridicule with imperturbable good humor" and remains
silent in "the face of insult and abuse" was not disparaging.
Nor were her rhetorical questions: "For why resent when
your object is to overcome? Why bluster and fight when
you may manipulate or control in secret?"[11] These sentences have been cited as "clearly anti-Semitic," in implying
something like a Jewish conspiracy against Western society.[12] But Webb was praising the Jew for doing exactly
what the Fabians preached: seeking to prevail by quiet per-
sistence, to "manipulate or control in secret."

"Every country," Beatrice Webb cited the familiar saying
(it was apparently familiar a century ago), "has the Jew it
deserves." That was not, however, true of England, which

had received its most recent contingent of Jews "ready-made" from a country diametrically different from itself, a country where oppression and restriction were pervasive. In Russia, no Jew could own land; in one place he could not enter a profession, in another could not establish a business, in still another had no right of domicile; and everywhere, he lived in terror of the petty tyranny of the governor. Yet in spite of this systematic oppression, the Jews in Russia multiplied and prospered in any trade or profession open to them. Even the penal laws were ineffectual against their "superior mental equipment," forcing them into activities where sometimes they survived to the detriment of their neighbors. It was only when the Russian government changed its tactics, deliberately encouraging mob violence as a means of expulsion, that the Jews finally fled the country.[13]

This was the formative experience of the latest generation of Jewish immigrants in England. Their adversities were the source of their virtues:

> Social isolation has perfected home life; persecution has intensified religious fervour, an existence of unremitting toil, and a rigid observance of the moral precepts and sanitary and dietary regulations of the Jewish religion have favoured the growth of sobriety, personal purity, and a consequent power of physical endurance.[14]

Having been deprived of a secular education, the Jews focused all their thoughts and feelings in their own literature: in the Old Testament, with its "magnificent promises of universal dominion," and in the Talmud, with its "minute instructions as to the means of gaining it." The Talmud was a veritable encyclopedia of law, civil and penal, human and divine—a Jewish *Corpus Juris*. Beyond that law, the pious

Jew recognized no obligations: "The laws and customs of the Christians are so many regulations to be obeyed, evaded, set at naught, or used according to the possibilities and expediencies of the hour."[15]

Here and throughout the essay, one finds a curious mixture of fanciful idealism and plainspoken realism. The child is described sitting on its mother's lap lisping passages from the Talmud; the old man is seen tottering to his grave still seeking in it the secret of existence. But the Jews are also said to have obeyed or evaded Christian laws as expediency dictated. To Webb, these characteristics were entirely compatible. The same circumstances that made the Jews so meticulous in the observance of their own laws and customs made them less than respectful of the laws and customs of Christian societies, where they had managed to survive a long history of persecution only by a strategy of obedience tempered by evasion. She hastened to add that she was speaking only of the recent immigrants whose habits had been formed in that hostile environment—not of the older Jewish community, which had long enjoyed the freedom, culture, and public spirit of English life.

Beatrice Webb had a strong religious streak, so it is not surprising to find her appreciative of Jewish religion—all the more because she saw it as her kind of religion, a this-worldly one. The strength of Judaism, as she described it, was that it provided "a law of life on this earth, sanctioned by the rewards and punishments of this world."[16] The Beth Din, the highest judicial authority of the Jewish community, adjudicated not only religious questions but also family quarrels, trade and labor disputes, and the other practical problems of everyday life. And the local community organizations, the Chevrahs—"self-creating, self-supporting, and self-governing"—were part synagogue, part school, part social center, part benefit club assisting their members in times of sickness or death. Although the poorest class of Jews did not belong to Chevrahs, they clung "with an almost superstitious tenacity to the habits and customs of their race." And although the class itself was permanent, the individuals were in a constant state of flux, the older immigrants rising out of it while newer immigrants entered it. Even the poorest Jews were not without resources, for they were united to the Jewish middle and upper classes by "a downward stream of charity and personal service, a benevolence at once so widespread and so thorough-going, that it fully justifies the saying, 'All Israel are brethren.' "[17]

Jewish benevolence was also of a distinctive kind. The Jewish Free School, the largest school of its kind in all of England, was an admirable example of Jewish charity. And the Jewish Board of Guardians compared favorably with its English equivalent in supervising public relief. Privately organized and financed, it raised £13,000–£14,000 annually, of which only £2,000 was given in the familiar form of poor relief—money or vouchers for the purchase of coal, clothes, or other necessities. Small sums went for emigration, sanitary inspection, and the like, but the bulk was given to individuals as capital for trade and business. The intention was to enable the recipients to become self-supporting, and the success of this policy was such that of the 3,313 cases dealt with by the board in 1887, only 268 had previously been applicants. As a result, there was not in the Jewish community, as there was in England at large, a "chronically parasitic class of 'paupers.' " Because of "the character of those who take" or "the method of those who give," Jewish charity did not have the demoralizing effects that relief had for the rest of the population.[18]

Most of the immigrants did not require communal assistance, or if they did, it was only briefly and intermittently, since the process of acculturation was usually rapid. The "greenest" of the immigrants eked out a bare existence either from the charity of coreligionists or by working long hours in return for a place to sleep and a loaf of bread. After a short while, having learned a trade, the worker found a job where he received some pittance of pay. Within a year he had joined a Chevrah, and if he managed to resist the "Jewish passion for gambling," he was on his way to becoming a "tiny capitalist," earning a living by his own labor and by that of a few employees. He and his family lived modestly and decently. He never went to a public house, although he did enjoy an occasional glass of rum and a game of cards with friends. He treated his wife with "courtesy and tenderness," and their chief concern was their children. "In short, he has become a law-abiding and self-respecting citizen of our great metropolis, and feels himself the equal of a Montefiore or a Rothschild."[19]

This achievement, Webb claimed, was all the greater because it was in stark contrast to the condition of many of the inhabitants of the East End. Why, in the midst of the "very refuse of our population," were the Jews so successful? In large part, she replied, because of their intellectual superiority. The Jews were not, to be sure, "cultured," in the sense of having a wide knowledge and appreciation of other cultures. But they did have a deep knowledge and appreciation of their own culture, which had stimulated their faculties of memory, reason, and calculation. Moreover, these faculties existed among all classes of Jews, for there was a striking equality among them and a uniformly high level of intellectual achievement. Unlike Christian nations with their sharp class distinctions, "the children of Israel are a nation of priests." Moreover, these intellectual accomplishments, originating in their religious training, had been intensified by a process of natural selection, the long history of persecution having had the effect of weeding out the less competent and the less intelligent. In contrast to their English neighbors, the Jews in the East End were a "race of brain-workers." Manual labor was only the first rung of the ladder, to be left behind by the enterprising manufacturer, merchant, or moneylender—provided, of course, that they did not fall prey to that "vice of the intellect," gambling.[20]

Their intellectual superiority was only one factor contributing to their success. More important was the "moral and physical regimen" that every pious Jew, male and female, was subjected to from birth. It was a regimen that "favours the full development of the bodily organs, protects them from abuse and disease, and stimulates the growth of physical self-control and mental endurance." Unlike Christianity and Buddhism, which seek spiritual exaltation through the mortification of the flesh, Jewish religious and dietary laws are intended not as a preparation for another world but as a means of surviving and thriving in this world. This moral discipline was centered on the family; it prescribed obedience toward parents, devotion to children, the chastity of girls, and the support and protection of wives. The religious Jew was "a being at once moral and sensual; a creature endowed with the power of physical endurance, but gifted with a highly-trained and well-regulated appetite for sensuous enjoyment."[21]

It was this unique combination—of intellectual aptitude, moral rectitude, and physical stamina—that accounted for the Jews' success. At a time when physical health, intellectual acquisition, and material prosperity were so highly esteemed, it was no wonder that "the chosen people, with three thousand years of training, should in some instances realize the promise made by Moses to their forefathers: 'Thou shalt drive out nations mightier than thyself, and thou shalt take their land as an inheritance.' "[22]

The success of the Jewish immigrants was naturally resented, as was the fact that, for all their virtues, they were
deficient in "that highest and latest development of human
sentiment—social morality." This did not mean that they
violated the laws of either society or commerce. On the
contrary, they were the most law-abiding inhabitants of the
East End. They were so for good reason, because they knew
that " 'law and order' and the 'sanctity of contract' are the
sine qua non of a full and free competition in the open market," and that they themselves could succeed "by competition, and by competition alone." But while they observed
the law and fulfilled their contracts, they were unrestrained
by considerations of personal dignity, class loyalty, or trade
integrity. The Jewish immigrant might accept less pay than
other workers, the small manufacturer might produce
shoddy goods, the moneylender might take advantage of
the weaknesses of his customers. But if they fell short of
that higher "social morality," they observed the strictest
standards of personal morality and of familial and communal obligations. This was the distinctively Jewish ethos, as
Webb saw it. And it was also the distinctively capitalist
ethos.

> Thus the immigrant Jew, fresh from the sorrowful ex-
> periences typical of the history of his race, seems to
> justify by his existence those strange assumptions
> which figured for *man* in the political economy of
> Ricardo—an Always Enlightened Selfishness, seeking
> employment or profit with an absolute mobility of
> body and mind, without pride, without preference,
> without interests outside the struggle for the existence
> and welfare of the individual and the family.[23]

*   *   *

The Jew as Ricardian man, economic man, *homo economicus*. Where have we heard that before? From Karl Marx, for one, whose essay "On the Jewish Question," published in 1844, has had more echoes in the socialist movement than some socialists would like to think. There has been much controversy about whether that essay is anti-Semitic or merely anticapitalist. But since Marx equated the Jew with the capitalist—not accidentally or circumstantially but metaphysically and religiously—the distinction is insignificant. Certainly the effect is unambiguously hostile.

> What is the profane basis of Judaism? Practical need, self-interest. What is the worldly cult of the Jew? Huckstering. What is his worldly god? Money. Very well: then in emancipating itself from huckstering and money, and thus from real and practical Judaism, our age would emancipate itself. . . .
>
>   Money is the jealous god of Israel, beside which no other god may exist. . . . The bill of exchange is the real god of the Jew. His god is only an illusory bill of exchange.[24]

It is interesting to compare Marx's image of the Jew with Beatrice Webb's. Both saw the Jew as the personification of economic man, but Webb's image of that man, unlike Marx's, is sympathetic, even admiring. This is all the more interesting because she was at this time, if not a full-fledged socialist, at least an incipient one. She was, however, a *Victorian* socialist, and a Victorian more than a socialist. It was the Victorian in her that responded favorably to those values—hard work, thrift, intelligence, rationality, sobriety, fidelity, self-reliance, self-discipline, respect for the law, devotion to family and community—that she saw as conducive to economic improvement and to a decent, moral existence. Her economic man, the economic man she identified with the Jew, exemplified an "Always Enlightened Selfishness": enlightened because his "selfishness" embraced his family and community (he took upon himself the care of the poorer members of his community); because it promoted values that were in the interest of society as well as of himself; and because those values were not only socially desirable but also good in themselves—they were virtues for all men at all times. She could have paid no greater tribute to the Jew *cum* economic man than to say of her own beloved father, a successful businessman (a "venture capitalist," we would now call him), that "he believed in the Jewish maxim—a maxim he often cited—that a bargain is not a good bargain unless it pays both sides."[25]*

There is nothing enlightened or commendable in Marx's portrait of the Jew as economic man. On the contrary, his Jew embodied the principle of "egoism" or "self-interest," which is an "antisocial element" and the primary source of "alienation." Money is the Jewish god, and "money is the alienated essence of man's work and existence; this essence dominates him and he worships it." Money deprives both humanity and nature of their "proper value"; it "abases" all other gods and turns everything into "commodities." Even the "species-relation itself, the relation between man and woman," is reduced to a commodity. This is what Marx made of the much vaunted Jewish family life. The wife,

---

* There is one ambivalent note in Webb's account. The socialist-to-be could not resist pointing out that the "Hebrew economist" who promoted this image of economic man also doomed most manual workers to a "bare subsistence wage." The allusion, of course, is to Ricardo's "iron law of wages." Socialists commonly cited David Ricardo as the archetypical political economist, rather than Adam Smith, who, so far from holding to an iron law of wages, believed that the wages of even the lowest class would rise in an expanding economy.

whom Beatrice Webb depicted as loved, protected, and respected, was for Marx nothing but an "object of commerce," a woman to be "bartered away."[26]

For both Marx and Webb, the Jew as economic man had the most intimate relationship to the Jew as religious man. But Marx saw in the Jew nothing but economic man; the "real Jew" was not the "sabbath Jew" but the "everyday Jew"—materialistic, egoistic, alienated, dehumanized.[27] For Webb, the Jew epitomized religious man as well as economic man; his religion had a spiritual integrity as well as a social utility. And it is this spiritual quality that she valued as much as the social ethos.

Webb respected the Jew *qua* religious man because she respected religion as such. One of the great tragedies of her early life was that she was unable to reconcile religion and socialism: the religion that she believed to be the end and purpose of existence, and the socialism that she saw as the rational means of reforming and reorganizing society. (She finally found that reconciliation in the Soviet Union, which made a "religion," as she saw it, of the new "scientific" socialist order.)[28] Yet her own sense of religiosity was as firm as her commitment to socialism. She regularly prayed at home and less regularly attended services and took communion at St. Paul's. She had a high regard, therefore, for the Jew who also prayed, attended services, and observed the laws and rites of his religion. Religion was no "illusion" to her—not her own religion or anyone else's.

She also appreciated, as even a great many nonbelieving Victorians did, the relationship between religion and morality. Valuing morality as highly as the Victorians did, they welcomed any support for morality. And traditionally the strongest support of morality and its ultimate sanction was religion. For Webb, Judaism was an especially effective instrument of morality precisely because it was this-worldly. In a sense, Judaism transcended the duality that she found so disturbing in her own life—the duality between the ends of life and the means of social organization, the first having its source in religion, the second, in reason and science. In Judaism, as she saw it, there was no such dichotomy. Life was all of a piece—religion and reason, ritual and law, the individual and the community, personal salvation and social obligation, moral conduct and economic well-being.

It would be interesting to inquire into the historical accuracy of Beatrice Webb's account of the Jewish immigrant community in England a century ago.[29] On the face of it, one must be skeptical of some of her more effusive statements and sweeping generalizations. There were surely Jews who were drunkards as well as gamblers, who abandoned or maltreated their wives and children, who did not support their poorer brethren, who could not read the Bible let alone the Talmud, who were not notably intelligent, or moral, or pious, or industrious, or successful. There were also, as she must have known, Jews for whom success was an invitation to cease being Jews. But however oversimplified and overdrawn her portrait might be, there is no doubt of the powerful impression made upon her by a community where, as she saw it, morality infused every aspect of life, including the most material and mundane. If there is any determinism in her account, it is an ethical rather than economic determinism. It was not the economic success of the Jews to which she attributed their superior moral character; it was their character that was responsible for their success.

Beatrice Webb was describing not so much the actual Jewish community of the East End as an "ideal type," a "Jewish ethic." In this respect she anticipated by many years the classic work of the genre. It was not until 1904 that Max

Weber wrote the first of the essays that were later translated under the title *The Protestant Ethic and the Spirit of Capitalism*. In that work Judaism was mentioned only in passing, and then only to distinguish between the Judaic ethic, which encouraged a "speculatively oriented adventurous capitalism," and the Protestant or Puritan ethic (Weber often used the terms interchangeably), which was the source of the more rational "bourgeois capitalistic ethic."[30] But his account of the Puritan ethic was very similar to Beatrice Webb's Jewish ethic: a "worldly asceticism" that prescribed a rigorous private as well as social morality.

Several years later, Werner Sombart described essentially the same ethic, this time assigning it specifically to the Jews. The thesis of *The Jews and Modern Capitalism* was that Judaism was the archetype of Puritanism: "The dominating ideas of Puritanism which were so powerful in capitalism were more perfectly developed in Judaism, and were also of course of much earlier date."[31] There is no evidence that Sombart was aware of Webb's essay; his book was a response to Weber's. (Nor is there any evidence that Webb, later in life, read either Weber or Sombart.)[32] Yet the similarities are uncanny. At greater length than Webb and supported by many quotations from the Bible, the Talmud, and the Jewish sages, Sombart described a religion and an ethic that were preeminently rational, based upon a profound respect for intellect, law, contract, morality, family, industry, energy, discipline, sexual restraint, this-worldly asceticism—all of which made for a "rationalization of life" that was peculiarly congenial to capitalism.[33]

The Weber-Sombart theses about the relation between religion and capitalism have become a staple of historical controversy (which makes it all the stranger that Webb has not figured in it, although she anticipated so much of it). The religious terms of the debate vary, focusing alternately on Protestantism and Puritanism, Calvinism and Methodism, Judaism and the Judaic-Christian tradition. And the causal relation between religion and capitalism varies: sometimes it is the religious ethic that is said to inspire the capitalist ethic; sometimes the capitalist ethic that is presumed to determine the religious ethic; sometimes a secular ethic (science or rationalism) that is said to shape both the religious and the capitalist ethic. Moreover, the religious ethic may be construed theologically, in terms of specific doctrinal beliefs, or socially, as a reflection of the practices of the community. But all these variations posit an "ethic" that defines the nature of the society, of the economy, and, more particularly, of that uniquely modern society and economy, capitalism.

It may seem ironic that so sympathetic an account of the Jew as economic man, the ideal type of the capitalist, should have been written by Beatrice Webb, who had long been attracted to the socialism of Auguste Comte and who was soon to become a convert to Fabian socialism. She read *Fabian Essays* as soon as it was published, shortly after her own essay on the Jews appeared, and was especially impressed by Sidney Webb's contribution. Several months later, after meeting with him, she triumphantly announced in her diary: "At last I am a socialist!"[34] But even after she became a socialist, she continued to cherish the values—capitalist values, as she herself recognized—she had found among those poor Jewish immigrants.

It is as if Webb wanted to superimpose those values upon socialism itself—as if the values that make for a successful and ethical capitalism are also the basis of a successful and ethical socialism. The very idea, of course, is self-contradictory. An ethic of "Always Enlightened Selfishness" predicates, as she said of Ricardo, "an absolute mobility of body and mind." And that mobility requires a free, competitive society that places no limits (apart from those set by law) upon the exertions or sacrifices an individual chooses to make and the commensurate rewards he expects to receive. The ethic encourages people to earn as much as they are capable of earning, to save as much of their earnings as they wish, to invest their savings in enterprises they hope will be profitable, to reap the profits of those enterprises and pass them on to their families, and to discharge their communal responsibilities in accord with their voluntary desires. Such an ethic is hardly compatible with the kind of planned, controlled, regulated—regimented, an unfriendly critic might call it—society that was the aim of Fabianism.

Beatrice Webb, as has been observed, was a moralist as well as a socialist. Indeed, she was a socialist because she was a moralist, because she thought that a moral society could come about only by the systematic imposition upon society of values that were in accord with the "Religion of Humanity." These were values that put the claims of society above those of individuals, that made "social values" preeminent over self-interest, and that made society the initiator, arbiter, and enforcer of values. In the Jewish community, she found a very different kind of society, one that was eminently moral but where moral values reposed in the individual, where individuals were encouraged to be responsible, self-reliant, and self-disciplined, and where those values were expressed in their relations to their family, their community, their religion, and, not least, their work.

It is interesting that in her autobiography, written many years later, Webb did not mention the essay on the Jews, although she did speak of her research in the East End (and although this essay was one of the most important products of the "apprenticeship" that was the theme of her autobiography). This curious omission may reflect her growing distrust of the individual—the "average sensual man," as she put it. Such a man could not be trusted to know his own interests, let alone those of society. Therefore he should not be given money when unemployed, lest he spend it "as he chose," and he should not be allowed to select his own doctor when he was sick because he would select one who "interferes least with his habits."[35] Or perhaps she did not mention the essay because, as the good socialist she then was, she did not want to be reminded that the Jewish ethic she had admired so much was also the capitalist ethic, that the same values that made the Jew an "economic man" also made him a moral man, and that capitalism itself had a moral as well as an economic dimension.

Socialists are apt to contrast a precapitalist "moral economy," complete with "just prices" and "just wages," with an amoral (if not immoral) capitalist economy, where prices and wages are determined in the market.[36] Most Victorians had a different conception of both morality and the economy, perhaps because they had more respect for the "average sensual man." Believing the average man to be a moral as well as a sensual man, they also believed that a society of free men was at least as capable of creating a moral economy as was a society governed by economic planners and moral guardians.

Like "Victorian values," the "Jewish values" described by Webb were mundane ones. An ethic of "Always Enlightened Selfishness" takes people as they are and as they always have been, as human beings capable of being enlightened as well as self-interested—enlightened precisely because they are self-interested, because their "self" ("properly understood," as Tocqueville would say, or their "better self," as T. H. Green would have it) naturally embraces family and community, economic interests and moral values. In this sense, Webb's "ideal type" of Jew was more Victorian than Webb herself, the quintessential Fabian.

The New Women and
the New Men

———◆———

From the height of his atheistic nihilism, Nietzsche looked
down on those "English flatheads," those "little moralistic
females à la Eliot," who thought it possible to have a morality without religion. "They are rid of the Christian God
and now believe all the more firmly that they must cling to
Christian morality"; they become "moral fanatics" to compensate for their religious emancipation. For the moment,
"morality is not yet a problem." But it would become a
problem once they discovered that without Christianity
there is no morality. "When one gives up the Christian
faith, one pulls the right to Christian morality out from
under one's feet."[1]

That prediction seemed to come to pass sooner than
Nietzsche might have expected. Even as he wrote, there
was emerging in England a group of men and women who
were not quite "free souls" as he understood the term—he
would have had no more use for them than for the "flatheads" and "fanatics" of an earlier generation—but who did
pride themselves on being liberated from the moral and

sexual conventions of their time. These were the "new" men and women of the 1880s and 1890s. It is fitting that one of these new men, Havelock Ellis, should have written the first serious appreciation of Nietzsche in English, commending him for making the most determined effort to "destroy modern morals" and hailing him as the "greatest spiritual force" since Goethe.[2]

Contemporaries did not use the term "new men," but they did speak of "new women." This expression came into use in the early 1890s, about the same time as "feminist," and like the latter, it can be read backward in time at least to the 1880s. While the two terms were sometimes used interchangeably, they were essentially different. The feminists were women with a cause—or with several causes: the suffrage, education, work, birth control, or some specific reform that was especially pertinent to women. The new women had no particular cause, only the larger, more general cause of social and sexual liberation.

Again, as with "feminist," "new women" was applied to a wide spectrum of women. In its broadest sense, it was used to describe the "fast" young women who wore bloomers, rode bicycles, played tennis and golf, smoked in public, read Shaw and Ibsen, and shocked their elders by conversing about "free love," before settling down to marriage, home, and children. Some contemporaries were aware of what historians are now discovering: that bicycles liberated more women than did the "advanced" ideas of the new women or even the reforms achieved by the feminists. Writing in 1895 in the *Lady Cyclist* (one of the scores of women's journals that flourished in the 1890s), one enthusiast said that cycling was responsible for "a new dawn, a dawn of emancipation."[3] Another woman, a trade union organizer, admitted that "the bicycle is doing more for the independence of women than anything expressly designed to that end." A woman could go cycling unaccompanied by chaperon or maid; it was perhaps the first amusement she took up to please herself and not a man; it required comfortable attire; and it was "absolutely independent, and yet not necessarily unsociable."[4]

There was another kind of woman, however, who wanted more by way of liberation than bicycling, smoking, or reading risqué books—who sought nothing less than sexual liberation—to whom the term "new woman" more pointedly applied. Like most such neologisms, it started as a derisive label and was then adopted by those who were meant to be denigrated by it. By January 1894, it was well established in the popular press. A ditty in one women's journal described the familiar process:

> As "New Woman" is she known.
> 'Tis her enemies have baptized her,
>   But she gladly claims the name;
> Hers it is to make a glory,
>   What was meant should be a shame.[5]

Two months later, the feminist novelist who wrote under the name Sarah Grand published an article in *North American Review* using "new woman" in a favorable sense. The title, "The New Aspect of the Woman Question," made it clear that "new woman" was not simply a new name for the old feminist. The article was widely read in England as well as America and provoked a good deal of controversy, including a hostile reply in a subsequent issue by another, better-known woman novelist, "Ouida," this under the title "The New Woman." Later that year, a play of the same name satirized those women who wanted to make girls into boys and men into maids. "Everything's New nowadays!" a colonel in the play complains. "We have a New Art . . .," whereupon three women chime in, "A New Journalism . . . A New Political Economy . . . A New Morality," to which the colonel adds, "A New Sex!"[6] A few weeks later, a popular penny paper, *Woman* (whose assistant editor was Arnold Bennett and whose motto was "Forward but not too fast"), ran a contest for the best definition of the New Woman. A prize was awarded to the verse:

> *She flouts Love's caresses,*
> *Reforms ladies' dresses,*
> *And scorns the Man-Monster's tirades;*
> *She seems scarcely human,*
> *This mannish "New Woman,"*
> *This "Queen of the Blushless Brigade."*[7]

The "new aspect of the woman question," as Sarah Grand put it, went beyond the old "separate spheres" question into the realm of marriage itself. It was in the 1880s that marriage became an issue—not, to be sure, for the old-style feminists but for the new women. In 1888, the *Westminster Review* (hardly a feminist, let alone a new-woman, organ) published an article by the novelist Mona Caird, describing marriage as a "vexatious failure" and comparing the relation of husband and wife to that of master and servant, without even "the cook's privilege of being able to give warning." The *Daily Telegraph* put the question to its readers: "Is Marriage a Failure?" and received 27,000 letters in reply.[8]

Scores of novels appeared on the subject, creating almost a new genre, the new-woman novel. The progenitor of the type was Olive Schreiner's *The Story of an African Farm* (1883). The main plot features a young woman, Lyndall, who leaves her respectable but weak and unmanly fiancé (a "man-woman") to go off with a romantic stranger whom she refuses to marry, in spite of her pregnancy, lest she lose her freedom. Her child dies shortly after birth, and she herself falls ill. The novel ends when her rejected fiancé (disguised as a female nurse) finds her dying, alone in a strange town, still refusing to marry her lover, firm in her resolve to be independent (although she does receive generous sums of money from him). Yet her passion for independence, which has proved so costly, is itself equivocal. "Will nothing free me from myself? . . . I want to love! I want something great and pure to lift me to itself! . . . One day I will love something utterly, and then I will be better." Hallucinating on her deathbed, she explains to her lover why she cannot marry him: "I must know and see, I cannot be bound to one whom I love as I love you." One day, however, she hopes to find "something nobler and stronger than I, before which I can kneel down . . . something to worship."[9]

The novel was a great favorite not only of the new women but of the old feminists as well. Feminists today tend to be less enthusiastic, some finding in it vestiges of racism and others complaining of unsympathetic, stereotypical women characters.[10] The introduction to a recent edition, referring to these criticisms, observes that "Politics and poetics seem not to have made a satisfying match."[11] Even at the time, the social implications of the book were sufficiently ambiguous to permit someone like Gladstone to be counted among its admirers; perhaps he was pleased by the thoroughly depressing denouement of the novel— hardly a recommendation for the kind of freedom espoused by the heroine.

Another vastly popular novel (it went through twenty printings within a few months) was by a man: Grant Allen's *The Woman Who Did* (1895). The heroine, Herminia Barton, falls in love with a man who wants to marry her, but, scorning marriage as a form of "vile slavery," she persuades him to live with her without going through the degrading wedding ceremony. She is not, however, the author assures us, one of "that blatant and decadent sect of 'advanced women' who talk as though motherhood were a disgrace and a burden, instead of being, as it is, the full realization of woman's faculties." On the contrary, she looks forward to having children who will enjoy "the unique and glorious birthright of being the only human beings ever born into the world as the deliberate result of a free union, contracted on philosophical and ethical principles." She gives birth to a child, soon after her lover's death, and rears her in her own principles, hoping that she will represent the "apostolate of women" destined to "regenerate humanity" from aeons of slavery. Encouraged to think for herself, her daughter does so by coming to value all the things her mother despises— respectability, convention, material goods, social status. In the climactic scene, the daughter informs her mother that she cannot marry the man she loves so long as her mother is alive, whereupon the mother commits suicide, thereby freeing her daughter to marry—an ironic conclusion to a book ostensibly praising liberation from marriage.[12]

The book was widely read and roundly denounced, not only by conventional reviewers but by some feminists for whom the very idea of sexual liberation was anathema. Millicent Fawcett accused Allen of contributing nothing to the true causes of women's emancipation—the suffrage, work, and social equality. The liberation he preached "would amount to libertinage, not to liberty; it would mean the immeasurable degradation of women; it would reduce to anarchy the most momentous of human relationships—the relation between husband and wife and parents and children."[13] A feminist critic today is outraged for the opposite reason. Speculating that Allen was really an "antifeminist," Elaine Showalter cites an article he had written a few years earlier, in which he had argued "for motherhood before self-fulfillment."[14] One might suspect him of writing a deliberate parody of the new woman, were it not for his evident contempt for the daughter and the "Mammon-worshipping" society she represents, whose religion is "the united worship of Success and Respectability." The mother, on the other hand, emerges as utopian and naive, but also as thoroughly principled and honorable, a "martyr to humanity."[15]

George Gissing's *The Odd Women* (1893) is of an entirely different order, both as a literary work and as a novel of ideas. One might not agree with George Orwell that it is "one of the best novels in English," but there is no question of its superiority to the typical new-woman novel.[16] The "odd women" of the title are odd in different ways. Two of the sisters are odd, Gissing later explained, in the sense in which one speaks of an "odd glove";[17] they are "redundant" women—unmarried and unemployed (or precariously and inadequately employed). A third sister, Monica, does get married, partly out of desperation, to an older man and finally leaves him when he proves to be obsessively possessive. An abortive love affair (it is never consummated) ends with her dying while giving birth to her husband's child, a child he refuses to acknowledge as his own.

The two other principal women characters, Mary Barfoot and Rhoda Nunn, run an agency designed to prepare redundant women like the sisters for gainful employment. Mary is a conventional feminist with strong feelings about women's work but not about marriage. It is Rhoda who carries the burden of the new-woman theme. Determined to be truly independent, she is wary of any emotional, let alone marital, ties, is almost ascetic in her mode of life and somewhat masculine in her demeanor. Rhoda becomes involved with Mary's cousin, Everard Barfoot, who would seem to be her perfect match. He is the new man to her new woman. "Marry in the legal sense I never shall," he informs her before there is any talk of a relationship between them. "My companion must be as independent of forms as I am myself."[18] She assures him that she too has no intention of marrying, that she wants only to devote herself to the odd women who require her help. When he later proposes that they live together without being married, she at first declines, suspecting (with good cause, in view of rumors about his past) that his refusal of marriage testifies to the shallow and ephemeral nature of his love. She then accepts, although only on the condition of marriage, ostensibly to test him but in fact betraying her own ideal as well as his. When he, in turn, concedes to marriage, she refuses, repeating her initial objections and implying that his reversal signifies a lack of faith. The denouement has her remaining a lonely, unmarried woman (an odd woman), while he promptly marries a conventional young woman of good social standing.

Thomas Hardy's *Jude the Obscure* (1896) is a more distinguished specimen of this genre. In the original preface to the book, Hardy tried to forestall criticism by insisting that while his novel dealt with "the strongest passion known to humanity," there was nothing in it "to which exception can be taken."[19] Exception was taken, however, and in the postscript to a later edition, instead of concealing his radical intentions, Hardy made the most of them. A German critic, he was pleased to report, had described the novel as the first fictional representation of "the woman of the feminist movement—the slight, pale 'bachelor' girl—the intellectualized, emancipated bundle of nerves that modern conditions were producing, mainly in cities."[20]

That is a good description of Sue Bridehead, the heroine

of the novel—not a feminist, however, but a new woman. When Sue quotes John Stuart Mill, it is not his essays on enfranchisement but *On Liberty*: "She, or he"—Sue improves upon Mill—"who lets the world, or his own portion of it, choose his plan of life for him, has no need of any other faculty than the ape-like one of imitation." Rejecting that conformist role, Sue feels free to leave her husband and live with Jude. She does not, however, live with him as man and wife. "Put it down to my timidity," she explains—by which she means, in spite of her brave professions of independence, her conventionality. After both Sue and Jude get divorces (Jude's wife having left him many years earlier), they continue to live together, although without going through a marriage ceremony and without having sexual relations—the former because she believes marriage to be a "hopelessly vulgar institution," an "iron contract" that would extinguish their love; and the latter because, Jude suggests, she has so little "animal passion" (or, the reader suspects, because of her lingering "timidity").[21] They do, finally, live together as man and wife, in fact although not in law (they pretend to be married, but she still refuses to go through the ceremony), and they have two children, in addition to the child from his former marriage whom they raise.

Because people suspect they are not married, Jude is fired from one job after another, the family is constantly on the move, and they are finally at the point of near-starvation and homelessness. The oldest boy, Jude's child, wanting to help and believing that it is the children's fault the family is in such dire condition, kills the other two children and himself. In a grotesque scene, Sue and Jude find their bodies hanging from clothes hooks on a door. This is not the end of the story, however, for it is followed by a series of anticlimaxes that come perilously close to reducing the tragedy to something like a farce. Sue, who had been a confirmed atheist (this had been part of her liberation), finds religion, returns to her husband, and forces herself to sleep with him in spite of her revulsion. Jude, who had earlier hoped to study for the ministry, becomes bitterly antireligious and is tricked into remarrying his former wife, who has also (after leading a rather disreputable life) found religion.

Starting as a free spirit, Sue turns out to be the unwitting evil spirit of the novel, blighting the lives of everyone she touches, driven not by "animal passion" but by ideological passion—a passion all the more destructive for being so inchoate and inconstant. Early in the novel, Sue describes herself as "a woman tossed about, all alone, with aberrant passions, and unaccountable antipathies"; and Jude, just before the terrible hanging scene, reflects: "I was, perhaps, after all, a paltry victim to the spirit of mental and social restlessness, that makes so many unhappy in these days!" Afterward Sue explains the tragedy:

> We went about loving each other too much—indulging ourselves to utter selfishness with each other! We said—do you remember?—that we would make a virtue of joy. I said it was Nature's intention, Nature's law and *raison d'être* that we should be joyful in what instincts she afforded us—instincts which civilization had taken upon itself to thwart. What dreadful things I said! And now Fate has given us this stab in the back for being such fools as to take Nature at her word![22]

Even here, however, Sue has not yet taken the full measure of the tragedy. For all her talk of nature, there is precious little that is natural, let alone joyous, in her life, either at the beginning or at the end. And Jude, for his part, while initially defending "civilization" (religion, convention, marriage) against her "nature," is finally so embittered that he turns against both civilization and nature.

If Sue's repudiation of nature makes the novel read like a polemic against the new woman, Jude's repudiation of civilization made contemporaries regard it as a profoundly subversive work. One reviewer dubbed it "Jude the Obscene," while another, the novelist Margaret Oliphant, attacked its "grossness, indecency, and horror"; it was, she said, "an assault on the stronghold of marriage, which is now beleaguered on every side."[23]* Hardy himself felt so beleaguered by the harsh criticism he received that he never wrote another novel.

There were real new women, as well as fictional ones, in late-Victorian England. If the heroine of *African Farm* was a dubious "role model" for the liberated woman, Olive Schreiner herself was no more satisfactory. Unlike her heroine, who thought that true love could be realized only outside of marriage, in a state of "perfect freedom," Schreiner professed to believe that it could, and ideally should, be realized in marriage. She could not imagine, she wrote—apparently forgetting Lyndall's passionate proclamations—how anyone could deduce from her writings that she thought lightly of marriage. "I think it to be the most holy, the most organic, the most important sacrament in life, and how men and women can enter into it with the lighthearted indifference they do, has always been, and is, a matter of endless wonder to me."[24]

---

* To that arch-antifeminist D. H. Lawrence, the novel was an assault not on marriage but on manhood. Sue represented everything in woman that he most hated and feared: "Her female spirit did not wed with the male spirit. . . . Her spirit . . . wished to become the male spirit. . . . One of the supremest products of our civilization is Sue, and a product that well frightens us."[25]

Unhappily, her ideals, both of love and of marriage, fell far short of the reality in her own life. When she left South Africa for England in 1881, she was twenty-six, having already written *African Farm* as well as the drafts of two other novels. She soon fell in with a set of like-minded free spirits, including the writer Havelock Ellis and the eugenicist Karl Pearson. Ellis, she soon discovered, had "advanced" theories about sex but was himself notably deficient in sexual desire or potency. Although he was married and had many "relationships" (the word is his),[26] it is not certain that he consummated any of them or, for that matter, his marriage (his wife was a lesbian); certainly his affair with Schreiner remained "platonic."* Another of her great friends in that circle was Edward Carpenter, who was homosexual.

Schreiner's most passionate attachment was to Pearson, founder of the Men and Women's Club, whose meetings she regularly attended and which prided itself on dealing with such issues as marriage and sexuality in a liberated spirit. Although she candidly expressed her feelings for Pearson, he made it clear that he did not reciprocate them, insisting that their relationship remain purely intellectual, "man to man," with no "sex element" in it.[27] She pretended to acquiesce in this arrangement but was deeply hurt,

---

* Such sexual impulses as Ellis had were aroused by the sight of women urinating; it was he who named this phenomenon: "undinism" or "urolagnia." To a disciple of Ellis, Freud said that "a certain degree of neurosis" was of inestimable value to a psychologist, and that Ellis must have had "some sexual abnormality, else he would never have devoted himself to the field of sex research." Freud hastened to add: "You might of course say the same of me, but I would answer that it is first of all nobody's business, and second of all it is not true." When this was reported to Ellis, he agreed that this was true of many "sex-obsessed" people but accepted Freud's assurance that it was not true of him, and "neither is it true of me!"[28]

all the more so because unlike some of her other men friends, Pearson was neither asexual nor homosexual. (He later married another member of the club.)

This unsatisfactory relationship undoubtedly contributed to Schreiner's breakdown in 1886. Her love for Pearson was probably also responsible for her rejection of the one suitor who presented himself at this time. Echoing Lyndall in *African Farm*, she explained: "I must be free, you know, I must be *free*. I've been free all my life." She did believe in marriage: "No kind of sex relationship can be good and pure but marriage." But she herself could marry only if she met a man "mentally, morally, emotionally, practically" stronger than she was—and her suitor patently was not that. To Pearson, however (perhaps to reassure him that she had no marital designs upon him), she confessed that marriage was not for her: "I am not a marrying woman; when it comes to the point my blood curdles and my heart is like stone."[29]

She did marry, however. Restless and discontented, she returned to South Africa in 1889, and at the age of thirty-nine married a devoted and docile man (not unlike the fiancé of her novel), who took her name, sold his farm, and otherwise tried to accommodate her needs and various ailments. (Her asthma afflicted her not only on the farm but elsewhere when they tried to live together, which suggests to some biographers that the condition was psychosomatic.) The death of her only child (life imitating art, her infant, like Lyndall's, lived only a few hours), several miscarriages, her inability to complete the novel that was meant to recoup her reputation and fortune, and her husband's growing resentment at the difficulties she placed in the way of his career put an intolerable strain on the marriage, and they lived apart even while they were both in South Africa. Just before the First World War she returned to England without him, while insisting, as she did until the end of her life, that they were truly and happily married.

Her only substantial book, apart from *African Farm,* was *Women and Labour* (1911), called by her biographers the "Bible of the Woman's Movement,"[30] but not at all the creative work that was expected of the author of *African Farm.* She did some other casual writing and continued to work on the two uncompleted novels that occupied her virtually her entire lifetime. She was so dissatisfied with them that she never published them; when they appeared posthumously, her judgment was vindicated. During the war she became involved in the pacifist movement, but for the most part she lived the lonely life of a semi-invalid. When her husband finally sought her out (again, a reprise of *African Farm*), he found her alone, ill, greatly aged, almost unrecognizable. That reunion too was short-lived, for she then decided to return, without him, to South Africa to die.

A good friend of Olive Schreiner and of the other liberated men and women in that circle was Eleanor Marx, Karl Marx's daughter. In a sense, she was a new woman more by default than by desire. While she had all the proper "advanced" ideas about sex and marriage, she herself would dearly have loved to be married and have children. Like George Eliot, she assumed the name of the man whom she would have married had he not already had a wife. But unlike Eliot, who had a loving and loyal (if not legal) mate, Eleanor Marx was unfortunate enough to become involved with a thoroughly disreputable and unscrupulous man—a "cad," the Victorians would have said. "Dr." Edward Aveling (as he called himself and as he was generally addressed, for no good reason) was a disciple of Marx and a figure of some importance in socialist circles. He was also an incorrigible philanderer, liar, debtor, schemer, and, probably, embezzler of party funds. (He was also, by all accounts, ugly—"repulsive," another socialist called him.)[31] After fourteen years of a miserable pseudo marriage in which Eleanor Marx was entirely faithful to him, Aveling's wife died, whereupon he promptly married another woman, concealing that marriage from Marx and continuing to harass her for money she did not have. Shortly afterward, probably when she found out about his new marriage, she committed suicide with chloroform, which had been purchased, it was suspected, by Aveling himself.* She died in 1898, at the age of forty-three, only two months before Aveling, who succumbed to the consumption that she had faithfully nursed him through earlier.

The disjunction between principle and practice was nowhere more conspicuous than here. In 1886, Eleanor Marx-Aveling (as she signed herself) and Edward Aveling collaborated on an essay, "The Woman Question," which appeared in the *Westminster Review* and was then published as a pamphlet. Taking as its text the English translation of a book by the German socialist August Bebel, *Woman—Past, Present and Future,* the essay presented the conventional Marxist view of marriage as a purely economic arrangement and women as an oppressed class. Just as workers were subject to the "organised tyranny of idlers," so women were to the "organised tyranny of men." Marriage was

---

* There were other suicides among the new women: the poet Adela Nicholson and the poet and novelist Amy Levy. Levy was a feminist and socialist whom Eleanor Marx befriended and whose novel, *Reuben Sachs,* she translated into German. Levy sought to be liberated not only from the conventional female role but also from everything else that defined her—her Jewishness, her family, her bourgeois background, even, it has been suggested, her sex. She was talented and extraordinarily prolific, having published three novels, three collections of poetry, and several essays and short stories by the time of her death, at the age of twenty-eight, in 1889.[32]

based upon "commercialism," weddings were "business transactions," and prostitution was the result of the "surplus labour population" produced by capitalism. Any deferral of marriage was as intolerable as marriage itself, since chastity was a crime against nature. (Here the authors cited the authority not of Bebel but of Shakespeare and Shelley).[33]

The only remedy to this inhuman state of affairs, the Avelings agreed, was a socialist revolution that would bring a new economic system and with it a total change in the condition of women. In that new era, "wage-slavery" would disappear, the state would be abolished, and women would be the equal of men, independent and free. There would be no public contract of marriage, no prostitution, and no need for divorce. Nor would there be "the hideous disguise, the constant lying, that makes the domestic life of almost all our English homes an organised hypocrisy." Whether monogamy or polygamy would prevail under socialism, they did not presume to predict, but they themselves believed that "monogamy will gain the day," for the highest ideal was "the complete, harmonious, lasting blending of two human lives," "the cleaving of one man to one woman." All that was necessary for the realization of that ideal were "love, respect, intellectual likeness, and command of the necessities of life."[34]

It is an extraordinary testament, first in its affirmation of monogamy rather than free love as the ideal of the future, and then in its description of the lying, hypocrisy, and commercialism characterizing conventional marriage—a description that was uncomfortably applicable to their own relationship. What is difficult to understand is why a strongminded, strong-willed woman like Eleanor Marx put up with it, why she denied herself the freedom that she espoused in principle and that was so readily attainable (it would not even have required the formality of a divorce, and there were no children to bind her)—why finally she chose death rather than freedom.

It is curious that another of the notorious philanderers in this circle, H. G. Wells, was also physically unprepossessing, although he had no difficulty attracting a series of talented and handsome young women, one of whom remained his long-suffering, good-natured wife (second wife, actually) for almost thirty years. During all that time, while he engaged in one affair after another, they maintained their marriage and household, which included their two sons. (He had two other, illegitimate children, with different women.) His wife met his mistresses socially and seemed not to object to his keeping their pictures in the house. At one time he was involved with two women at the same time, so that his friends were not certain which one he had run off with to the Continent. His most celebrated relationship, with Rebecca West, came later, shortly before the war. West thought of herself as a new woman, until she found, to her dismay, that the position of a single mother was distinctly unliberating—indeed, more confining and abasing than that of the conventionally married woman, for she and her child were tucked away in a cottage in the countryside, without friends and, for long periods, without the companionship of Wells.

Earlier in his career, soon after his second marriage, Wells wrote a sharp critique of Grant Allen's *The Woman Who Did,* which he interpreted as a defense of free love. But it was monogamy, Wells protested, not free love, that was in the best interests of women. Monogamy had always been regarded as a restraint primarily upon men, "a fetter upon virile instincts." What women needed was freedom not from monogamy or marriage but from "the narrowness, the sexual savagery, the want of charity" of some marriages.

His [Allen's] proposal is to abolish cohabitation, to abolish the family—that school of all human gentleness—and to provide support for women who may have children at the expense of the State. We are all to be foundlings together, and it will be an inquisitive child who knows its own father.[35]

Quoting this review many years later in his *Autobiography*, Wells was reminded of the very harsh notice Rebecca West had written of one of his own books; it was this that had first brought her to his attention. It did not occur to him that his comments on marriage and monogamy were prescient of his own relationships, not only with West but with his other lovers, who were ill served by a doctrine of free love that liberated his "virile instincts" far more than their feminine ones. Even more pertinent were his comments on the abolition of the family, when it would be "an inquisitive child who knows its own father"—a poignant reminder of the child he had with West, who did not, in fact, know his father until his adolescence. (The child was also told that his mother was his "aunt.")[36]

The other new women in this circle adapted to liberation in other ways. Edith Bland, better known as Edith Nisbet, the famous author of children's stories, managed to be a prolific writer and, like her husband, an active member of the Fabian Society, at the same time that she carried on a succession of love affairs and coped with her husband's castoffs. She befriended one of his former lovers and brought up the child he had with another; when Wells later tried to seduce that child, he was repulsed by an outraged father.

This saga of sexual liberation and betrayal is the subject of a recent book by Ruth Brandon, *The New Women and the Old Men*, which might more accurately have been entitled

"The New Women and the New Men." The men these women were involved with were not, in fact, "old men"— the familiar Victorian patresfamilias. They were "new men" who rejected that conventional role even as the women rejected theirs. The paterfamilias, whatever other shortcomings he might have, did assume the responsibilities and obligations that, in the traditional ethos, had the effect of mitigating authority and patriarchy. The new man disavowed those responsibilities and obligations together with the ethos that sustained them.

Fortunately for those women (including most feminists) who found satisfaction as well as security within marriage, the gospel of sexual liberation was confined to a very small circle. Even within that circle, it was recognized that that mode of life was appropriate for only a select few, those superior souls capable of throwing off the shackles of bourgeois convention. When Everard Barfoot, the archetypical new man in Gissing's novel, declared that he would never marry, that his companion must be as "independent of forms" as he himself was, he quickly added: "I don't advocate this liberty for all mankind. Only for those who are worthy of it."[37] But even for the worthiest, as he himself, and Rhoda still more, eventually realized, that ideal was fraught with difficulty and finally abandoned.

What the new women, in life as in fiction, too often discovered was that their sexual liberation was not very liberating, that what promised to be freedom turned out to be a new and possibly worse form of oppression. They would have agreed with Jude that Sue had suffered even more than he had. "The woman mostly gets the worst of it in the long run!"[38]

If the old feminists disapproved of these new women (to say nothing of the new men), the father of feminism would have been still more appalled by them. When John Stuart Mill spoke admiringly in *On Liberty* of "experiments in living," he did not have in mind sexual experiments, still less anything like sexual libertinism. Shortly before his death in 1873 (a few years before the emergence of the new women), Mill declared himself confident that the "force of natural passions" had been greatly exaggerated and that the advance of civilization would bring with it a diminution of sexuality.

> I think it most probable that this particular passion will become with men, as it is already with a larger number of women, completely under the control of the reason. It has become so with women because its becoming so has been the condition upon which women hoped to obtain the strongest love and admiration of men. . . . Men are by nature capable of as thorough a control over these passions as women are.[39]

Mill went on to say that he knew "eminent medical men, and lawyers of logical mind" who agreed with him. He might have been thinking of his own father, whom he elsewhere described as looking forward to "a considerable increase of freedom in the relations between the sexes"—a freedom, however, that had no connection with "sensuality either of a theoretical or of a practical kind." One of the beneficial effects of freedom, his father anticipated, would be to liberate the imagination and feelings from dwelling upon "the physical relation and its adjuncts," which was "one of the deepest seated and most pervading evils in the human mind."[40]

This is the ultimate paradox in a saga replete with paradoxes: that one of the most progressive and enlightened men of the time should have been so much more puritanical than the conventional Victorian, that the author of the most

famous work celebrating liberty should have been so censorious of sexual liberation, and that the most distinguished
advocate of women's emancipation should have been so
unsympathetic to the kind of sexual emancipation sought
by a new generation of new women.*

Mill would have been even more appalled by the liberation sought by another species of new men—the liberation
not only from marriage and monogamy but from conventional morality and, for many, from conventional sexuality.
These free souls called themselves "aesthetes," or, more
provocatively, "decadents." Today they are known as the
fin de siècle movement. Their inspiration, as the name sug-

---

* One is reminded of another eminently progressive and enlightened man, William Godwin, who also believed that the progress
of civilization would culminate in the triumph of reason over
passion. "The tendency of a cultivated and virtuous mind," Godwin wrote in 1793, "is to render us indifferent to the gratification
of sense," and especially to the gratification of a "mere animal
function." Thus enlightened mankind could happily look forward
to the diminution and eventual elimination of all sexuality.[41]
    Godwin also recalls an earlier circle of new men and new
women. His wife, Mary Wollstonecraft, author of *Vindication of
the Rights of Woman,* is a much honored figure in the history of
feminism. She was also a notable new woman in her time, having
had several lovers before meeting Godwin and having twice at-
tempted suicide after being abandoned and left with an illegitimate child. When their daughter later ran off with Shelley, a
married man, Godwin denounced their "licentious love." Shelley
then proceeded to have an affair simultaneously with one of Godwin's stepdaughters (who then took up with Byron and bore his
child), while another of his stepdaughters (Wollstonecraft's child
by an earlier marriage) committed suicide because of her unre-
quited love for Shelley.[42]

gests, came from the French—Baudelaire, Rimbaud, Mallarmé, Huysmans.* Their lineage can also be traced to the English aesthetes of an earlier generation, the Pre-Raphaelites, and more particularly to Walter Pater, whose *Renaissance,* Oscar Wilde told his friend William Butler Yeats, was his own "golden book . . . the very flower of decadence."[43] Pater's aestheticism, however—the cultivation of experience, sensuality, passion, the exotic—although possessing an obvious affinity to the decadents, had a high seriousness, even an ultimate sense of morality, that was lacking in the decadents.[44]

The *fin de siècle* was ushered in with the publication in 1891 of Wilde's *The Picture of Dorian Gray,* which was as close to pure decadence as the movement was to achieve. The book opens almost in a spirit of innocence, a naïve, childlike pleasure in beauty and self. But even then, in that seemingly artless narcissism, there are intimations of tragedy, of "exquisite joys and exquisite sorrows."[45] When Lord Henry, early in the novel, comments on the extraordinary beauty of Dorian as portrayed in the painting, the artist warns him, "We shall all suffer for what the gods have given us, suffer terribly."[46] The gods exact their terrible vengeance, Dorian's narcissism degenerating into extreme hedonism and sensualism and ending with a corruption of mind, soul, and body. Unable to bear the visible evidence of his evil in the painting, Dorian finally slashes it with the

---

* The name "decadents" also came from the French *"décadents."* Their journal, *Le décadent,* ceased publication in 1889, about the time that the English took over that term. Wilde visited the *décadents* in Paris but had difficulty communicating with them since his French accent was so bad. It was Wilde who gave currency, in *The Picture of Dorian Gray,* to the expression *fin de siècle:* " 'Fin de siècle,' murmured Lord Henry. 'Fin du globe,' answered his hostess."[47]

same knife he had used to stab the painter, thus restoring the picture to its original youth and beauty but himself dying in the process, putting the knife in his own heart as his face becomes aged and hideous.

If that final scene was intended to placate public sensibilities by exposing and punishing evil, it failed of its purpose. Dorian's death does not undo or redeem the evil, for it persists in the person of Lord Henry, the satanic tempter, who is still, at the end of the novel, alive and well, witty and urbane, making the rounds in polite society, corrupting others without himself suffering the consequences of his corruption.

Wilde was surely being disingenuous when he wrote Conan Doyle, who had been with him when the story was commissioned by *Lippincott's*: "I cannot understand how they can treat *Dorian Gray* as immoral." And Doyle himself was being, if not disingenuous, then naïve when he described the book as "surely upon a high moral plane."[48] Most of the reviewers thought otherwise, denouncing the book as vicious and, worse, as a sad imitation of the French. They also sensed what the book feebly tried to obscure: the motif of homosexuality. One reviewer went so far as to say that Wilde could write only for "outlawed noblemen and perverted telegraph boys"—an allusion to a recent scandal involving a lord and some post office employees in a male brothel.[49] Wilde had deleted from an earlier version one sentence that was explicitly homosexual and was careful to give the main characters wives or women lovers. Lord Henry (like Wilde himself) is nominally married, at least early in the novel; and Dorian is at first much attracted to Sibyl and is disillusioned only when the real woman emerges from behind the mask of the actress. "Why is your friendship so fatal to young men?" the painter asks Dorian, adding, as if in afterthought, that it was also fatal to young women.[50]

The powerful aura of evil in the book does not come from the barely disguised intimations of homosexuality; it comes from a corruption of soul and spirit that transcends sex. Nor is it the kind of nihilism that might be associated with Nietzsche. Nietzsche went "beyond good and evil" to an affirmation of will and life. Dorian can only affirm evil itself and is thus doomed to decay and death.

The fate of Dorian Gray presaged the fate of Oscar Wilde, and the theme that was veiled in the novel was glaringly exposed in his trials. It was a tragic end for Wilde but not a heroic one. His downfall was precipitated by a libel suit he himself brought, refusing to heed the advice of friends, against the Marquess of Queensberry, Lord Alfred Douglas's father, who had accused him of corrupting his son. Wilde's profession of innocence was belied by the testimony of several young men who admitted blackmailing him, whereupon he himself was arrested and charged with offenses under the Criminal Law Amendment Act (passed only ten years earlier), which prohibited "indecencies" between males.

There was one moment of grace toward the end of the trial when Wilde tried to redeem himself in an eloquent speech on "the love that dare not speak its name." But even then he did not dare speak its name, pretending that it was nothing more than platonic love, "that deep, spiritual affection that is as pure as it is perfect."[51] It was a stirring performance but not quite to the point, for the charge brought against him was not of "spiritual" but of carnal love. The trial was deadlocked by a hung jury, and Wilde had to submit to yet another, when he was convicted and sentenced to two years at hard labor. His best-known poem, written in jail, "The Ballad of Reading Gaol," was not a defense of homosexuality, even in its platonic form, but a passionate indictment of the prison system.

Wilde's conviction was the climactic event in the *fin de siècle* movement, but it did not epitomize the movement as a whole or signal its end. Nor was *Dorian Gray* representative of the movement. *The Yellow Book* was, and that was quite a different matter. The title of the journal, like the name of the movement, was inspired by the French, an allusion to the yellow paperback French novels that the English assumed to be highly salacious.* Although Wilde never wrote for *The Yellow Book,* he was generally identified with it, partly because of the reputation he enjoyed as the archdecadent of the movement and partly because of his association with the art editor, Aubrey Beardsley, who had earlier illustrated his *Salome.* The two had fallen out, however, which was why Wilde was not invited to contribute to the journal. It is ironic that a by-product of Wilde's disgrace was Beardsley's dismissal from the magazine. When Wilde was arrested in 1895, he was reported as carrying *The Yellow Book* under his arm, and the publishers, fearful of the effect of the scandal, decided to sacrifice Beardsley. (In fact, Wilde was carrying a yellow-covered French novel.)

After *Dorian Gray, The Yellow Book* was an anticlimax. The first issue, in April 1894, had a story by Henry James and contributions by such other respectable members of the intellectual establishment as the president of the Royal Academy and an Eton schoolmaster. The only parts of it that could possibly have given offense were a short poem by Arthur Symons alluding to an encounter with a prostitute, a facetious piece by Max Beerbohm, "A Defence of Cosmetics," professing to find artifice superior to nature, and Beardsley's cover drawing of an aged prostitute instructing a young one in the tricks of the trade. Although one critic

---

* In *Dorian Gray,* Lord Henry sends Dorian a "yellow book" to further his corruption. Clearly modeled on Huysmans's *À Rebours,* the book is repeatedly described as "poisonous," belying Lord Henry's assertion that no one can be poisoned by a book.[52]

called for an act of Parliament "to make this kind of thing illegal," others were more derisive than outraged, even the straitlaced *Times* dismissing it as a mixture of "English rowdyism and French lubricity."[53] Wilde, having had no part in it, judged it "dull and loathsome, a great failure . . . not yellow at all."[54]

Later issues had the same combination of stories and essays by literary notables of the time—James, Gissing, Wells, Yeats—leavened by frivolities and somewhat risqué poems and squibs. Beerbohm, as irreverent about the journal as about everything else, mocked the pretensions of evil in "the lurid verses written by young men, who in real life, know no haunt more lurid than a literary public-house."[55] (Beerbohm himself was still an undergraduate when he started to contribute to *The Yellow Book*.) The preface to a later anthology of selections from *The Yellow Book* describes its dominant theme as the "sense of sin."[56] But the contents of the anthology hardly bear that out. At worst the articles were "naughty," as was said at the time, deriding the hypocrisies of polite society or satirizing some social situation; more often they were conventional commentaries on social problems or perfectly respectable stories. More provocative were some (by no means all) of the illustrations, especially those by Beardsley and Beerbohm, which caricatured women in somewhat erotic postures and states of deshabille and men in dandy dress and effete poses. A comment by David Cecil, Beerbohm's biographer, on the *fin de siècle* as a whole is especially pertinent to *The Yellow Book*: "a feeble English version of a French phenomenon; languid little poems and stories in which half a grain of Baudelaire is diluted in many gallons of London water."[57]

The movement was well named; it did not survive the *siècle*. *The Yellow Book* expired in 1897, after only a few years of publication. Beardsley died the following year and Wilde two years later, both in exile appropriately in France, and both having received the last rites of the Catholic Church, Beardsley as a convert, Wilde as a penitent. Wilde had earlier said that "Catholicism is the only religion to die in," and shortly before his death he had blamed his "moral obliquity" on the fact that his father would not allow him to be a Catholic. "The artistic side of the Church and the fragrance of its teaching would have cured my degeneracies. I intend to be received before long."[58]* It is not clear that he was actually conscious when the priest administered the last rites. Nor is it likely that Catholicism would have cured his "degeneracies" (or that he would have wished them cured); he could just as well have enlisted the "artistic side" of the Church and the "fragrance" of its teaching in the service of those degeneracies. Dorian Gray too was fascinated by the rituals performed by a Catholic priest but made of it a purely aesthetic, even decadent experience, not at all an occasion for moral or spiritual redemption.

It is interesting that from the beginning the movement was known under the French label, as if to suggest how alien it was to England—rather like the "French flu" or the "French pox." A character in a novel remarks, in a Cockney accent, "It's *fang-de-seeaycle* that does it, my dear, and education, and reading French."[59] If there is any temptation to think of the *fin de siècle* as Nietzschean, *The Yellow Book* and the career of Wilde should disabuse us of it. One can imagine Nietzsche's contempt for those free souls whose notion of decadence was dandyism, who had no higher aspiration than to *épater le bourgeois,* whose great sin against society was homosexuality—and who then thought to redeem themselves by converting to Catholicism. In his last and

---

* Not only Wilde and Beardsley but Lord Douglas and others associated with the movement (including John Gray, who is assumed to have been the model for Dorian Gray) later became converts to Catholicism.

perhaps best play, *The Importance of Being Earnest,* Wilde delivered himself of a witticism that Nietzsche would have appreciated. "I hope," a young woman says, "you have not been leading a double life, pretending to be wicked and being really good all the time. That would be hypocrisy."[60]

There are obvious affinities—and as obvious disparities—between the new men and women in what might be called the Schreiner circle and the new men (there were no new women there) among the decadents. Together the two groups may be said to constitute the late-Victorian "counterculture," a period of "sexual anarchy," as Gissing called it, when traditional sexual roles and identities were being challenged without any clear sense of what would take their place.[61] While the Schreiner group flouted the conventions of marriage, the Wilde circle flaunted their homosexuality. But there were homosexuals and lesbians among the former (Edward Carpenter, Edith Ellis) and heterosexuals among the latter (Beerbohm was not a homosexual, though he was very much a dandy, which was sometimes assumed to be much the same thing). And some of the homosexuals were not exclusively that; Wilde himself was married, had two sons, and remained on good terms with his wife until almost the end. The two groups overlapped in other ways. *The Yellow Book* published articles and stories (such as Gissing's "The Foolish Virgin," on the theme of the "redundant woman") that could well have appeared in a new-woman's journal. Wilde himself, ironically, edited such a journal, *Woman's World,* in which he published stories and essays by Olive Schreiner, Amy Levy, and other new women.

Within that "anarchic" world, however, there were serious tensions, for if they shared a common antipathy toward the bourgeoisie, they also had an ill-concealed antipathy toward each other.[62] The aesthetes, exalting art and artifice over nature and biology, identified women with coarse, bodily nature and men with art and spirit. None of the English were as outspokenly, brutally misogynist as the French—as Baudelaire, for example:

Woman is the opposite of the dandy. Therefore she inspires horror. Woman is hungry so she must eat; thirsty, so she must drink. She is in heat, so she must be fucked. How admirable! Woman is natural, which is to say abominable.[63]

There are muted echoes of this in *Dorian Gray,* when Lord Henry disabuses Dorian of the idea that Sibyl Vane, his actress friend, is a genius. Women cannot be geniuses, he explains; they are purely decorative; they have nothing to say, but say it charmingly. "Women represent the triumph of matter over mind, just as men represent the triumph of mind over morals."[64] As if to confirm his words, Sibyl fails as an actress and then commits suicide when she realizes that she has lost Dorian as well. When Dorian expresses some guilt about having been cruel to her, Lord Henry assures him that that is just what women want.

I am afraid that women appreciate cruelty, downright cruelty, more than anything else. They have wonderfully primitive instincts. We have emancipated them, but they remain slaves looking for their masters, all the same. They love being dominated.[65]

The women caricatured in *The Yellow Book* (or at least the most memorable of them) are very different from those fantasized by Lord Henry. They are neither charming, mindless creatures nor slaves yearning to be mastered. The old, ugly, obese, overpowering woman on the cover of the first issue is repulsive and fearsome, all the more so by contrast to the young, slim, pretty girl standing beside her; it is perfectly clear, however, that the young woman will grow up to be exactly like the old.

If the aesthetes had little use for any women, let alone the assertive new women, the latter, for their part, had no reason to be better disposed to these men. Having waged their own war against conventional society, which had sought to confine them to their separate sphere of home and children, the new women had no desire to be relegated to the no less inferior sphere of nature and matter in contrast to art and spirit. Their goal was not only sexual and social liberation but sexual and social equality as well, and this was denied them as surely by the aesthetes as by the bourgeois. Moreover, sexual liberation, for all save a very small number of the new women, meant sexual—which is to say, heterosexual—fulfillment; and here too they could find little sympathy and still less satisfaction from men who professed to admire only platonic love, the love that is "as pure as it is perfect"—and pure and perfect because it is between men.

"Sexual anarchy" is an apt description of the *fin de siècle,* so long as both expressions are understood to apply to particular groups and movements in that period and not the period as a whole. *"Fin de siècle,"* conjuring up, as it does, images of decadence and scandal, is so dramatic that in retrospect it tends to dominate and define the entire period. And it is still more compelling because it seems to presage the future. In contemplating the "sexual anarchy" of the late nineteenth century, one can hardly fail to see in it portents of the "sexual revolution" of the late twentieth century.

There are indeed significant resemblances between that time and ours. But there is also one overriding difference. A century ago the "advanced" souls were just that, well in advance of the culture, whereas now they pervade the entire culture. This is the significance of our "sexual revolution": it is a revolution democratized and legitimized. The "free spirits" of the late-Victorian period had no such democratic or revolutionary aspirations. They thought of themselves as rare beings, capable of a degree of independence and nonconformity that most people did not aspire to and could not attain. By their dress and demeanor as much as their sexual predilections, the decadents consciously and proudly defined themselves in opposition to the bourgeoisie and to the common people. They did not want to convert the enemy; nor did they want to be accepted by, still less assimilated into, society. In the language of our day, they were content to be "marginalized." Indeed, they insisted upon it as the condition of their own distinctiveness—and of their decadence. In this sense they were anarchistic rather than revolutionary.

The new women had a different agenda. They did want to liberate all women, at least to a degree, to free them from the tyranny, as they saw it, of domesticity, even to release them from sexual inhibitions. But whatever their own experiments in "free love," they did not preach that gospel for others; indeed, most of them did not prefer it even for themselves, except as a last resort. However much they and their mates engaged in extramarital affairs, they did not make a virtue of that. If they thought of marriage as an intolerable restriction on their freedom, they idealized a love outside marriage as more devoted, more constant, more faithful, than any conventional marriage. Even the socialists among them, denouncing bourgeois marriage as a form of prostitution, looked forward to a socialist society where, as Eleanor Marx and Aveling said, "monogamy will gain the day."

The *fin de siècle,* then, was part of late-Victorian England, but only a small part of it, circumscribed by the larger world in which Victorian values still prevailed—among some classes more firmly than ever. This is not to say that the larger world was unaffected by the dissidence within it. The Wilde case brought into the open what had long been concealed, familiarizing people with a subculture, or counterculture, of which they had been ignorant or only vaguely aware. But it also dramatized the most sordid aspects of that subculture, thus confirming their worst suspicions about social nonconformity and sexual deviancy. Similarly, the new-woman novels had an ambiguous effect, portraying the liberated woman in such a way as to make her seem sympathetic and even heroic, but also tragic, condemned to loneliness, betrayal, and death.

There was much else going on in the culture to put this counterculture in perspective, for contemporaries as for historians. Late-Victorian England produced not only the writers associated with the *fin de siècle* but a host of others who were not: Henry James, George Meredith, Robert Louis Stevenson, Robert Bridges, Rudyard Kipling, Joseph Conrad, George Bernard Shaw, Conan Doyle, A. E. Housman. And there were other, younger writers who were just beginning to make their name: John Galsworthy, Arnold Bennett, John Buchan, Hilaire Belloc, G. K. Chesterton.* The culture, it was evident, was not the exclusive province of the aesthetes; nor was the "new" the exclusive domain of the new women and new men.

There were other new movements that occupied the minds and lives of people and that had little or no relationship to what we now think of as the *fin de siècle*. The 1880s and 1890s saw the emergence of a social consciousness that

---

* It is noteworthy that although there were so many women writers at this time, including many best-selling ones, there was no one as memorable as Jane Austen or George Eliot earlier in the century.

was far more widespread and, it may be argued, consequential than any idea of sexual liberation. This was as fertile a period in ideas and institutions as any in modern English history, spawning a variety of socialist organizations and philanthropic societies, research and scientific enterprises, educational and reform movements, philosophical and scientific theories. And these new ideas and institutions supported and reinforced most of the traditional Victorian values, even when they proposed to reform society.

Nietzsche's predictions about the fate of a morality divorced from religion had to await a future age. Late-Victorian England, in spite of the new men and new women of the time—perhaps even in reaction against them—remained invincibly Victorian.

A De-Moralized Society

"The past is a foreign country," it has been said. But it is not an unrecognizable country. Indeed, we sometimes experience a "shock of recognition" as we confront some aspect of the past in the present. One does not need to have had a Victorian grandmother, as did Margaret Thatcher, to be reminded of "Victorian values." One does not even have to be English; "Victorian America," as it has been called, was not all that different, at least in terms of values, from Victorian England. Vestigial remains of that Victorianism are everywhere around us. And memories of them persist even when the realities are gone, rather like an amputated limb that still seems to throb when the weather is bad. The sense of values lost may be as palpable as the values we do have.

How can we not think of our present condition when we read Thomas Carlyle on the "Condition of England" a hundred and fifty years ago? While his contemporaries were debating "the standard of living question"—the "pessimists" arguing then (as some historians do today) that the standard of living of the working classes had declined in that early period of industrialization, and the "optimists" (then as now) that it had improved—Carlyle reformulated the issue as "the condition of England question." That question, he insisted, could not be resolved by citing "figures of arithmetic" about wages and prices, earnings and expenditures. What was important was the "condition" and "disposition" of the people: their beliefs and feelings, their sense of right and wrong, the attitudes and habits that would dispose them either to a "wholesome composure, frugality, and prosperity," or to an "acrid unrest, recklessness, gin-drinking, and gradual ruin."[1]

In fact, the Victorians, like us, did have "figures of arithmetic" bearing upon the "condition" and "disposition" of the people as well as upon their economic and physical state. They called these figures "moral and social statistics"; we call them "social indices" or "social indicators."[2] Their statistics dealt with crime, illiteracy, drunkenness, illegitimacy, pauperism, vagrancy. If they did not have, as we do, statistics on drugs, divorce, or teenage suicide, it is because these problems were then so negligible as not to constitute "social problems."

It is in this historical context that we may address our own "condition of the people question." And it is by comparison with the Victorians that we may find even more reason for concern. For the current statistics are not only more troubling than those a century ago; they constitute a trend that bodes even worse for the future than for the present. Where the Victorians had the satisfaction of witnessing a significant improvement in their condition, we are confronting a considerable deterioration in ours.

In nineteenth-century England, the illegitimacy ratio—the proportion of out-of-wedlock births to total births—rose from a little over 5 percent at the beginning of the century to a peak of 7 percent in 1845.[3] It then fell steadily until it was less than 4 percent at the turn of the century. (See Figure 1, page 229.) In East London, the poorest section of the city, the figures are more dramatic because more unexpected; illegitimacy there was consistently well below the average: 4.5 percent in midcentury and slightly under 3 percent by the end of the century.* Apart from a temporary increase during both world wars, the ratio continued to hover around 5 percent until 1960. It then started a rapid rise: to over 8 percent in 1970, 12 percent in 1980, and then, precipitously, to more than 32 percent by the end of 1992—a two-and-a-half times increase in the last decade alone and a sixfold rise in three decades.[4] (See Figure 2, page 229.) In 1981 a married woman was half as likely to have a child as she was in 1901, while an unmarried woman was three times as likely.[5]

In the United States, the figures are no less dramatic. Starting at 3 percent in 1920 (the first year for which there are national statistics),[6] the illegitimacy ratio rose gradually to slightly over 5 percent by 1960, after which it grew rapidly: to almost 11 percent in 1970, over 18 percent in 1980, and 30 percent by 1991—a tenfold increase from 1920, and a sixfold increase from 1960. (See Figure 3, page 230.) For whites alone the ratio went up only slightly between 1920 and 1960 (from 1.5 percent to a little over 2 percent) and

---

* The contrast with France is striking. At the beginning of the nineteenth century, France's illegitimacy ratio was slightly under that of England; it rose steadily in the course of the century, reaching almost 9 percent by 1900, more than double that of England. In midcentury, London's ratio was a little over 4 percent, lower than that in the country as a whole; in Paris it was almost 33 percent, much higher than in the rest of the country. In other capital cities it was higher still: Stockholm 46 percent, Vienna 49 percent.[7] Victorianism, it is evident, was peculiarly English—or, perhaps, Anglo-Saxon; one can speak of Victorian America, not of Victorian France.

then advanced at an even steeper rate than that of blacks: to almost 6 percent in 1970, 11 percent in 1980, and just under 22 percent in 1991—fourteen times the 1920 figure and eleven times that of 1960. If the black illegitimacy ratio did not accelerate as much, it was because it started at a much higher level: from 12 percent in 1920 to 22 percent in 1960, over 37 percent in 1970, 55 percent in 1980, and 68 percent by 1991.[8] (See Figure 4, page 230.)

In teenage illegitimacy the United States has earned the dubious distinction of ranking first among all industrialized nations.[9] The rate tripled between 1960 and 1991: for whites it increased almost fivefold; for blacks the increase was less spectacular, but the final rate was almost four times that of the whites.[10] In 1990, one in ten teenage girls got pregnant, half of them giving birth and the other half having abortions.[11] England is second only to the United States in teenage illegitimacy, but the rate of increase in the past three decades has been even more rapid.[12] In both countries, teenagers are far more "sexually active" (as the current expression has it) than ever before, and at an earlier age. In 1970, 5 percent of fifteen-year-old girls in the United States had had sexual intercourse; in 1988, 25 percent had.[13]

Public opinion polls in both England and the United States show crime as the major concern of the people, and for good reason, as the statistics suggest. Again, the historical pattern is dramatic and disquieting. In England between 1857 and 1901, the rate of indictable offenses decreased from about 480 per 100,000 population to 250—a decline of almost 50 percent in four decades.* (See Figure 5, page 231.)

* Indictable offenses are equated with serious crimes; they do not include simple assault, drunkenness, vagrancy, and the like— "vices, rather than crimes," as the Criminal Registrar put it in 1857.[14]

The absolute numbers are even more graphic: while the population grew from about 19 million to 33 million, the number of serious crimes fell from 92,000 to 81,000.[15] Moreover, 1857 was not the peak year; it is simply the year when the most reliable and consistent series of statistics starts. The decline (according to earlier statistics) actually started in the mid- or late 1840s—at about the same time as the beginning of the decline in illegitimacy. It is also interesting that just as the illegitimacy rate in the middle of the century was lower in the metropolis than in the rest of the country, so was the crime rate. Even allowing for a considerable margin of error, these trends are unmistakable, all the more because they are confirmed by the accounts of contemporaries. In 1847 an article in the journal of the Statistical Society of London noted the lower crime rate in London and correlated it with the greater literacy of the population. "The results," the author commented, "completely extinguish our belief in rural innocence."[16]

The considerable decrease in crime is often attributed to the establishment of the police force, first in London in 1829, then in the counties, and, by 1856, in the country at large. Although this undoubtedly had the effect of deterring crime, it also improved the recording of crime and the apprehension of criminals, which makes the lower crime rates even more notable. One criminologist, analyzing these statistics, concludes that deterrence alone cannot account for the decline, that the explanation has to be sought in "heavy generalizations about the 'civilizing' effects of religion, education, and environmental reform."[17] (His own initial discomfort with this explanation can be seen in the quotation marks around "civilizing.")

The low crime rate persisted until shortly before the First World War, when it rose very slightly. It fell during the war and started a steady rise in the mid-twenties, reaching 400 per 100,000 population in 1931 (somewhat less than the

1861 rate) and 900 in 1941. During the Second World War, unlike the First (and contrary to popular opinion), crime increased, leveling off or declining slightly in the early 1950s. The largest rise occurred in the late fifties, from under 1,000 in 1955 to 1,750 in 1961, 3,400 in 1971, 5,600 in 1981, and a staggering 10,000 in 1991—ten times the rate of 1955 and forty times that of 1901. Violent crimes alone almost doubled in each decade after 1950.[18]* (See Figure 6, page 231.) Recently the English have been obliged to add a new statistic: the number of crimes involving guns rose more than 50 percent from 1982 to 1992. The absolute numbers are infinitesimal compared with the United States, but they are shocking in a country where the gun-control laws are strict and where, until very recently, police officers carried nothing more than a nightstick. (Today a few dozen specified officers have been authorized to carry guns.)

There are no national crime statistics for the United States for the nineteenth century and only partial ones (for homicides) for the early twentieth century. Local statistics, however, suggest that as in England the decrease in crime started in the latter part of the nineteenth century (except for a few years following the Civil War) and continued into the early twentieth century. There was even a decline of homicides in the larger cities, where they were most common; in Philadelphia, for example, the rate fell from 3.3 per 100,000 population in midcentury to 2.1 by the end of the century.[19]

National crime statistics became available in 1960, when

---

* On the eve of this rise, in 1955, the anthropologist Geoffrey Gorer remarked upon the extraordinary degree of civility exhibited in England, where "football crowds are as orderly as church meetings."[20] Within a few years, those games became notorious as the scene of mayhem and riots.

the rate was under 1,900 per 100,000 population. That figure doubled within the decade and tripled by 1980. A decline in the early 1980s, from almost 6,000 to 5,200, was followed by an increase to 5,800 in 1990; the latest figure, for 1992, is somewhat under 5,700. (See Figure 7, page 232.) The rate of violent crime (murder, rape, robbery, and aggravated assault) followed a similar pattern, except that the increase after 1985 was more precipitous and continued until 1992, making for an almost fivefold rise from 1960.[21]* In 1987, the Department of Justice estimated that eight of every ten Americans would be a victim of violent crime at least once in their lives.[22] The incidence of nonviolent crime is obviously greater; in 1992 alone, one in four households experienced such a crime.[23]

Homicide statistics go back to the beginning of the century, when the national rate was 1.2 per 100,000 population. That figure skyrocketed during Prohibition, reaching as high as 9.7 by one account (6.5 by another) in 1933, when Prohibition was repealed. The rate dropped to between 5 and 6 during the 1940s and to under 5 in the fifties and early sixties. In the mid-sixties, it started to climb rapidly, more than doubling between 1965 and 1980. A decline in the early eighties was followed by another rise; in 1991 it was just short of its 1980 peak.[24]† The rate among blacks, especially in the cities, was considerably higher than among

---

* Because of differences in the definition and reporting of crimes, the American index of crime is not equivalent to the English rate of indictable offenses. The English rate of 10,000 in 1991 does not mean that England experienced almost twice as many crimes per capita as America did. It is the trend lines in both countries that are significant, and those lines are comparable.

† The most dramatic difference between England and the United States is in the homicide rate. In 1980 the rate in the United States was almost ten times that of England.[25]

whites—at one point in the 1920s, as much as 8 times higher. In the 1970s and early 1980s, the black rate fell by more than one-fourth (from over 40 to under 30), while the white rose by one-third (from 4.3 to 5.6); since then, however, the rate for young black males has tripled, while that for young white males rose by 50 percent.[26] Homicide is now the leading cause of death among black youths.[27]

For all kinds of crimes the figures for blacks are far higher than for whites—for blacks both as victims and as perpetrators of crime. Criminologists have coined the term "criminogenic" to describe this phenomenon:

> In essence, the inner city has become a criminogenic community, a place where the social forces that create predatory criminals are far more numerous and overwhelmingly stronger than the social forces that create virtuous citizens. At core, the problem is that most inner city children grow up surrounded by teenagers and adults who are themselves deviant, delinquent, or criminal. At best, these teenagers and adults misshape the characters and lives of the young in their midst. At worst, they abuse, neglect, or criminally prey upon the young.[28]

There are brave souls, inveterate optimists, who try to put the best gloss on the statistics. But it is not much consolation to be told that the overall crime rate in the United States has declined slightly from its peak in the early 1980s, if the violent crime rate has risen in the same period—and increased still more among juveniles and girls (an ominous trend, since the teenage population is also growing). Nor that the divorce rate has fallen somewhat in the past decade, if it doubled in the previous two decades; if more people, including parents, are cohabiting without benefit of mar-

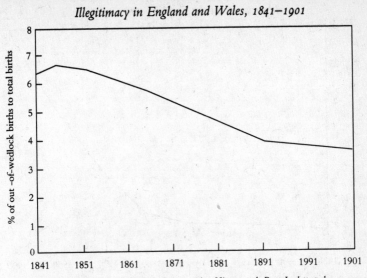

FIGURE 1

Illegitimacy in England and Wales, 1841–1901

Source: For 1800–1840: Bastardy and Its Comparative History, ed. Peter Laslett et al.
(Cambridge, Mass., 1980); for 1841–1992: United Kingdom Office of Population Censuses and Surveys.

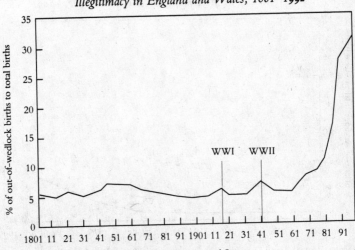

FIGURE 2

Illegitimacy in England and Wales, 1801–1992

Source: United Kingdom Office of Population Censuses and Surveys.

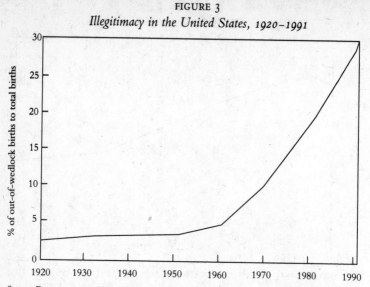

FIGURE 3

Illegitimacy in the United States, 1920–1991

Source: For 1920–1930: U.S. Bureau of the Census, Vital Statistics of the United States, 1940; for 1940–1991: U.S. Department of Health and Human Services, National Center for Health Statistics.

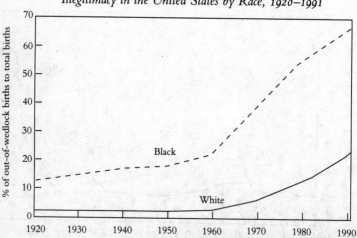

FIGURE 4

Illegitimacy in the United States by Race, 1920–1991

Source: For 1920–1930: U.S. Bureau of the Census, Vital Statistics of the United States, 1940; for 1940–1991: U.S. Department of Health and Human Services, National Center for Health Statistics.
Note: Until 1970 data are for nonwhites.

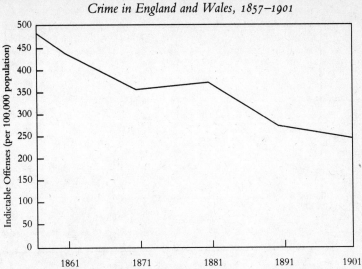

FIGURE 5
Crime in England and Wales, 1857–1901

Source: For 1857–1980: B. R. Mitchell, British Historical Statistics (Cambridge, England, 1988),
pp. 776–778; for 1981–1991: Home Office Criminal Statistics.
Note: I have converted absolute numbers into rate per 100,000 population.

FIGURE 6
Crime in England and Wales, 1857–1991

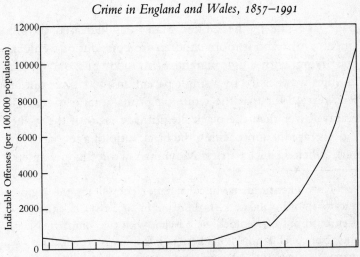

Source: For 1857–1980: B. R. Mitchell, British Historical Statistics (Cambridge, England, 1988),
pp. 776–778; for 1981–1991: Home Office Criminal Statistics.
Note: I have converted absolute numbers into rate per 100,000 population.

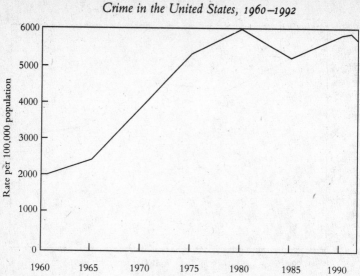

FIGURE 7

Crime in the United States, 1960–1992

Source: *U.S. Department of Justice, Federal Bureau of Investigation.*
Note: *Because of differences in the definition and reporting of crimes, the American index of crime is not equivalent to the English rate of indictable offenses. It is only the trend lines in the two countries that are comparable.*

riage (the rate in the United States has increased sixfold since 1970);* and if more children are born out of wedlock and living with single parents. (In 1970, one out of ten families was headed by a single parent; in 1990, three out of ten were.) Nor that the white illegitimacy ratio is considerably lower than the black illegitimacy ratio, if the white ratio is rapidly approaching the black ratio of a few decades ago, when Daniel Patrick Moynihan wrote his percipient

---

* The higher incidence of cohabitation complicates this picture but does not invalidate it. In England in 1992 over half the children born out of wedlock were living with two unmarried parents. But cohabitation, it has been pointed out, is no substitute for marriage, since such arrangements are far less stable than marriages, only 16 percent lasting more than five years. This compares with a ten-year average for marriages that end in divorce—and, of course, most marriages do not end in divorce.[29]

report about the breakdown of the black family. (The black ratio in 1964, when that report was issued, was 24.5 percent; the white ratio now is 22 percent. In 1964, 50 percent of black teenage mothers were single; in 1991, 55 percent of white teenage mothers were single.)

Nor is it reassuring to be told that two-thirds of new welfare recipients are off the rolls within two years, if half of those soon return, and a quarter of all recipients remain on for more than eight years. Nor that divorced mothers leave the welfare rolls after an average of five years, if never-married mothers remain for more than nine years, and un-married mothers who bore their children as teenagers stay on for ten or more years. (Forty-three percent of the longest-term welfare recipients started their families as un-wed teenagers.)[30]

Nor is the cause of racial equality promoted by the news of an emerging "white underclass," smaller and less con-spicuous than the black (partly because it is more dispersed) but rapidly increasing. If, as has been conclusively demon-strated, the single-parent family is the most important factor associated with the "pathology of poverty"[31]— welfare dependency, crime, drugs, illiteracy, homeless-ness—a white illegitimacy rate of 22 percent, and twice that for white women below the poverty line, signifies a new and dangerous trend. This has already reached a "tipping point" in some working-class communities, creating a white underclass with all the characteristics of such a class.[32] (Charles Murray finds a similar underclass developing in England, with twice the illegitimacy rate of the rest of the population; there it is a purely class rather than racial phe-nomenon.[33])

Nor can one be sanguine about statistics suggesting that drug use in the United States has fallen among casual users, if it has risen among habitual users; or that heroin addiction is decreasing, if crack-cocaine addiction is increasing (or, as more recent statistics show, both are on the rise); or that drug addiction among juveniles is lagging behind alcoholism. Nor can one take much satisfaction in the knowledge that the infant mortality rate has fallen, if it is disproportionately high in some groups, not because prenatal care is unavailable, but because single parents often do not avail themselves of it or because their drug or alcohol addiction has affected their infants.

The English sociologist Christie Davies has described a "U-curve model of deviance," which applies to both Britain and the United States. The curve shows the drop in crime, violence, illegitimacy, and alcoholism in the last half of the nineteenth century, reaching a low at the turn of the century, and a sharp rise in the latter part of the twentieth century, reaching a peak in the present.[34] The curve is actually more skewed than this image suggests. It might more accurately be described as a "J-curve," for the height of deviancy in the nineteenth century was considerably lower than it is today—an illegitimacy ratio of 7 percent in England in the mid-nineteenth century, compared with over 30 percent toward the end of the twentieth; or a crime rate of about 500 per 100,000 population then compared with 10,000 now. (See Figures 2 and 6, pages 229, 231.)

In his essay "Defining Deviancy Down," Senator Moynihan has taken the idea of deviancy a step further by describing the downward curve of the *concept* of deviancy.[35] What was once regarded as deviant behavior is no longer so regarded; what was once deemed abnormal has been normalized. As deviancy is defined downward, so the threshold of deviancy rises: behavior once stigmatized as deviant is now tolerated and even sanctioned. Mental patients can rarely be institutionalized or even medicated against their will; free to live on the street, they are now treated, and appear in the statistics, not as mentally incapacitated but as "homeless." Divorce and illegitimacy, once seen as betokening the breakdown of the family, are now viewed benignly as "alternative life styles"; illegitimacy has been officially rebaptized as "nonmarital childbearing"; and divorced and unmarried mothers are lumped together in the category of "single parent families." And violent crime has become so endemic that we have practically become inured to it. The St. Valentine's Day Massacre in Chicago in 1929, when four gangsters killed seven other gangsters, shocked the nation and became legendary, immortalized in encyclopedias and history books; in Los Angeles today as many people are killed every weekend.

It is ironic to recall that only a short while ago criminologists were accounting for the rise of the crime rates in terms of our "sensitization to violence." As a result of the century-long decline of violence, they reasoned, we had become more sensitive to "residual violence"; thus more crimes were being reported and apprehended.[36] This "residual violence" has by now become so overwhelming that, as Moynihan points out, we are being desensitized to it.*

Charles Krauthammer has proposed a complementary concept: "Defining Deviancy Up."[37] As deviancy is normalized, so the normal becomes deviant. The kind of family that has been regarded for centuries as natural and moral—

---

* An illustration of "defining deviancy down" is Jose Harris's observation that in 1912–13, one-quarter of males between the ages of sixteen and twenty-one imprisoned in London were serving seven-day sentences for such offenses as drunkenness, playing games in the street, riding a bicycle without lights, gambling, obscene language, and sleeping outdoors. "If late-twentieth-century standards of policing and sentencing had been applied in Edwardian Britain, then prisons would have been virtually empty; conversely, if Edwardian standards were applied in the 1990s then most of the youth of Britain would be in gaol."[38]

the "bourgeois" family, as it is invidiously called—is now seen as pathological, concealing behind the facade of respectability the new "original sin," child abuse. While crime is underreported because we have become desensitized to it, child abuse is grossly overreported, including fantasies imagined (often inspired by therapists and social workers) long after the supposed events. Similarly, rape has been "defined up" as "date rape," to include sexual relations that the participants themselves may not have perceived as rape at the time.

The combined effect of defining deviancy up and defining it down has been to normalize and legitimize what was once regarded as abnormal and illegitimate, and, conversely, to stigmatize and discredit what was once normal and respectable. This process, too, has occurred with startling rapidity. One might expect that attitudes and values would lag behind the reality, that people would continue to pay lip service to the moral principles they were brought up with, even while violating those principles in practice. What is striking about the 1960s "sexual revolution," as it has properly been called, is how revolutionary it was, in sensibility as well as reality. In 1965, 69 percent of American women and 65 percent of men under the age of thirty said that premarital sex was always or almost always wrong; by 1972, those figures had plummeted to 24 percent and 21 percent. For women over the age of thirty, the figures dropped from 91 percent to 62 percent, and for men from 62 percent to 47 percent—this in seven short years.[39] In 1990, only 6 percent of British men and women under the age of thirty-four believed that it was always or almost always wrong.[40]*

---

* Attitudes toward extramarital sex—sexual relations between a married person and someone other than his or her spouse—appear to be more traditional; 84 percent in 1973 believe it to be always or almost always wrong, and as many as 90 percent in 1993.[41]

Language, sensibility, and social policy conspire together to redefine deviancy. But the true effect may better be conveyed by an almost random array of facts. In his book on the underclass, Myron Magnet presents a sampling of statistics:

> By 1970 a baby born and raised in a big city had a greater chance of being murdered than a World War II GI had of dying in battle. Today, a twelve-year-old American boy has an 89% chance of becoming a victim of violent crime in his lifetime. . . . In mid-1989, one out of every four young black American males was either in jail or on probation—a larger proportion than was in college.[42]

For a long time social critics and policy-makers have found it hard to face up to the realities of our moral condition, in spite of the statistical evidence. They criticize the statistics themselves or try to explain them away. The crime figures, they say, reflect not a real increase of crime but an increase in the reporting of crime; or the increase is a temporary aberration, a blip on the demographic curve representing the "baby-boomers" who will soon outgrow their infantile, antisocial behavior; or criminal behavior is a cry for help from individuals desperately seeking recognition and self-esteem; or crime is the unfortunate result of poverty, unemployment, and racism, to be overcome by a more generous welfare system, a more equitable distribution of

---

These figures may be as high as they are precisely because there is so much more tolerance for premarital sex and cohabitation outside of marriage, to say nothing of divorce. With all these options available to people, extramarital sex may appear unnecessary and therefore more objectionable.

wealth, and a more aggressive policy against discrimination.

A few theorists have taken refuge in massive denial. Adapting the "social control" thesis that has been applied to the nineteenth century, they maintain that all the talk of crime and disorder is designed to create a "moral panic," thus justifying an increase in the power of the state and of the police. There is no crisis in crime, they argue—the only crisis is in capitalism, which seeks to weaken the solidarity of the repressed classes by isolating and stigmatizing the most exploited as an "underclass."*

Some of these explanations are plausible. The rise and fall of crime sometimes, though not always, corresponds to the increase and decrease of the age group most prone to criminal behavior. And there is an occasional, though not consistent, correlation between crime and economic depression and poverty. In England in the 1890s, in a period of severe unemployment, crime (including property crime) fell. Indeed, the inverse relationship between crime and poverty at the end of the nineteenth century suggests to some historians that "poverty-based crime" had given way to "prosperity-based crime."[43]

In the twentieth century, the correlation between crime and unemployment has been no less erratic. While crime did increase in England during the depression of the 1930s, that increase had started some years earlier. A graph of unemployment and crime between 1950 and 1980 shows no significant correlation in the first fifteen years and only a rough correlation thereafter. The crime figures, the author of that study observes, would correlate equally well, or even better, with other kinds of data. "Indeed, the consumption of

---

* This thesis has recently been subjected to criticism by some radicals who dismiss it as a form of "left idealism." What is required, they say, is a new "left realism," which will start with the proposition, "Crime really is a problem."[44]

alcohol, the consumption of ice cream, the number of cars on the road, and the Gross National Product are highly correlated with rising crime over 1950–1980."[45]

The situation is similar in the United States. In the high-unemployment years of 1949, 1958, and 1961, when unemployment was 6 or 7 percent, crime was less than 2 percent; in the low-unemployment years of 1966 to 1969, with unemployment between 3 and 4 percent, crime was almost 4 percent.[46] Today in the inner cities there is a correlation between unemployment and crime, but it is not a causal one. Or if it is causal, it is not unemployment that causes crime so much as a culture that denigrates or discourages employment, making crime seem more normal, natural, and desirable than employment. The "culture of criminality," it is evident, is very different from the "culture of poverty" as we once understood that concept.

Nor can the decline of the two-parent family be attributed, as is sometimes suggested, to the economic recession of recent times. Neither illegitimacy nor divorce increased during the far more serious depression of the 1930s—or, for that matter, in previous depressions, either in England or in the United States. In England in the 1980s, illegitimacy actually increased more in areas where the employment situation improved than in those where it got worse. Nor is there a necessary correlation between illegitimacy and poverty; in the latter part of the nineteenth century, illegitimacy was significantly lower in the East End of London than in the rest of the country. Today there is a correlation between illegitimacy and poverty, but not a causal one; just as crime has become part of the culture of poverty, so has the single-parent family.

These realities have been difficult to confront because they violate the dominant ethos, which assumes that moral progress is a necessary by-product of material progress. It seems incomprehensible that in this age of free, compulsory education, illiteracy should be a problem, not among immigrants but among native-born Americans; or illegitimacy, at a time when sex education, birth control, and abortion are widely available; or drug addiction, once associated with primitive cultures and bohemian individuals. We rarely question that assumption about moral progress because we are suspicious of the very idea of morality. Moral principles, still more moral judgments, are thought to be at best an intellectual embarrassment, at worst evidence of an illiberal and repressive disposition. It is this reluctance to speak the language of morality, far more than any specific values, that separates us from the Victorians.

Most of us are uncomfortable with the idea of making moral judgments even in our private lives, let alone with the "intrusion," as we say, of moral judgments into public affairs. We are uncomfortable not only because we have come to feel that we have no right to make such judgments and impose them upon others, but because we have no confidence in the judgments themselves, no assurance that our principles are true and right for us, let alone for others. We are constantly beseeched to be "nonjudgmental," to be wary of crediting our beliefs with any greater validity than anyone else's, to be conscious of how "Eurocentric" and "culture-bound" we are. "*Chacun à son goût*," we say of morals, as of taste; indeed, morals have become a matter of taste.

Public officials in particular shy away from the word "immoral," lest they be accused of racism, sexism, elitism, or simply a lack of compassion. When members of the president's cabinet were asked whether it is immoral for people to have children out of wedlock, they drew back from that distasteful word. The Secretary of Health and Human Services replied, "I don't like to put this in moral terms, but I do believe that having children out of wedlock is just wrong." The Surgeon General was more forthright: "No. Everyone has different moral standards. . . . You can't impose your standards on someone else."[47]

It is not only our political and cultural leaders who are prone to this failure of moral nerve. Everyone has been infected by it, to one degree or another. A moving testimonial to this comes from an unlikely source: Richard Hoggart, the British literary critic and very much a man of the left, not given to celebrating Victorian values. It was in the course of criticizing a book espousing traditional virtues that Hoggart observed about his own hometown:

> In Hunslet, a working-class district of Leeds, within which I was brought up, old people will still enunciate, as guides to living, the moral rules they learned at Sunday School and Chapel. Then they almost always add, these days: "But it's only my opinion, of course." A late-twentieth-century insurance clause, a recognition that times have changed towards the always shiftingly relativist. In that same council estate, any idea of parental guidance has in many homes been lost. Most of the children there live in, take for granted, a violent, jungle world.[48]

"But it's only my opinion, of course." That is hardly a stirring faith by which to order one's private life. Still less is it a creed for public life. In Victorian England, moral principles and judgments were as much a part of social discourse as of private discourse, and as much a part of public policy as of personal life. They were not only deeply ingrained in tradition; they were also embedded in two powerful strains of Victorian thought: Utilitarianism on the one hand, Evangelicalism and Methodism on the other. These may not have been philosophically compatible, but in practice they complemented and reinforced each other, the Benthamite calculus of pleasure and pain, rewards and punishments, being the secular equivalent of the virtues and vices that Evangelicalism and Methodism derived from religion.

It was this alliance of a secular ethos and a religious one that determined social policy, so that every measure of poor relief or philanthropy, for example, had to justify itself by showing that it would promote the moral as well as the material well-being of the poor. The principle of "less eligibility," the "workhouse test," the distinction between "pauper" and "poor," the stigma attached to the "able-bodied pauper," indeed, the word "pauper" itself—all of which figured so largely in the New Poor Law—today seem invidious and inhumane. At the time, however, they were the result of a conscious moral decision: an effort to discourage dependency and preserve the respectability of the independent poor, while providing at least minimal sustenance for the indigent.[49]

In recent decades we have so completely rejected any kind of moral calculus that we have deliberately, systematically divorced welfare—no longer called "relief"—from moral sanctions or incentives. This reflects in part the theory that society is responsible for all social problems and should therefore assume the task of solving them; and in part the prevailing spirit of relativism, which makes it difficult to pass any moral judgments or impose any moral conditions upon the recipients of relief. We are now confronting the consequences of this policy of moral neutrality. Having made the most valiant attempt to "objectify" the problem of poverty, to see it as the product of impersonal economic and social forces, we are discovering that the economic and social aspects of that problem are inseparable from the moral and personal ones. And having made the most determined effort to devise social policies that are "value-free," we find that these policies imperil both the moral and the material well-being of their intended beneficiaries.

In de-moralizing social policy—divorcing it from any moral criteria, requirements, even expectations—we have demoralized, in the more familiar sense, both the individuals receiving relief and society as a whole. Our welfare system is counterproductive not only because it aggravates the problem of welfare, creating more incentives to enter and remain within it than to try to avoid or escape from it. It also has the effect of exacerbating other more serious social problems. Chronic dependency is an integral part of the "social pathology" that now constitutes almost a single "social problem."

The Supplemental Security Income Program in the United States is a case in point. Introduced in 1972 to provide a minimum income for the blind, the elderly, and the disabled poor, the program has been extended to drug addicts and alcoholics because of an earlier ruling defining "substance abusers" as "disabled" and therefore eligible for public assistance. Apart from encouraging these "disabilities" ("vices," the Victorians would have called them), the program has the effect of rewarding those who remain addicts while penalizing (by cutting off their funds) those who try to overcome their addiction. This is the reverse of the principle of "less eligibility" that was the keystone of Victorian social policy. One might say that we are now operating under a principle of "more eligibility," the recipient of relief being in a more eligible, more favorable, position than the self-supporting person.

Just as many intellectuals, social critics, and policymakers were reluctant for so long to credit the unpalatable facts about crime, illegitimacy, or dependency, so they find it difficult to appreciate the extent to which these facts themselves are a function of values—the extent to which "social pathology" is a function of "moral pathology" and social policy a function of moral principle.

*   *   *

The moral divide has become a class divide. The "new class," as it has been called, is not in fact all that new; it is by now firmly established in the media, the academy, the professions, and the government. In a curious way, it is the mirror image of the "underclass." One might almost say that the two have a symbiotic relationship to each other. In its denigration of "bourgeois values" and the "Puritan ethic," the new class has legitimated, as it were, the values of the underclass and illegitimated those of the working class, who are still committed to bourgeois values and the Puritan ethic.

In a powerfully argued book, Myron Magnet has analyzed the dual revolution that led to this strange alliance between what he calls the "Haves" and the "Have-Nots." The first was a social revolution intended to liberate the poor from the political, economic, and racial oppression that kept them in bondage. The second was a cultural revolution liberating them (as the Haves themselves were being liberated) from the moral restraints of bourgeois values. The first created the welfare programs of the Great Society, which provided counterincentives to leaving poverty. And the second disparaged the behavior and attitudes that traditionally made for economic improvement—"deferral of gratification, sobriety, thrift, dogged industry, and so on through the whole catalogue of antique-sounding bourgeois virtues."[50] Together these revolutions had the unintended effect of miring the poor in their poverty—a poverty even more demoralizing and self-perpetuating than the old poverty.

The underclass is not only the victim of its own culture, the "culture of poverty." It is also the victim of the upper-class culture around it. The kind of "delinquency" that a white suburban teenager can absorb with relative (only relative) impunity may be literally fatal to a black inner city teenager. Similarly, the child in a single-parent family headed by an affluent professional woman is obviously in a very different condition from the child (more often, children) of a woman on welfare. The effects of the culture, however, are felt at all levels. It was only a matter of time before there should have emerged a white underclass with much the same pathology as the black. And not only a white underclass but a white upper class; the most affluent suburbs are beginning to exhibit the same pathological symptoms: teenage alcoholism, drug addiction, crime, and illegitimacy.

By now this "liberated," anti-bourgeois ethic no longer seems so liberating. The moral and social statistics have become so egregious that it is now finally permissible to speak of the need for "family values." Under the headline "Courage to Say the Obvious," the black liberal columnist William Raspberry explained that he meant no disrespect for the many admirable single women who raise decent families, but he was worried about social policies that were likely to produce more single mothers.[51] This column, and others like it, appeared in April 1993, soon after *The Atlantic* featured a long article by Barbara Dafoe Whitehead summarizing the recent work of social scientists about the family. The article created a sensation, partly because of the provocative title, "Dan Quayle Was Right," and partly because of the message encapsulated on the cover: "After decades of public dispute about so-called family diversity, the evidence from social-science research is coming in: The dissolution of two-parent families, though it may benefit the adults involved, is harmful to many children, and dramatically undermines our society."[52]

A similar furor in the British press a few months later greeted the reissue of a booklet, *Families Without Fatherhood*, by Norman Dennis and George Erdos, which makes much the same argument for Britain. What particularly caught the attention of the press was the fact that the authors are long-time socialists ("ethical socialists," they call themselves) and members of the Labour Party.

President Clinton himself has put the official seal of approval on family values, even going so far as to concede—a year after the event—that there were "a lot of very good things" in Quayle's famous speech about family values (although, he was quick to add, the "Murphy Brown thing" was a mistake).[53]* Children, he agrees, are better off in two-parent than in one-parent families.

If liberals have much rethinking to do, so do conservatives, for the familiar conservative responses to social problems are inadequate to the present situation. It is not enough to say that if only the failed welfare policies are abandoned and the resources of the free market released, economic growth and incentives will break the cycle of dependency and produce stable families. There is an element of truth in this view, but not the entire truth, for it underestimates the moral and cultural dimensions of the problem. In Britain, as in America, more and more conservatives are returning to an older Burkean tradition, which appreciates the material advantages of a free-market economy (Edmund Burke himself was a disciple of Adam Smith), but also recognizes that such an economy does not automatically produce the moral and social goods that they value—that it may even subvert

---

* The "Murphy Brown thing," Clinton said, was "too cute because this woman is not symbolic of the real problem in society." In his speech, Quayle had deplored the example set by Murphy Brown, the character in a much publicized television series who gave birth to an illegitimate child. Quayle's point was that Murphy Brown, precisely because she was so successful, beautiful, and affluent, had made illegitimacy respectable and even glamorous, thus contributing to the "real problem in society."

those goods. Some Conservatives have criticized "Thatcherism" for fostering a free-market expansionist economy totally dominated by economic concerns with no room for moral and cultural values, forgetting that it was Mrs. Thatcher who first raised the issue of "Victorian values," to the discomfort of many of her present critics.[54]

For the promotion of moral values, conservatives have always looked to individuals, families, churches, communities, and all the other voluntary associations that Tocqueville saw as the genius of American society. Today they have more need than ever to do that as the dominant culture—the "counterculture" of yesteryear—becomes increasingly uncongenial. They support "school choice," permitting parents to send their children to schools of their liking; or they employ private security guards to police their neighborhoods; or they form associations of fathers in inner cities to help fatherless children; or they create organizations to encourage "puritan" virtues and family values. They look, in short, to civil society to do what the state cannot do—or, more often, to undo the evil that the state has done.

Yet here too conservatives are caught in a bind, for the values imparted by the reigning culture have by now received the sanction of the state. This is reflected in the official rhetoric ("nonmarital childbearing" or "alternative lifestyle"), in the distribution of condoms in schools, in the prohibition of school prayer, in social policies that are determinedly "nonjudgmental," and in myriad other ways. Against such a pervasive system of state-supported and state-sanctioned values, the traditional conservative recourse to private groups and voluntary initiatives may seem inadequate.

Individuals, families, churches, and communities cannot operate in isolation, cannot long maintain values at odds with those legitimated by the state and popularized by the culture. It takes a great effort of will and intellect for the individual to decide for himself that something is immoral and to act on that belief, when the law declares it legal and the culture deems it acceptable. It takes an even greater effort for parents to inculcate that belief in their children, when school officials contravene it and authorize behavior in violation of it. Values, even traditional values, require legitimation. At the very least, they require not to be illegitimated. And in a secular society, legitimation or illegitimation is in the hands of the dominant culture, the state, and the courts.

You cannot legislate morality, it is often said. Yet we have done just that. Civil rights legislation prohibiting racial discrimination has succeeded in proscribing racist conduct not only legally but morally as well. Today moral issues are constantly being legislated, adjudicated, or resolved by administrative fiat (by the educational establishment, for instance). Those who want to resist the dominant culture cannot merely opt out of it; it impinges too powerfully upon their own lives and their families. They may be obliged, however reluctantly, to invoke the power of the law and the state, if only to protect those private institutions and associations that are the best repositories of traditional values.

One of the most effective weapons in the arsenal of the "counter-counterculture" is history—the memory not only of a time before the counterculture but also of the evolution of the counterculture itself. In 1968, the English playwright and member of Parliament A. P. Herbert had the satisfaction of witnessing the passage of the act he had sponsored abolishing censorship on the stage. Only two years later, he complained that what had started as a "worthy struggle for reasonable liberty for honest writers" had ended as the "right to represent copulation, veraciously, on the public stage."[55] About the same time, a leading American civil-liberties lawyer, Morris Ernst, was moved to protest that he had meant to ensure the publication of Joyce's *Ulysses*, not the public performance of sodomy.[56]

In the last two decades, the movements for cultural and sexual liberation in both countries have progressed far beyond their original intentions. Yet few people are able to resist their momentum or to recall their initial principles. In an unhistorical age such as ours, even the immediate past seems so remote as to be antediluvian; thus anything short of the present state of "liberation" is regarded as illiberal. And in a thoroughly relativistic age such as ours, any assertion of value—any distinction between the publication of *Ulysses* and the public performance of sodomy—is thought to be arbitrary and authoritarian.

It is in this situation that history may be instructive, to remind us of a time, not so long ago, when all societies, liberal as well as conservative, affirmed values different from our own. (One need not go back to the Victorian age; several decades will suffice.) To say that history is instructive is not to suggest that it provides us with models for emulation. One could not, even if one so desired, emulate a society—Victorian society, for example—at a different stage of economic, technological, social, political, and cultural development. Moreover, if there is much in the ethos of our own times that one may deplore, there is no less in Victorian times. Late-Victorian society was more open, liberal, and humane than early-Victorian society, but it was less open, liberal, and humane than most people today would think desirable. Social and sexual discriminations, class rigidities and political inequalities, autocratic men, submissive women, and overly disciplined children, constraints, restrictions, and abuses of all kinds—there is enough to give pause to the most ardent Victoriaphile. Yet there is also much that might appeal to even a modern, liberated spirit.

The main thing the Victorians can teach us is the importance of values—or, as they would have said, "virtues"—in our public as well as private lives. And not so much the specifically Victorian virtues that we may well value today, as the importance of an ethos that does not denigrate or so thoroughly relativize values as to make them ineffectual and meaningless.

The Victorians were, candidly and proudly, "moralists." In recent decades that has almost become a term of derision. Yet contemplating our own society, we may be more respectful of Victorian moralism. We may even be on the verge of assimilating some of that moralism into our own thinking. It is not only "values" that are being rediscovered, but "virtues" as well. That long neglected word is appearing in the most unlikely places: in books, newspaper columns, journal articles, and scholarly discourse.

An article in the *Times Literary Supplement*, reporting on a spate of books and articles from "virtue revivalists" on both the right and the left of the political spectrum, observes that "even if the news that Virtue is back is not in itself particularly exciting to American pragmatism, the news that Virtue is good for you most emphatically is."[57] A liberal American philosopher, Martha Nussbaum, reviewing the state of Anglo-American philosophy, focuses upon the subject of "Virtue Revived." Her opening sentence suggests a return not to classical ethics but to Victorian ethics.

Anglo-American moral philosophy is turning from an ethics based on enlightenment ideals of universality to an ethics based on tradition and particularity; from an ethics based on principle to an ethics based on virtue; from an ethics dedicated to the elaboration of systematic theoretical justifications to an ethics suspicious of theory and respectful of local wisdom; from an ethics based on the isolated individual to an ethics based on affiliation and care; from an ahistorical detached ethics to an ethics rooted in the concreteness of history.[58]

If anything was lacking to give virtue the imprimatur of American liberalism, it was the endorsement of the White House, which came when Hillary Rodham Clinton declared her support for a "Politics of Virtue." If she is notably vague about the idea (and if, as even friendly critics have pointed out, some of her policies seem to belie it), her eagerness to embrace the term is itself significant.

In fact, the idea of virtue has been implicit in our thinking about social policy even while it was being denied. When we speak of the "social pathology" of crime, drugs, violence, illegitimacy, promiscuity, pornography, illiteracy, are we not making a moral judgment about that "pathology"? Or when we describe the "cycle of welfare dependency," or the "culture of poverty," or the "demoralization of the underclass," are we not defining that class and that culture in moral terms, and finding them wanting in those terms? Or when we propose to replace the welfare system by a "workfare" system, or to provide "role models" for fatherless children, or to introduce "moral education" into the school curriculum, are we not testifying to the enduring importance of moral principles that we had, surely prematurely, consigned to the dustbin of history? Or when we are told that organizations are being formed in black communities to "inculcate values" in the children and that "the concept of self-help is reemerging," or that campaigns are being conducted among young people to promote sexual abstinence and that "chastity seems to be making a comeback," are we not witnessing the return of those quintessentially Victorian virtues?[59]

*   *   *

It cannot be said too often: No one, not even the most ardent "virtue revivalist," is proposing to revive Victorianism. Those "good-old"/"bad-old" days are irrevocably gone. Children are not about to return to that docile condition in which they are seen but not heard, nor workers to that deferential state where they tip their caps to their betters (a custom that was already becoming obsolete by the end of the nineteenth century). Nor are men and women going to retreat to their "separate spheres"; nor blacks and whites to a state of segregation and discrimination. But if the past cannot—and should not—be replicated, it can serve to put the present in better perspective.

In this perspective, it appears that the present, not the past, is the anomaly, the aberration. Those two powerful indexes of social pathology, illegitimacy and crime, show not only the disparity between the Victorian period and our own but also, more significantly, the endurance of the Victorian ethos long after the Victorian age—indeed, until well into the present century. The 4-5 percent illegitimacy ratio was sustained (in both Britain and the United States) until 1960—a time span that encompasses two world wars, the most serious depression in modern times, the traumatic experiences of Nazism and Communism, the growth of a consumer economy that almost rivals the industrial revolution in its moral as well as material consequences, the continuing decline of the rural population, the unprecedented expansion of mass education and popular culture, and a host of other economic, political, social, and cultural changes. In this sense "Victorian values" may be said to have survived not only the formative years of industrialism and urbanism but some of the most disruptive experiences of our times.

It is from this perspective, not so much of the Victorians as of our own recent past, that we must come to terms with such facts as a sixfold rise of illegitimacy in only three decades (in both Britain and the United States);* or a nearly sixfold rise of crime in England and over threefold in the United States; or all the other indicators of social pathology that are no less disquieting. We are accustomed to speak of the sexual revolution of this period, but that revolution, we are now discovering, is part of a larger, more ominous, moral revolution.

The historical perspective is useful in reminding us of our gains and losses—our considerable gains in material goods, political liberty, social mobility, racial and sexual equality—and our no less considerable losses in moral well-being. There are those who say that it is all of a piece, that what we have lost is the necessary price of what we have gained. ("No pain, no gain," as the motto has it.) In this view, liberal democracy, capitalism, affluence, and modernity are thought to carry with them the "contradictions" that are their undoing. The very qualities that encourage economic and social progress—individuality, boldness, the spirit of enterprise and innovation—are said to undermine conven-

---

* The present illegitimacy ratio is not only unprecedented in the past two centuries; it is unprecedented, so far as we know, in American history going back to colonial times, and in English history from Tudor times. The American evidence is scanty, but the English is more conclusive. English parish records in the mid-sixteenth century give an illegitimacy ratio of 2.4 percent; by the early seventeenth century it reached 3.4 percent; in the Cromwellian period it fell to 1 percent; during the eighteenth century it rose from 3.1 percent to 5.3 percent; it reached its peak of 7 percent in 1845, and then declined to under 4 percent by the end of the nineteenth century.[60] It is against this background that the present rate of over 30 percent must be viewed.

tional manners and morals, traditions and authorities.[61] This echoes a famous passage in *The Communist Manifesto*:

> The bourgeoisie, wherever it has got the upper hand, has put an end to all feudal, patriarchal, idyllic relations. It has pitilessly torn asunder the motley feudal ties that bound man to his "natural superior," and has left no other bond between man and man than naked self-interest, than callous "cash payment."[62]

Marx was as wrong about this as he was about so many things. Victorian England was a crucial test case for him because it was the first country to experience the industrial-capitalist-bourgeois revolution in its most highly developed form. Yet that revolution did not have the effects he attributed to it. It did not destroy all social relations, tear asunder the ties that bound man to man, and reduce everything to "cash payment" (the "cash nexus," in other translations). It did not do this, in part because the free market was never as free or as pervasive as Marx thought (laissez-faire, historians now agree, was less rigorous, both in theory and practice, than was once supposed); and in part because traditional values and institutions continued to play an important role in society, even in those industrial and urban areas most affected by the economic and social revolution.

Among the many myths belied by the facts (myths shared by many Victorians) is the vision of the Victorian city as a hell-hole of degradation and iniquity—filthy, pestilent, home to every vice and disease, destructive of all traditional authority, conducive to "anomie" and "alienation." It is fascinating, therefore, to find that illegitimacy, which might be expected to be the by-product of these inhumane conditions, was actually less prevalent in urban and industrial areas than in rural ones. In the middle of the nineteenth century, when the illegitimacy ratio for the whole of England was 7 percent, that for East London, the poorest and most overcrowded part of the city, was 4.5 percent; at the end of the century, when it was just under 4 percent for the rest of the country, it was under 3 percent for East London. Manchester enjoyed a notoriety second only to that of London; if London was the "Great Wen," as William Cobbett called it, Manchester, Asa Briggs reminds us, was the "shock city" of industrial England.[63] Yet Manchester had an illegitimacy ratio of a little over 5 percent in mid-century, declining to 4 percent at the end of the century. Rural Cumberland, on the other hand, during the same period, had a ratio of 17-18 percent. In Scotland as well, illegitimacy was higher in the rural areas than in the towns.[64]*

Industrialism and urbanism—"modernism," as it is now known—so far from contributing to the de-moralization of the poor, seems to have had the opposite effect. At the end of the nineteenth century, England was a more civil, more pacific, more humane society than it had been in the beginning. "Middle-class" manners and morals had penetrated into large sections of the working classes. The traditional family was as firmly established as ever, even as feminist movements proliferated and women began to be liberated from their "separate spheres." Voluntary associations and public agencies mitigated some of the worst effects of industrialism and urbanism. And religion continued to thrive, in spite of the premature reports of its death. (It even managed to beget two of the most important institutions of the twentieth century, the British trade-union movement and the Labour Party, both of which were virtually born in the chapel.)

---

* Nor does the conventional urban/rural thesis apply to black illegitimacy in the United States. Since the 1940s, a larger proportion of black women had illegitimate children in rural areas than in metropolitan ones.[65]

*   *   *

If Victorian England did not succumb to the moral and cultural anarchy that is said to be the inevitable consequence of economic individualism, it is because of a powerful ethos that kept that individualism in check, as it also kept in check the anarchic impulses in human nature. For the Victorians, the individual, or "self," was the ally rather than the adversary of society. Self-help was seen in the context of the community as well as the family; among the working classes this was reflected in the virtue of "neighbourliness," among the middle classes, of philanthropy. Self-interest stood not in opposition to the general interest but, as Adam Smith had it, as the instrument of the general interest. Self-discipline and self-control were thought of as the source of self-respect and self-betterment; and self-respect as the precondition for the respect and approbation of others. The individual, in short, was assumed to have responsibilities as well as rights, duties as well as privileges.

That Victorian "self" was very different from the "self" that is celebrated today. Unlike "self-help," "self-esteem" does not depend upon the individual's actions or achievements; it is presumed to adhere to the individual regardless of how he behaves or what he accomplishes. Moreover, it adheres to him regardless of the esteem in which he is held by others, unlike the Victorian's self-respect which always entailed the respect of others. The current notions of self-fulfillment, self-expression, and self-realization derive from a self that does not have to prove itself by reference to any values, purposes, or persons outside itself—that simply is, and by reason of that alone deserves to be fulfilled and realized. This is truly a self divorced from others, narcissistic and solipsistic. It is this self that is extolled in the movement against "co-dependency," which aspires to free the self from any dependency upon others and, even more, from any responsibility to others. Where the interrelationship of dependency and responsibility was once regarded as a natural human condition, the source of such virtues as love, friendship, loyalty, and sociability, "co-dependency" is now seen as a pathological condition, a disease requiring a radical cure.

This is the final lesson we may learn from the Victorians: that the ethos of a society, its moral and spiritual character, cannot be reduced to economic, material, political, or other factors, that values—or better yet, virtues—are a determining factor in their own right. So far from being a "reflection," as the Marxist says, of the economic realities, they are themselves, as often as not, the crucial agent in shaping those realities. If in a period of rapid economic and social change, the Victorians managed to achieve a substantial improvement in their "condition" and "disposition," it may be that economic and social change do not necessarily result in personal and public disarray. If they could retain and even strengthen an ethos that had its roots in religion and tradition, it may be that we are not as constrained by the material circumstances of our time as we have thought. A postindustrial economy, we may conclude, does not necessarily entail a postmodernist society or culture.

It is often said that there is in human beings an irrepressible need for spiritual and moral sustenance. Just as England experienced a resurgence of religion when it seemed most unlikely (the rise of Puritanism in the aftermath of the Renaissance, or of Wesleyanism in the age of deism), so there emerged, at the very height of the Enlightenment, the movement for "moral reformation." Today, confronted with an increasingly de-moralized society, we may be ready for a new reformation, which will restore not so much Victorian values as a more abiding sense of moral and civic virtues.

The "New Victorians" and the Old

———◆◆———

We have long been familiar with the paradox of contemporary society: the increasing individualism and libertarianism in the moral realm ("values" or "lifestyles"), and at the same time the increasing involvement of the government in economic and material affairs (industry, health, the environment). The English jurist Lord Devlin once called this a combination of "physical paternalism and moral individualism."[1] In recent years that paternalistic area has been extended to such matters as racial integration, sexual equality, affirmative action, and multicultural education—"social paternalism," one might call it.

More recently still, efforts have been made to expand paternalism still further: to prohibit pornography, "hate speech," "sexual harassment," and "date rape," and to require employees, students, and professors to attend "sensitivity" and "consciousness-raising" sessions to correct their supposed racism, sexism, and homophobia. At this point we seem to be embarking upon a new form of paternalism—"moralistic paternalism," one might call it.

These new paternalists (or maternalists, as is more often the case, for they are most prominent among the feminists) have been called the "New Victorians."[2] In fact, they are a travesty of Victorianism. There is a world of difference between the Victorian code of manners and morals, so deeply embedded in tradition and convention that it was largely internalized, and that of the New Victorians, which is novel and contrived, officially legislated and coercively enforced. The Victorians would have been as distressed by the overtness and formality of college regulations governing sexual conduct (with explicit consent required at every stage of the sexual relation) as by the kind of conduct—promiscuity, they would have called it—implicitly sanctioned by those regulations. They would have been astonished to observe universities acting *in loco parentis,* not by encouraging students to exercise any degree of sexual restraint, but rather by requiring them to exhibit the greatest degree of tolerance for the greatest variety of sexuality, provided only that the proper precautions are taken.

The Victorians would also have derided the new moral guardians presiding over this new code of manners and morals, who bear an uncanny resemblance to Mrs. Grundy. But Mrs. Grundy was a figure of mockery in the play in which she first appeared (a pre-Victorian play, at that), and was immortalized in the language as a symbol of the narrow-minded, self-righteous, self-appointed social censor. The Mrs. Grundys of our day, vigilantly supervising the proprieties of conduct and speech, command the respect of many of those who profess to be in the vanguard of enlightened thought. Some of them, appointed to direct "sensitivity" and "consciousness" sessions—"facilitators," they are sometimes called—enjoy the status and perquisites of well paid administrators in corporations and universities.

The New Victorian brings to mind another fictional character, Mrs. Jellyby of *Bleak House,* who was too engrossed in the affairs of a tribe on the banks of the Niger to attend to her own brood of hungry, dirty, neglected children. For Dickens she was the exemplar of "telescopic philanthropy," her eyes having the "curious habit of seeming to look a long way off, as if . . . they could see nothing nearer than Africa!"[3]

Today's moralists have that same far-away, fanatical glint in their eye—"telescopic morality," we might call it. Telescopic morality disdains the mundane values of everyday life as experienced by ordinary people—the "bourgeois values" of family, fidelity, chastity, sobriety, personal responsibility. Instead it embodies a new moral code that is more intrusive and repressive than the old because it is based not on familiar, accepted principles but on new and recondite ones, as if designed for another culture or tribe.

The New Victorians do not condemn promiscuity; they only condemn those men who fail to obtain the requisite consent for every phase of sexual intercourse. They do not denounce drunkenness; they only denounce those who take "advantage" of their partners' drunkenness. They do not expend their indignation upon the brutal rapes that are all too common in our society; instead they trivialize rape by associating it with "date rape," defined so loosely as to include consensual intercourse that is belatedly regretted by the woman. They are not concerned with the kinds of crime that agitate most citizens—violent, irrational, repeated, and repeatedly unpunished crime; they only propose to pass new legislation to punish speech or conduct normally deemed uncivil rather than illegal.

Telescopic morality has the effect not only of distancing the new morality from the old; it also distances moral responsibility from the moral agent. We have become accustomed to the transference of responsibility from the individual to society—from the criminal to the economic and social conditions that are the presumptive causes of his criminality. What is new about the new morality is the shift of responsibility from one individual to another. In cases of rape or racial disputes, the New Victorian almost invariably places the burden of guilt upon the "privileged" or "hegemonic" person—the man rather than the woman, the white rather than the black. By the same token the "victim" is defined as such by virtue of his (or, more often, her) "unprivileged" status. The individual thus functions not as an independent, responsible moral agent but as a surrogate for gender or race.

Victorian moralists were of a very different order. They did not presume to create a new set of values to be imposed upon society. They sought rather to sustain those traditional values that encouraged the individual to be virtuous. Responsibility, respectability, sobriety, independence were the common values of everyday life. And it was because they were commonplace that they could be naturally and confidently applied to public affairs. T. H. Green, who firmly believed in the moral character of the state, was just as adamantly opposed to any sort of "paternal government." The state should promote morality, he insisted, only by strengthening the "moral disposition" of the individual, not by subjecting the individual to any kind of "moral tutelage."[4]

The New Victorians are engaged in just this kind of paternalism. They do not trust the natural "moral disposition" of people; instead they propose to submit them to a new form of "moral tutelage" designed to promote a new moral code. The movement against "hate speech" is not intended, as is sometimes claimed, merely to revive the old rules of civility. It has invented entirely new rules, defining as violations of civil rights, and therefore punishable, remarks that were formerly regarded as boorish or vulgar.

Similarly, the campaign against pornography launched by some feminists is not meant to restore the local regulations and voluntary arrangements that once restricted or prohibited pornography. Instead it redefines and expands the concept of pornography to include anything that may offend a particular feminist sensibility, thus taking it well beyond the old "prevailing community standards"—and taking it as well beyond the authority of the local community, making of it a national issue to be resolved at the highest legislative or judicial level.

The New Victorians, it is evident, have little in common with the old. Their euphemisms are even more obfuscatory than the old; "limbs" instead of "legs" is relatively innocuous compared with "phallocentric" or "vertical" thinking in place of "reason." And the code of behavior they zealously monitor is at once more permissive and more repressive than the old; casual sexual intercourse is condoned, while a flirtatious remark may be grounds for legal action. It is a curious combination of prudery and promiscuity that is enshrined in the new moral code. An old Victorian would call it censorship without morality.

What the New Victorians have created is a species of "moral correctness" designed to complement the prevailing "political correctness." Their real kinship is not to the Victorians but to George Orwell's "Big Brothers" (or "Big Sisters," it may be). One need look no further back than to *1984* to find their place in history.

NOTES

Complete bibliographical information for each reference appears in the first citation of that source in each chapter.

Prologue: From Virtues to Values

1. *Weekend World,* January 16, 1983, quoted by Eric M. Sigsworth, *In Search of Victorian Values: Aspects of Nineteenth-Century Thought and Society,* ed. Sigsworth (Manchester, 1988), p. 1. (The interview is mistakenly dated 1982.) See also Raphael Samuel, "Mrs. Thatcher's Return to Victorian Values," in *Victorian Values: A Joint Symposium of the Royal Society of Edinburgh and the British Academy December 1990,* ed. T. C. Smout (Oxford, 1992), p. 12; Ferdinand Mount, *Daily Telegraph,* May 22, 1987.
2. Samuel, "Mrs. Thatcher's Return," p. 12.
3. *Evening Standard,* April 15, 1983, quoted by Raphael Samuel, "Soft Focus Nostalgia," in *Victorian Values,* a supplement to *The New Statesman,* May 27, 1983, p. iii; Samuel, "Mrs. Thatcher's Return," p. 14.

4. Speech released by the White House Press Secretary, November 13, 1993, pp. 4, 7.

5. *Daily Telegraph* and *Guardian,* January 29, 1983, quoted by Samuel in "Mrs. Thatcher's Return," p. 12; Margaret Thatcher, *The Revival of Britain: Speeches on Home and European Affairs 1975–1988* (London, 1989), p. 248 (speech of May 13, 1988), and pp. 250–55 (speech of May 21, 1988).

6. Thomas Morton, *Speed the Plough* (London, 1800 [1st ed., 1798]), p. 6 (act 1, sc. 1).

7. Aristotle, *Politics,* in *The Basic Works of Aristotle,* trans. W. D. Ross, ed. Richard McKeon (New York, 1941), pp. 1138–39 (1257).

8. Margaret Thatcher, *The Downing Street Years* (New York, 1993), p. 627; Marghanita Laski, "Victorian Virtues and Vices," *Country Life,* May 7, 1987, p. 136. A fine book on Thatcher's career and ideas, Shirley Letwin's *The Anatomy of Thatcherism* (London, 1992), speaks of her as supporting "the vigorous virtues," but this is the author's expression, not Thatcher's.

9. Augustine, *The City of God,* trans. John Healey (London, 1945), p. 265 (bk. XIX, chap. 25).

10. Reinhard Bendix and Guenther Roth, *Scholarship and Partisanship: Essays on Max Weber* (Berkeley, 1971), p. 22.

11. Christina Hoff Sommers, "Teaching the Virtues," *The Public Interest,* Spring 1993, p. 9.

12. *Daily Telegraph,* April 23, 1983, quoted by Samuel in "Mrs. Thatcher's Return," p. 13.

13. James Walvin, *Victorian Values* (Athens, Ga., 1987), p. 161.

14. Charles Dickens, *The Old Curiosity Shop* (Oxford ed., London, n.d. [1st ed., 1840–41]), p. 111; Dickens, *David Copperfield* (Modern Library ed., New York, n.d. [1st ed., 1849–50]), p. 31.

15. Allan Bloom quotes this, without attributing it to Leo Strauss, in the preface to his translation of Plato's *Republic* (New York, 1968), p. xii.

16. Edward Glover, "Victorian Ideas of Sex," in *Ideas and Beliefs of the Victorians: An Historic Revaluation of the Victorian Age*

(New York, 1966 [1st ed., 1949]), p. 363. Glover parenthetically adds: "(This particular manifestation was, by the way, American in origin, but no matter.)" Other historians have been more skeptical. See Smith, "Sexuality in Britain," p. 183; Degler, "What Ought to Be," p. 1467; Peter Gay, *The Bourgeois Experience; Victoria to Freud,* vol. I, *Education of the Senses* (New York, 1984), p. 495.

17. F. Barry Smith, "Sexuality in Britain, 1800–1900: Some Suggested Revisions," in Martha Vicinus, ed., *A Widening Sphere: Changing Roles of Victorian Women* (Bloomington, Ind., 1977), p. 182; Carl N. Degler, "What Ought to Be and What Was: Women's Sexuality in the Nineteenth Century," *American Historical Review,* December 1974, p. 1467.

18. James Q. Wilson, *The Moral Sense* (New York, 1993), p. x.

19. Thomas Mann, *The Magic Mountain,* trans. H. T. Lowe-Porter (New York, 1939 [1st Ger. ed., 1924]), p. 131.

20. William J. Bennett, *The Book of Virtues: A Treasury of Great Moral Stories* (New York, 1993). See Epilogue, pp. 250–51, for other examples of "virtue revivalism."

21. Max Weber, *On Charisma and Institution Building: Selected Papers,* ed. S. N. Eisenstadt (Chicago, 1968).

22. *From Max Weber: Essays in Sociology,* trans. and ed. H. H. Gerth and C. Wright Mills (New York, 1946), p. 489.

23. Max Weber, *The Sociology of Religion,* trans. Ephraim Fischoff (Boston, 1963 [1st Ger. ed., 1922]), pp. 164–65, 175, 177, 244.

24. Thomas Hill Green, *Prolegomena to Ethics,* ed. A. C. Bradley (New York, 1969 [1st ed., 1883]), p. 261.

Chapter I: Manners and Morals

1. In France, of course, they were one word: *"mœurs,"* as Montesquieu used it, meaning both morals and manners.

2. John Milton, *Areopagitica* (1644), in *The Prose of John Milton,* ed. J. Max Patrick (New York, 1968), p. 272.

3. Thomas Hobbes, *Leviathan* (1651), (Everyman ed., London, 1943), p. 49.

4. William Makepeace Thackeray, "On Tailoring—and Toilets in General," in *The Four Georges [and] Sketches and Travels in London* (Boston, 1891), p. 148.

5. W. L. Burn, *The Age of Equipoise: A Study of the Mid-Victorian Generation* (London, 1964), p. 44.

6. Phyllis Rose, *Parallel Lives: Five Victorian Marriages* (New York, 1983), p. 221.

7. *The Gladstone Diaries*, ed. H. C. G. Matthew (Oxford, 1982), VIII, 163. One of the few sympathetic accounts of the diaries is Barbara C. Malament, "W. E. Gladstone: An Other Victorian?" *British Studies Monitor*, Winter 1978, pp. 22–38.

8. Ibid., III, xlvi–vii.

9. Ibid., p. xlvii.

10. *Life and Letters of Charles Darwin*, ed. Francis Darwin (London, 1887), I, 307 (April 2, 1873).

11. *Life and Letters of Leslie Stephen*, ed. F. W. Maitland (London, 1906), pp. 144–45.

12. Gordon S. Haight, *George Eliot: A Biography* (Oxford, 1968), p. 464.

13. See Thomas Walter Laqueur, *Religion and Respectability: Sunday Schools and Working Class Culture, 1780–1850* (New Haven, 1976).

14. Hippolyte Taine, *Notes on England*, trans. Edward Hyams (London, 1957 [1st French ed., 1860–70]), pp. 11–12.

15. Ibid., pp. 157, 276.

16. The most sophisticated forms of this thesis are modeled on Michel Foucault's *Discipline and Punish: The Birth of the Prison*, trans. Alan Sheridan (New York, 1977). Some examples of the theory applied to Victorian England are A. P. Donajgrodzki, ed., *Social Control in Nineteenth Century Britain* (Totowa, N.J., 1977); Phillip McCann, *Popular Education and Socialization in the Nineteenth Century* (London, 1979); Peter Bailey, *Leisure and Class in Victorian England: Rational Recreation and the Contest for Control, 1830–1885* (London, 1987); Paul Johnson, "Class Law in Victorian England," *Past and Present*, November 1993. For critical discussions of this theory and additional bibliography, see Gertrude Himmelfarb,

The Idea of Poverty: England in the Early Industrial Age (New York, 1983), pp. 29, 41, 59, 178, 537, n. 18, 553, n. 2; Himmelfarb, *Poverty and Compassion: The Moral Imagination of the Late Victorians* (New York, 1991), 200–1, 431–32, n. 52; F. M. L. Thompson, "Social Control in Victorian Britain," *Economic History Review*, May 1981; Thomas L. Haskell, "Capitalism and the Origins of the Humanitarian Sensibility," *The American Historical Review*, April 1985; "Humanitarianism or Control: A Symposium on Aspects of Nineteenth-Century Social Reform in Britain and America," *Rice University Studies*, Winter 1981. Martin Wiener, "Social Control in Nineteenth Century Britain," *Journal of Social History*, 1978–79.

17. John F. Kasson, *Rudeness and Civility: Manners in Nineteenth-Century Urban America* (New York, 1990), p. 165.

18. E. P. Thompson, *The Making of the English Working Class* (New York, 1964), p. 12.

19. Gareth Stedman Jones, *Outcast London: A Study in the Relationship Between Classes in Victorian Society* (Oxford, 1971), p. 196.

20. Enid Gauldie, *Cruel Habitations: A History of Working-Class Housing, 1780–1918* (London, 1974), p. 22.

21. See note 16 above. Some historians have recently begun to speak more respectfully of respectability. The word even appears in the titles of books and articles: F. M. L. Thompson, *The Rise of Respectable Society: A Social History of Victorian Britain, 1830–1900* (Cambridge, Mass., 1988); Laqueur, *Religion and Respectability;* P. Bailey, " 'Will the Real Bill Banks Please Stand Up?' Towards a Role Analysis of Mid-Victorian Working-Class Respectability," *Journal of Social History*, 1978–79, p. 343. See also Brian Harrison, *Peaceable Kingdom: Stability and Change in Modern Britain* (Oxford, 1982), pp. 157 ff.; Elizabeth Roberts, *A Woman's Place: An Oral History of Working-Class Women, 1890–1940* (Oxford, 1984), passim; Michael J. Childs, *Labour's Apprentices: Working-Class Lads in Late Victorian and Edwardian England* (Montreal, 1992), passim.

22. This mistaken idea is encapsulated in the title of a recent essay, "How to Join the Middle Classes: With the Help of Dr. Smiles and Mrs. Beeton," by Christopher Clausen, *American Scholar,* Summer 1993.

23. Richard Ellmann, *Oscar Wilde* (New York, 1988), p. 9.

24. Eric M. Sigsmouth, ed., *In Search of Victorian Values: Aspects of Nineteenth-Century Thought and Society* (Manchester, 1988), p. 2.

25. Standish Meacham, *A Life Apart: The English Working Class, 1890–1914* (Cambridge, Mass., 1977), p. 89. See also Roberts, *A Woman's Place,* for abundant evidence to the same effect.

26. Jeffrey Richards, "Victorian Values Revisited," *Encounter,* March 1887.

27. Thomas Carlyle, *Past and Present* (Everyman ed., London, n.d.), pp. 193–99.

28. Childs, *Labour's Apprentices,* p. 15.

29. Meacham, *A Life Apart,* p. 27.

30. Charles Booth, *Life and Labour of the People in London* (London, 1892), I, 174.

31. "General" William Booth, *In Darkest England and the Way Out* (London, 1970 [1st ed., 1890]), p. 24.

32. It is interesting that it is Mayhew and "General" Booth, but not Charles Booth, who are cited in a book that is equally skewed because it is based entirely on the records of a foundling hospital that dealt only with illegitimate children: Françoise Barret-Ducrocq, *Love in the Time of Victoria: Sexuality and Desire Among Working-Class Men and Women in Nineteenth-Century London,* trans. John Howe (London, 1992 [French ed., 1989]).

33. Brian Harrison, *Drink and the Victorians: The Temperance Question in England, 1815–1872* (Pittsburgh, 1971), p. 401.

34. Ibid., p. 96.

35. Thompson, *The Rise of Respectable Society,* p. 312.

36. Samuel Smiles, *Duty: With Illustrations of Courage, Patience, and Endurance* (London, 1880), p. 319.

37. Taine, *Notes on England,* p. 25.

38. For more complete statistics, see Epilogue, pp. 224, 231. An

excellent short discussion of crime and violence in the late-Victorian and Edwardian periods is Jose Harris, *Private Lives, Public Spirit: A Social History of Britain, 1870–1914* (Oxford, 1993), pp. 208–15.

39. Matthew Arnold, *Culture and Anarchy*, ed. J. Dover Wilson (Cambridge, Eng., 1966 [1st ed., 1869]), p. 203.

40. Ibid., p. xxvi.

41. James Walvin, *Victorian Values* (Athens, Ga., 1987), p. 79. A temporary rise in drunkenness arrests in the third quarter of the century was more a reflection of the growing intolerance for drunkenness and the larger number of police to give effect to that intolerance than of an increase in drunkenness itself.

42. Stedman Jones, *Outcast London*, p. 346.

43. Bentley B. Gilbert, *The Evolution of National Insurance in Great Britain: The Origins of the Welfare State* (London, 1966), p. 24.

44. Quoted by V. A. C. Gatrell, "The Decline of Theft and Violence in Victorian and Edwardian England," in *Crime and the Law: The Social History of Crime in Western Europe Since 1500*, ed. V. A. C. Gatrell, Bruce Lenman, and Geoffrey Parker (London, 1980), p. 241.

45. Michael Anderson, "The Social Implications of Demographic Change," in *The Cambridge Social History of Britain 1750–1950*, ed. F. M. L. Thompson (Cambridge, Eng., 1990), II, 36; Joan Perkin, *Victorian Women* (London, 1993), pp. 59–60.

46. See Chapter III, p. 114.

47. Edmund Burke, letter to William Smith, January 29, 1795, in *The Works of Edmund Burke* (London, 1909–12), VI, 52.

48. A similar statement is sometimes attributed to Charles II.

49. Taine, *Notes on England*, pp. 145–46.

50. George Bernard Shaw, "The Revolutionist's Handbook," appended to *Man and Superman*, in *Plays by George Bernard Shaw*, ed. Eric Bentley (New York, 1960), p. 443.

51. Dinah Craik, *John Halifax, Gentleman* (London, 1906 [1st ed., 1856]), p. viii.

52. K. C. Phillipps, *Language and Class in Victorian England* (London, 1984), p. 5 (quoting Robert P. Ward, *De Vere; or the Man of Independence* [1827]).

53. Samuel Smiles, *Self-Help: With Illustrations of Conduct and Perseverance* (London, 1908 [1st ed., 1859]), p. 467.

54. Smiles, *Life and Labor, or Characteristics of Men of Industry, Culture and Genius* (New York, 1888), pp. 35, 38.

55. W. M. Thackeray, *The Four Georges and the English Humourists of the Eighteenth Century* (London, 1909 [delivered as lectures, 1851–52]), p. 138. Smiles paraphrased this passage in *Life and Labor*, p. 31.

56. Thackeray, *The Four Georges*, p. 138.

57. Smiles, *Life and Labor*, p. 43.

58. Anthony Trollope, *Doctor Thorne* (Oxf., World's Classics ed., 1951 [1st ed., 1858]), p. 85.

59. Trollope, *Phineas Finn: The Irish Member* (Oxf., World's Classics ed., 1951 [1st ed., 1869]). For an excellent account of this reading of Trollope, see Shirley Robin Letwin, *The Gentleman in Trollope: Individuality and Moral Conduct* (Cambridge, Mass., 1982).

60. Alfred Marshall, "The Future of the Working Classes," in *Memorials*, ed. A. C. Pigou (London, 1925), p. 102.

61. Smiles, *Self-Help*, p. 346.

62. Burke, "A Letter to a Member of the National Assembly" (January 19, 1791), in *Works*, II, 555.

63. Niccolò Machiavelli, *Political Discourses*, in *The Works of Nicholas Machiavel*, trans. Ellis Farneworth (London, 1762), II, 56 (bk. 1, chap. 18).

64. Burke, "Letters on a Regicide Peace" (1796), in *Works*, V, 208.

65. Smiles, *Self-Help*, p. 461. For a modern defense of "etiquette" in much these terms, see Judith Martin, "A Philosophy of Etiquette," *Proceedings of the American Philosophical Society*, 1993, no. 3.

Chapter II: Household Gods and Goddesses

1. Karl Marx and Friedrich Engels, *The Communist Manifesto*, ed. Samuel H. Beer (New York, 1955), pp. 12, 28–29.

2. For qualifications of this generalization, see Chapter III, pp. 104–08. Leonore Davidoff and Catherine Hall maintain that "well into the nineteenth century the family remained the basis for most economic activity." (*Family Fortunes: Men and Women of the English Middle Class, 1780–1850* [Chicago, 1987], p. 32.) This does not imply that all the members of the family were involved in that activity, only that the "family enterprise" was a typical form of economic activity.

3. Leonore Davidoff and Catherine Hall, "Home Sweet Home," "Victorian Values" supplement to *The New Statesman*, May 27, 1983, p. xiv.

4. E.g., Peter Laslett, *The World We Have Lost* (London, 1965); Peter Laslett and R. Wall, eds., *Household and Family in Past Time* (Cambridge, Eng., 1972); Zvi Razi, "The Myth of the Immutable English Family," *Past and Present*, August 1993. There were, of course, exceptions to the nuclear family. Michael Anderson, in his study of Lancashire, suggests that the extended family appeared there when grandparents were brought into the household to care for the children of working parents. He also points out that industrial families were more nuclear than agricultural ones, where the children were often sent out of the home, the girls going into domestic service and the boys sent out to work on other farms or to become apprentices in other trades. (Anderson, *Family Structure in Nineteenth Century Lancashire* [Cambridge, Eng., 1971].)

5. Edward Coke, *The Third Part of the Institutes of the Laws of England* (1644).

6. Lawrence Stone attributes the spirit of "moral regeneration and repression" to the sense of crisis fostered by the French Revolution, the fear that "the impoverished and alienated masses in the industrial cities would rise up in bloody revolution." (*The Family, Sex and Marriage in England, 1500–1800* [New York, 1977], p. 677.) But the "moral reformation" was inspired by the religious revival long before the outbreak of the French Revolution and before the concentration in industrial cities of those "impoverished and alienated masses."

7. Walter Bagehot, *The English Constitution* (London, 1964 [1st ed., 1867]), p. 96 (italics in the original).

8. *The Nineteenth-Century Constitution, 1815–1914: Documents and Commentary*, ed. H. J. Hanham (Cambridge, Eng., 1969), p. 39 (speech by Disraeli, April 3, 1872).

9. John Ruskin, "Lamp of Memory," in *The Seven Lamps of Architecture* (London, 1956 [1st ed., 1849]), p. 184; *Sesame and Lilies* (Everyman ed., London, 1917 [1st ed., 1865]), p. 59.

10. Asa Briggs, *A Social History of England* (New York, 1983), p. 240.

11. Anthony S. Wohl, ed., *The Victorian Family: Structure and Stresses* (London, 1978), p. 10 (quoting *City Press*, September 12, 1857).

12. Briggs, *A Social History*, p. 240.

13. Edmund Burke, *Reflections on the Revolution in France* (World's Classics ed., Oxford, 1950 [1st ed., 1790–91]), p. 50.

14. Ibid., p. 218.

15. Wohl, *The Victorian Family*, p. 9.

16. Frederic Harrison, *On Society* (New York, 1971 [1st ed., 1918, lecture delivered in 1893]), pp. 33, 42.

17. J. A. Froude, *The Nemesis of Faith* (New York, 1879), pp. 114, 117.

18. G. M. Young, *Victorian England: Portrait of an Age* (New York, 1954 [1st ed., 1936]), pp. 224, 227–28.

19. Froude, *The Nemesis of Faith*, p. 15.

20. Davidoff and Hall, *Family Fortunes*, p. 116 (quoting from T. Binney, *Address on the Subject of Middle Class Female Education* [1873]).

21. Coventry Patmore, *The Angel in the House* (London, 1885 [1st ed., 1854–63]), pp. 40–42 (canto 5).

22. Alfred Tennyson, "The Princess," in *The Works of Alfred Lord Tennyson* (London, 1894), pp. 198, 202. John W. Dodds prefaces his quotation of this passage with the comment that Tennyson "gave poetic authority to accepted doctrines." (*The Age of Paradox: A Biography of England, 1841–1851* [London, 1953], p. 70.)

23. Tennyson, p. 214.

24. Frederic Harrison, *Realities and Ideals: Social, Political, Literary and Artistic* (New York, 1970), pp. 103–4, 77. (Although the volume was first published in 1908, the essays had been written over a period of forty years.)

25. Ruskin, *Sesame and Lilies*, pp. 58–59.

26. Ibid., p. 62.

27. Ibid., p. 63.

28. Ibid., p. 59.

29. Quoted by David Rubinstein, *Before the Suffragettes: Women's Emancipation in the 1890s* (New York, 1986), p. 4.

30. Ruskin, *Sesame and Lilies*, p. 59.

31. Ibid., pp. 50–53.

32. Charles Kingsley, *Letters and Memories* (New York, 1973 [1st ed., 1877]), II, 330. I am indebted to Walter E. Houghton, *The Victorian Frame of Mind, 1830–1870* (New Haven, 1957), for suggesting this and several other sources. This book is an invaluable compilation of quotations and, more important, bibliographical references.

33. *The Diary of Beatrice Webb*, ed. Norman and Jeanne Mac-Kenzie (Cambridge, Mass., 1983), II, 52 (July 25, 1894).

34. Beatrice Webb, *My Apprenticeship* (Penguin ed., London, 1971 [1st ed., 1926]), p. 223; *Diary*, I, 214 (August 29, 1887).

35. Webb, *Diary*, II, 52 (July 25, 1894). Some years later, she seemed more reconciled to her motherless state, saying that "on the whole" she did not regret the decision not to have children. But this was expressed with great diffidence and reservations (ibid., p. 193 [Jan. 1, 1901]). See also the quotation on motherhood as the "special service of women," Chapter III, p. 101.

36. T. H. Huxley, "Emancipation—Black and White" (1865), in *The Essence of T. H. Huxley*, ed. Cyril Bibby (New York, 1967), pp. 194–96.

37. Virginia Woolf, "Professions for Women," in *Collected Essays* (New York, 1967), II, 285–86.

38. Tennyson, "Idylls of the King," in *Works*, p. 463.

39. Ibid., pp. 451, 473.

40. Mark Girouard, *The Return to Camelot: Chivalry and the English Gentleman* (New Haven, 1981), p. 184.

41. Ralph Waldo Emerson, *English Traits* (Boston, 1858 [1st ed., 1856]), pp. 112–13. The idea that the climate was responsible for the Englishman's love of home was common at the time. Samuel Smiles gave the same explanation: "It is said that comfort is the household god in England—that the English worship comfort. Perhaps this comes from the raw and changeable weather, which drives people within-doors." (*Life and Labor, or Characteristics of Men of Industry, Culture and Genius* [New York, 1888], p. 376.)

42. Hippolyte Taine, *Notes on England,* trans. Edward Hyams (London, 1957), pp. 79–80, 197–98.

43. Smiles, *Life and Labor,* pp. 373, 377.

44. Taine, *Notes on England,* pp. 81–82.

45. Peter T. Cominos, "Innocent Femina Sensualis in Unconscious Conflict," in *Suffer and Be Still: Women in the Victorian Age,* ed. Martha Vicinus (Bloomington, Ind., 1972), p. 168.

46. Steven Marcus, *The Other Victorians: A Study of Sexuality and Pornography in Mid-Nineteenth-Century England* (New York, 1964), p. 31.

47. Ibid., pp. 29, 31.

48. Ibid., p. xiii.

49. Lawrence Stone, "Sex in the West: The Strange History of Human Sexuality," *New Republic,* July 8, 1985, p. 35.

50. Cominos, "Innocent Femina," p. 167. See also Cominos, "Late Victorian Sexual Respectability and the Social System," *International Review of Social History,* 1963, pp. 18–48, 216–50.

51. On prostitution, see Chapter III, pp. 114–19.

52. For this revisionist view, see R. S. Neale, *Class and Ideology in the Nineteenth Century* (London, 1972), pp. 124–25; F. Barry Smith, "Sexuality in Britain, 1800–1900: Some Suggested Revisions," in *A Widening Sphere: Changing Roles of Victorian Women,* ed. Martha Vicinus (Bloomington, Ind., 1977); John Maynard, *Charlotte Brontë and Sexuality* (Cambridge, Eng., 1984); Norman Gash, *Robert Surtees and Early Victorian Society* (Oxford, 1993). Carl N. Degler makes out a similar case for

the United States: "What Ought to Be and What Was: Women's Sexuality in the Nineteenth Century," *American Historical Review,* December 1974, pp. 1467–90. Peter Gay applies the same theory to middle-class women in Europe and America, but his evidence is almost entirely from America (*The Bourgeois Experience: Victoria to Freud,* vol. I, *Education of the Senses* [Oxford, 1984]). A counter-revisionist view has been proposed by Carol Z. Stearns and Peter N. Stearns, "Victorian Sexuality: Can Historians Do It Better?" *Journal of Social History,* Summer 1985, pp. 625–34. But this essay too, although it starts by quoting writers on Victorian England, disputes them with evidence from America; after the opening paragraph, "Victorian" is used entirely in the sense of American Victorian. Michael Mason, *The Making of Victorian Sexuality* (Oxford, 1994), appeared after this book had gone to press, but his findings regarding female sexuality, illegitimacy, prostitution, and premarital pregnancy are consistent with those presented here.

53. See M. Jeanne Peterson, "Dr. Acton's Enemy: Medicine, Sex, and Society in Victorian England," in *Energy and Entropy: Science and Culture in Victorian Britain,* ed. Patrick Brantlinger (Bloomington, Ind., 1989).

54. Mrs. Ellis, *The Daughters of England* (London, 1845), quoted by Vicinus, in *Suffer and Be Still,* p. x.

55. Smith, "Sexuality in Britain," pp. 194–95.

56. Davidoff and Hall maintain that the commitment to a common "moral code" and the proper domestic setting for that code bound together the "middle class" of all regions, religions, professions, and occupations (*Family Fortunes,* p. 25). The same might be said of most of the working classes.

57. Marx, *The Communist Manifesto,* p. 28.

58. Briggs, *A Social History,* p. 242.

59. Elizabeth Roberts, *A Woman's Place: An Oral History of Working-Class Women, 1890–1940* (Oxford, 1984), p. 12.

60. Ibid., p. 51. (Italics in the original.)

61. One of the few divergences between Roberts's book and an earlier one by Standish Meacham, *A Life Apart: The English*

Working Class, 1890–1914 (Cambridge, Mass., 1977), is the greater amount of truancy reported in the latter (p. 172).

62. Roberts, *A Woman's Place*, p. 73.

63. Ibid., p. 79.

64. Françoise Barret-Ducrocq, *Love in the Time of Victoria: Sexuality and Desire Among Working-Class Men and Women in Nineteenth-Century London,* trans. John Howe (London, 1992 [French ed., 1989]), p. 180.

65. Roberts, *A Woman's Place*, p. 1. Roberts's approach is very different from that of another feminist historian, Carol Dyhouse, who finds it difficult to credit another account of a happy childhood. Molly Hughes's *A London Child of the Seventies* (London, 1934) is a witty and charming memoir of growing up in a middle-class household. The youngest child and only girl in the family, she was petted and patronized by her four brothers and happily waited upon them. Dyhouse is suspicious of her claim to have harbored no resentment against them, and concludes that her memoir is "a rather idealized account of her childhood and family life." (Carol Dyhouse, "Mothers and Daughters in the Middle-Class Home, c. 1870–1914," in *Labour and Love: Women's Experience of Home and Family, 1850–1940,* ed. Jane Lewis [Oxford, 1986], p. 41.)

66. Roberts, *A Woman's Place*, pp. 2–3.

67. Ibid., p. 83.

68. Joan Perkin, *Women and Marriage in Nineteenth-Century England* (Chicago, 1989), p. 3.

69. Roberts, *A Woman's Place*, pp. 2–3.

70. Ibid., p. 117 (quoting Helen Bosanquet, *The Family* [1906]).

71. Ibid., p. 84.

72. Michael J. Childs, *Labour's Apprentices: Working-Class Lads in Late Victorian and Edwardian England* (Montreal, 1992), pp. 11, 13. On the subject of working-class women's control of the family finances, most historians are in agreement. See, for example, Peter N. Stearns, "Working-Class Women in Britain, 1890–1914," in *Suffer and Be Still,* pp. 104–5.

73. Roberts, *A Woman's Place*, p. 203.

74. It is unfortunate that Roberts's book has not received the attention it deserves. It has not been reviewed in some of the major feminist journals, and has been too briefly reviewed in others.

75. See, for example, Childs, *Labour's Apprentices;* Meacham, *A Life Apart;* John Burnett, ed., *Annals of Labour: Autobiographies of British Working-Class People, 1820–1920* (Bloomington, Ind., 1974); Perkin, *Women and Marriage* and *Victorian Women.* Robert Roberts, *The Classic Slum: Salford Life in the First Quarter of the Century* (Manchester, 1971), and Paul Thompson, *The Edwardians: The Remaking of British Society* (Bloomington, Ind., 1975), deal with the Edwardian period primarily but have implications for the late-Victorian period as well.

76. Quoted by F. M. L. Thompson, *The Rise of Respectable Society: A Social History of Victorian Britain* (Cambridge, Mass., 1988), p. 151.

77. Brian Harrison, *Peaceable Kingdom: Stability and Change in Modern Britain* (Oxford, 1982), p. 172.

78. *Annals of Labour,* p. 290.

Chapter III: Feminism, Victorian Style

1. E. L. Woodward, *The Age of Reform, 1815–1870* (Oxford, 1938). See also Asa Briggs, *The Age of Improvement* (London, 1959).

2. The 1901 edition of the *Oxford English Dictionary* has no entry for "feminist." "Feminism," characterized as "rare," is briefly defined as "the qualities of females"; neither of the two citations (from 1846 and 1892) corresponds to the present meaning of the word. Later editions of the *OED* derive the word from the French and cite, as the earliest usage of "feminist," a passage in 1894 referring to a "Feminist group" in the French parliament. The earliest example of "feminism," the following year, has the word in quotation marks.

3. One historian goes so far as to say that "the views and beliefs held by feminists reflected, for the most part, those of society

at large." (Susan Kingsley Kent, *Sex and Suffrage in Britain, 1860–1914* [Princeton, 1987], p. 17.) This is surely an exaggeration. The largest women's organization was the Mothers' Union, which was not feminist at all; on the contrary, its aim was to preserve the traditional role of women in their "proper sphere."

4. For a discussion of the authorship of the earlier essay, see Gertrude Himmelfarb, *On Liberty and Liberalism: The Case of John Stuart Mill* (New York, 1974), pp. 183–86.

5. John Stuart Mill, *Enfranchisement of Women* (London, 1983 [1st ed., 1851]), p. 42.

6. John Stuart Mill, *The Subjection of Women* (London, 1983 [1st ed., 1869]), p. 76.

7. Ibid., pp. 159–63.

8. Mill, *Enfranchisement,* p. 35.

9. Mill, *Subjection,* p. 71.

10. Ibid., p. 167.

11. Francis Bacon, "Of Marriage and Single Life," in *Essays* (Oxford, 1949 [1st ed., 1597]), p. 29. (I have modernized the spelling and punctuation.)

12. John Stuart Mill, *Autobiography,* ed. John Jacob Coss (New York, 1924 [1st ed., 1873]), pp. 131–33. On the relationship between Mill and his wife, see Gertrude Himmelfarb, *On Liberty and Liberalism,* pp. 208 ff. and passim.

13. Mill, *Subjection,* pp. 175–76.

14. *The Letters of George Gissing to Eduard Bertz, 1887–1903,* ed. Arthur C. Young (New Brunswick, N.J., 1961), p. 171 (June 2, 1983). Also quoted by Elaine Showalter, *Sexual Anarchy: Gender and Culture at the Fin de Siècle* (New York, 1990), p. 30.

15. John C. Hawley, "The Muscular Christian as Schoolmarm," in *Victorian Scandals: Representations of Gender and Class,* ed. Kristine Ottesen Garrigan (Athens, Ohio, 1992), p. 137.

16. Samuel Butler, *The Way of All Flesh* (New York, 1944 [1st ed., 1903]), p. 3; Charles Dickens, *The Adventures of Oliver Twist* (London, n.d. [1st ed., 1837]), p. 481 (chap. 51).

17. Barbara Caine, *Victorian Feminists* (Oxford, 1992), pp. 37–38.

18. Lord Acton, *Selections from the Correspondence of the First Lord Acton* (London, 1917), p. 235 (April 26, 1891).

19. Jeffrey Weeks, *Sex, Politics and Society: The Regulation of Sexuality Since 1800* (London, 1981), p. 68.

20. *The George Eliot Letters*, ed. Gordon S. Haight (New Haven, 1975 [1st ed., 1954]), IV, 364 (May 14, 1867).

21. Cecil Woodham-Smith, *Florence Nightingale: 1820–1910* (London, 1950), pp. 486–88.

22. Deborah Epstein Nord, " 'Neither Pairs Nor Odd': Female Community in Late Nineteenth-Century London," *Signs,* Summer 1990, p. 753.

23. "Women's Suffrage: A Reply," *Fortnightly Review,* July 1889, p. 131.

24. Ibid., p. 126.

25. *The Diary of Beatrice Webb,* ed. Norman and Jeanne MacKenzie (Cambridge, Mass., 1983), II, 53–54 (July 25, 1894). See also Chapter II, pp. 66–67.

26. Margaret Cole, *The Story of Fabian Socialism* (New York, 1964 [1st ed., 1961]), p. 128.

27. Beatrice Webb, *Our Partnership,* ed. Barbara Drake and Margaret I. Cole (London, 1948), p. 361; *Beatrice Webb's Diaries, 1912–1924,* ed. Margaret I. Cole (London, 1952), p. 122 (June 16, 1918).

28. Brian Harrison, *Separate Spheres: The Opposition to Women's Suffrage in Britain* (London, 1978), pp. 111–12.

29. E. Moberly Bell, *Octavia Hill: A Biography* (London, 1942), p. 270.

30. Linda Colley, *Britons: Forging the Nation, 1707–1837* (New Haven, 1992), p. 281.

31. Anne Digby, "Victorian Values and Women in Public and Private," in *Victorian Values,* ed. T. C. Smout (Oxford, 1992), pp. 208 ff.

32. Webb, *Diary,* I, 136–37 (August 12, 1885).

33. Ibid.

34. Claire Midgley, *Women Against Slavery: The British Campaigns, 1780–1870* (London, 1992), p. 48.

35. Geoffrey Best, *Mid-Victorian Britain, 1851–1875* (New York,

1972), pp. 103–4; S. G. Checkland, *The Rise of Industrial Society in England, 1815–1885* (London, 1964); Michael Anderson, "The Social Implications of Demographic Change," in *The Cambridge Social History of Britain, 1750–1950*, ed. F. M. L. Thompson (Cambridge, Eng., 1990), pp. 62–63.

36. E.g., Richard D. Altick, *Victorian People and Ideas* (New York, 1973), p. 51.

37. See Anderson, "The Social Implications of Demographic Change," pp. 8–10; Anderson, "The Social Position of the Spinster in Mid-Victorian Britain," *Journal of Family History*, 1984.

38. Amy Cruse, *The Victorians and Their Reading* (Boston, 1935), p. 341.

39. Quoted by Joan N. Burstyn, *Victorian Education and the Ideal of Womanhood* (London, 1980), p. 66.

40. Rosemary Feurer, "The Meaning of 'Sisterhood': The British Women's Movement and Protective Labor Legislation, 1870–1900," *Victorian Studies*, Winter 1988, p. 235 (quoting *English Woman's Journal*, September 1859).

41. On Davies and the suffrage, see Rita McWilliams-Tullberg, "Women and Degrees at Cambridge University, 1862–1897," in *A Widening Sphere: Changing Roles of Victorian Women*, ed. Martha Vicinus (Bloomington, Ind., 1977), pp. 137–38 and p. 297, n. 45.

42. *The Later Letters of John Stuart Mill, 1849–1873*, ed. Francis E. Mineka and Dwight N. Lindley, in *Collected Works* (Toronto, 1972), I, 500 (ca. November 9, 1855).

43. John Stuart Mill, *On Liberty* (Everyman ed., London, 1940), p. 159.

44. *The Later Letters of Mill*, IV, 1634 (August 18, 1869).

45. Gail L. Savage, " 'Intended Only for the Husband': Gender, Class, and the Provision for Divorce in England, 1858–1868," in *Victorian Scandals: Representations of Gender and Class*, ed. Kristine Ottesen Garrigan (Athens, Ohio, 1992), pp. 11–42.

46. Mary Lyndon Shanley, " 'One Must Ride Behind': Married Women's Rights and the Divorce Act of 1857," *Victorian Studies*, Spring 1982, p. 364.

47. Lee Holcombe, *Wives and Property: Reform of the Married*

Women's Property Law in Nineteenth-Century England (Toronto, 1983), p. 154. A reviewer chastises Holcombe for ignoring the "misogynism" that was an important factor in that struggle. (Mary Lyndon Shanley in *Victorian Studies,* Spring 1985, p. 529.)

48. A. V. Dicey, *Lectures on the Relation Between Law and Public Opinion in England During the Nineteenth Century* (London, 1962 [1st ed., 1905]), pp. 394–95.

49. Judith R. Walkowitz, *Prostitution and Victorian Society: Women, Class, and the State* (Cambridge, Eng., 1980), p. 75.

50. Matthew Arnold, *Culture and Anarchy,* ed. J. Dover Wilson (Cambridge, Eng., 1966), pp. xxxi–xxxii, 181.

51. Ibid., p. 93.

52. The first edition of Acton's book appeared in 1857, the revised edition in 1870. The full title of the latter is *Prostitution, Considered in its Moral, Social, and Sanitary Aspects, in London and Other Large Cities and Garrison Towns, with Proposals for the Control and Prevention of Its Attendant Evils.*

53. One historian characterizes Josephine Butler's movement as "forward-looking in its feminism and its attack on the double standard, backward-looking in its fear of bureaucracy and state control." (Brian Harrison, "Underneath the Victorians," *Victorian Studies,* March 1967, p. 254.) This is a classic example of the "Whig fallacy," the imposition upon the past of present-minded views of what is progressive or regressive. Curiously, in this same essay, Harrison rebukes Steven Marcus for a "Whiggish outlook" in imposing his own judgments upon the nineteenth century (p. 249).

54. J. A. Banks and Olive Banks, *Feminism and Family Planning in Victorian England* (New York, 1964), p. 95.

55. E. M. Sigsworth and T. J. Wyke, "A Study of Victorian Prostitution and Venereal Disease," in *Suffer and Be Still: Women in the Victorian Age,* ed. Martha Vicinus (Bloomington, Ind., 1972), p. 97.

56. Priscilla Robertson, *An Experience of Women: Pattern and Change in Nineteenth-Century Europe* (Philadelphia, 1982), p. 495 n.

57. Kent, *Sex and Suffrage,* pp. 78–79.

58. Henry Mayhew, *London Labour and the London Poor* (New York, 1968 [1st ed., 1861–62]), IV, 211; Sigsworth and Wyke, pp. 78–79.

59. *The Bitter Cry of Outcast London: An Inquiry into the Condition of the Abject Poor* (London, 1883), pp. 9–10. For the authorship of this pamphlet, see Gertrude Himmelfarb, *Poverty and Compassion: The Moral Imagination of the Late Victorians* (New York, 1991), pp. 57–62.

60. Alfred Tennyson, "Locksley Hall Sixty Years After," in *The Works of Alfred Lord Tennyson* (London, 1894), p. 566.

61. Beatrice Webb, *My Apprenticeship* (Penguin ed., 1971 [1st ed., 1926]), p. 324.

62. Raymond L. Schults, *Crusader in Babylon: W. T. Stead and the Pall Mall Gazette* (Lincoln, Neb., 1972), p. 145. For a post-structuralist analysis of "The Maiden Tribute," see Walkowitz, *City of Dreadful Delight*.

63. William L. Langer, "The Origins of the Birth Control Movement in England in the Early Nineteenth Century," *Journal of Interdisciplinary History*, Spring 1975, p. 685.

64. Ibid.

65. Banks, *Feminism and Family Planning*, p. 90.

66. Ibid., pp. 89–90.

67. This thesis was developed and modified in a series of books by J. A. Banks and Olive Banks, *Prosperity and Parenthood* (1954), *Feminism and Family Planning* (1964), and *Victorian Values: Secularism and the Size of Families* (1981).

68. Banks, *Feminism and Family Planning*, p. 93. (Italics in the original.)

69. Lucy Bland, "Marriage Laid Bare: Middle-Class Women and Marital Sex, 1880–1914," in *Labour and Love: Women's Experience of Home and Family, 1850–1940*, ed. Jane Lewis (Oxford, 1986), p. 129.

70. Caine, *Victorian Feminists*, pp. 223, 234.

71. See Chapter VI.

Chapter IV: "The Mischievous Ambiguity of the Word Poor"

1. *Tocqueville and Beaumont on Social Reform,* ed. Seymour Drescher (New York, 1968), pp. 1–2. The "Memoir" was originally delivered to the Royal Academic Society of Cherbourg in 1835 and was printed in the proceedings of the society.

2. Ibid., p. 10.

3. Ibid., pp. 12–14, 17, 24–25.

4. William Cobbett, *A Legacy to Labourers* (London, 1872 [1st ed., 1834]), p. 97.

5. Rates in aid of wages had occasionally been used before Speenhamland, but the principle had not been formulated as explicitly and the system had not been applied as extensively.

6. There has been much controversy about the actual causes and effects of this system. See Mark Blaug, "The Myth of the Old Poor Law and the Making of the New," *Journal of Economic History,* 1963; Blaug, "The Poor Law Report Reexamined," ibid., 1964; James Stephen Taylor, "The Mythology of the Old Poor Law," ibid., 1969; Gertrude Himmelfarb, *The Idea of Poverty: England in the Early Industrial Age* (New York, 1984), pp. 65–6, 135–38, and passim. A revised version of Blaug's thesis is presented by George R. Boyer, *An Economic History of the English Poor Law, 1750–1850* (Cambridge, Eng., 1990).

7. Thomas Robert Malthus, *On Population,* ed. Gertrude Himmelfarb (New York, 1960), p. 33.

8. Ibid., pp. 367, 530.

9. J. R. Poynter is one of the few historians to make much of this, in the final chapter of *Society and Pauperism: English Ideas on Poor Relief, 1795–1834* (London, 1969).

10. *Report from His Majesty's Commissioners for Inquiring into the Administration and Practical Operation of the Poor Laws* (London, 1834), p. 127.

11. Ibid., p. 148. See Himmelfarb, *The Idea of Poverty,* pp. 147–76, for a more extensive discussion of the *Report* and of the New Poor Law.

12. For a summary of the main interpretations of the social im-

plications of the New Poor Law—the classes that it "empowered" and the interests reflected in it—see Peter Mandler, "The Making of the New Poor Law *Redivivus,*" *Past and Present,* November 1987, and the replies by Anthony Brundage, David Eastwood, and Peter Mandler, ibid., May 1990.

13. John Walter, *A Letter to the Electors of Berkshire* (London, 1834), p. 37.

14. *The Times* (London), February 25, 1834.

15. W. F. Monypenny and G. E. Buckle, *The Life of Benjamin Disraeli, Earl of Beaconsfield* (London, 1929 [1st ed., 1910]), I, 378 (election address, 1837).

16. Charles Dickens, *The Adventures of Oliver Twist* (Oxford ed., n.d.), pp. 20–29.

17. Anthony Brundage, *The Making of the New Poor Law: The Politics of Inquiry, Enactment, and Implementation, 1832–1839* (New Brunswick, N.J., 1978), p. 160.

18. See David Roberts, "How Cruel Was the Victorian Poor Law?" *Historical Journal,* 1963; Ursula Henriques, "How Cruel Was the Victorian Poor Law?" ibid., 1968.

19. Hippolyte Taine, *Notes on England,* trans. Edward Hyams (London, 1957 [1st French ed., 1860–70]), pp. 237–38.

20. Anne Digby, "The Rural Poor Law," in *The New Poor Law in the Nineteenth Century,* ed. Derek Fraser (London, 1976), table 7, p. 162.

21. David Ashforth, "The Urban Poor Law," in ibid., p. 135.

22. Ibid., p. 132.

23. Ibid.

24. Karl de Schweinitz, *England's Road to Social Security: From the Statute of Laborers in 1349 to the Beveridge Report of 1942* (New York, 1961 [1st ed., 1943]), p. 158 (quoting the *1st Annual Report of the Local Government Board,* 1871–72).

25. Josef Redlich and Francis W. Hirst, *The History of Local Government in England,* ed. Bryan Keith-Lucas (London, 1958), p. 115.

26. Ibid., p. 108; Best, *Mid-Victorian Britain,* p. 140.

27. For poor rates, see Best, *Mid-Victorian Britain,* pp. 138–40, and J. F. C. Harrison, *Late Victorian Britain, 1875–1901* (Lon-

don, 1990), p. 80. I have correlated this with the population for the relevant years.

28. See Gertrude Himmelfarb, *Poverty and Compassion: The Moral Imagination of the Late Victorians* (New York, 1991), pp. 23–28, for an account both of contemporary estimates of wages and of the historical evidence. For the difficulties in extrapolating from the earnings and standard of living of the working class to the conditions of paupers, see Mary MacKinnon, "Poor Law Policy, Unemployment, and Pauperism," *Explorations in Economic History,* 1986.

29. See Geoffrey Best, *Mid-Victorian Britain, 1851–1875* (New York, 1972), p. 147. Best's table starts in 1850 and goes up to 1880. I have projected it to 1890 from the same sources and assumptions. Best multiplies the official daily figure by three or three and a half to arrive at the annual figure. Other historians multiply it by two. See, for example, C. G. Hanson, "Welfare Before the Welfare State," in *The Long Debate on Poverty: Eight Essays on Industrialization and "The Condition of England"* (London, 1972), p. 116.

30. Best, *Mid-Victorian Britain,* p. 145.

31. Himmelfarb, *Poverty and Compassion,* pp. 102 ff.

32. Alfred Marshall, *Official Papers* (London, 1926), pp. 199, 244–45.

33. "Alfred Marshall's Lectures on Progress and Poverty," *Journal of Law and Economics,* 1969, pp. 188–90.

34. Quoted by Redlich and Hirst, *The History of Local Government,* p. 26.

Chapter V: "Gain All You Can. . . . Give All You Can"

1. John Wesley, "The Use of Money," *Works* (Grand Rapids, Mich., 1872), VI, 126, 136.

2. Max Weber, *The Protestant Ethic and the Spirit of Capitalism,* trans. Talcott Parsons (New York, 1976 [1st ed., 1904–5]), pp. 175–76.

3. Margaret Thatcher, speech to the Conservative Women's

Conference, May 25, 1988, reported in *Daily Telegraph,* May 26, 1988, p. 1.

4. M. G. Jones, *The Charity School Movement: A Study of Eighteenth Century Puritanism in Action* (Cambridge, Eng., 1938), p. 3.

5. M. Dorothy George, *England in Transition: Life and Work in the Eighteenth Century* (London, 1965 [1st ed., 1931]), pp. 73–74.

6. Hippolyte Taine, *Notes on England,* trans. Edward Hyams (London, 1957 [1st French ed., 1860–70]), pp. 167–68.

7. Helen Bosanquet, *Social Work in London, 1869–1912* (London, 1914), p. 74.

8. Beatrice Webb, *My Apprenticeship* (London, 1971 [1st ed., 1926]), p. 164.

9. Ibid., pp. 158 ff.

10. Brian Harrison, *Peaceable Kingdom: Stability and Change in Modern Britain* (Oxford, 1982), p. 241.

11. Gertrude Himmelfarb, *Poverty and Compassion: The Moral Imagination of the Late Victorians* (New York, 1991), pp. 83–84.

12. Arnold Toynbee, *"Progress and Poverty": A Criticism of Mr. Henry George* (London, 1884), p. 54.

13. T. H. Green, "Liberal Legislation and Freedom of Contract" (1881), in *The Political Theory of T. H. Green: Selected Writings,* ed. John R. Rodman (New York, 1964), pp. 51–52; Green, "On the Different Senses of 'Freedom' as Applied to Will and to the Moral Progress of Man," in *The Works of Thomas Hill Green,* ed. R. L. Nettleship (London, 1885–88), II, 322–23.

14. T. H. Green, *Lectures on the Principles of Political Obligation* (London, 1941 [1st ed., 1882]), pp. 39–40.

15. Asa Briggs and Anne Macartney, *Toynbee Hall: The First Hundred Years* (London, 1984), p. 22.

16. Standish Meacham, *Toynbee Hall and Social Reform, 1880–1914: The Search for Community* (New Haven, 1987), p. 58.

17. Ibid., p. 238.

18. William Beveridge, *Voluntary Action* (New York, 1948), p. 131.

19. Jane Addams, *Twenty Years at Hull-House* (New York, 1910), pp. 90 ff; Louise W. Knight, "Jane Addams' Views on the Responsibilities of Wealth" (unpublished paper delivered in June 1989, quoting Starr Papers, Sophia Smith collection, Smith College).

20. Beatrice Webb, Ms. of the Diaries, May 18, 1883 (Webb Ms. Collection, London School of Economics). (The published version omits an important part of this quotation.)

21. Meacham, *Toynbee Hall*, p. 80.

22. Jane Addams, *Democracy and Social Ethics,* ed. Anne Firor Scott (Cambridge, Mass., 1964 [reprint of 1907 ed., 1st ed., 1902]), p. 15.

23. Arnold Toynbee, "Are Radicals Socialists?" (1882), in *Lectures on the Industrial Revolution of the Eighteenth Century in England: Popular Addresses, Notes, and Other Fragments* (London, 1908 [1st ed., 1884]), p. 233.

24. Judith R. Walkowitz, *City of Dreadful Delight: Narratives of Sexual Danger in Late-Victorian London* (Chicago, 1992), p. 33.

25. Octavia Hill, "Colour, Space and Music for the People" (1884), in *Nineteenth-Century Opinion: An Anthology of Extracts from the First Fifty Volumes of the "Nineteenth Century,"* *1877–1901* (London, 1951), pp. 45–46.

26. Melvin Richter, *The Politics of Conscience: T. H. Green and His Age* (Cambridge, Mass., 1964), pp. 24, 250, 259, 266–67, 283, and passim; Andrew Vincent and Raymond Plant, *Philosophy, Politics and Citizenship: The Life and Thought of the British Idealists* (Oxford, 1984), pp. 29, 32, 67, 86; Stefan Colini, "Political Theory and the 'Science of Society' in Victorian Britain," *Historical Journal,* 1980, p. 227; Peter Clarke, *Liberals and Social Democrats* (Cambridge, Eng., 1978), pp. 14–15.

27. Brian Harrison, "Miss Butler's Oxford Survey," in *Traditions of Social Policy: Essays in Honour of Violet Butler,* ed. A. H. Halsey (Oxford, 1976), p. 56.

28. Helen Bosanquet, *Rich and Poor* (New York, 1970 [reprint of 2nd ed., 1898]), p. 120.

29. Kathleen Woodroofe, *From Charity to Social Work in England and the United States* (London, 1968 [1st ed., 1962]), p. 23.

30. Thomas Carlyle, *Sartor Resartus* (Everyman ed., London, 1940 [1st ed., 1833–34]), p. 87; *Heroes, Hero Worship and the Heroic in History* (New York, n.d. [1st ed., 1841]), p. 85. In *Westward Ho* (1855), Charles Kingsley used the word "self-helpful." And in 1857, George Holyoake, the militant atheist, claimed that he had coined the expression. (F. B. Smith, "The Atheist Mission, 1840–1900," in Robert Robson, ed., *Ideas and Institutions of Victorian Britain* [London, 1967], p. 219, quoting Holyoake in *The Reasoner*, May 17, 1857.)

31. Samuel Smiles, *Self-Help: With Illustrations of Conduct and Perseverance* (London, 1908 [1st ed., 1859]), p. 120. There are numerous other references to and quotations from Carlyle: e.g., Smiles, *Duty: With Illustrations of Courage, Patience, and Endurance* (London, 1880), pp. 18, 29; *Thrift* (London, 1876), pp. 185, 222–23, 303; *Life and Labor, or Characteristics of Men of Industry, Culture and Genius* (New York, 1888), passim.

32. Smiles, *Self-Help*, pp. v–viii.

33. Ibid., pp. x–xi.

34. Smiles, *Duty*, p. 261.

35. Smiles, *Self-Help*, pp. 111–12. "Genius" also appears in the subtitle of *Life and Labor:* "Characteristics of Men of Industry, Culture and Genius."

36. E.g., Walter E. Houghton, *The Victorian Frame of Mind, 1830–1870* (New Haven, 1957), p. 117.

37. Royden Harrison, Afterword to Smiles, *Self-Help* (London, 1968), p. 262.

38. Smiles, *Self-Help*, pp. 341–52.

Chapter VI: The Jew as Victorian

1. Irwin M. Stelzer, "What Thatcher Wrought," *The Public Interest,* Spring 1992, p. 27, n. 1.

2. Hugo Young, *One of Us: A Biography of Margaret Thatcher* (London, 1989), p. 423.

3. R. W. Johnson, in *London Review of Books,* April 20, 1989, p. 3.

4. Margaret Cole, *The Story of Fabian Socialism* (New York, 1964 [1st ed., 1961]), p. 83.

5. Yosef Gorni, "Beatrice Webb's Views on Judaism and Zionism," *Jewish Social Studies*, Spring 1978; Deborah Epstein Nord, *The Apprenticeship of Beatrice Webb* (Amherst, Mass., 1985), pp. 173–76, p. 276, n. 53.

6. Chushichi Tsuzuki, *H. M. Hyndman and British Socialism* (Oxford, 1961), pp. 126, 128.

7. Beatrice Webb, *My Apprenticeship* (London, 1971 [1st ed., 1926]), p. 38. There may be an allusion to this belief in a letter written while she was preparing this essay. She had been meeting with Jews "of all classes," she said, "and on the whole I like and respect them—I almost think I have a *true* feeling for them." (*The Letters of Sidney and Beatrice Webb*, ed. Norman MacKenzie [Cambridge, Eng., 1978], I, 64 [April 30, 1888].)

8. Webb, *My Apprenticeship*, p. 81.

9. Beatrice Potter, "The Jewish Community," in Charles Booth, *Labour and Life of the People* (3rd ed., London, 1891), I, 565. This was republished under the more familiar title *Life and Labour of the People in London*.

10. Beatrice Webb, *Our Partnership*, ed. Barbara Drake and Margaret I. Cole (London, 1948), p. 12.

11. Webb, "The Jewish Community," p. 588.

12. Gorni, "Beatrice Webb's Views," p. 104.

13. Webb, "The Jewish Community," pp. 577–78.

14. Ibid., p. 147.

15. Ibid., pp. 579–80.

16. Ibid., p. 566.

17. Ibid., pp. 570–71.

18. Ibid., pp. 573–74.

19. Ibid., pp. 583–84.

20. Ibid., pp. 585–87.

21. Ibid., pp. 587–88.

22. Ibid., p. 588.

23. Ibid., pp. 589–90.

24. Karl Marx, *Early Writings*, trans. and ed. T. B. Bottomore (New York, 1964), pp. 34–37. (I have eliminated the many italics in these passages.)

25. Webb, *My Apprenticeship,* p. 32.

26. Marx, *Early Writings,* pp. 34, 37.

27. Ibid., p. 34.

28. Sidney and Beatrice Webb, *Soviet Communism: A New Civilization* (London, 1947), pp. 901, 908–9. (In the first edition, the title ended with a question mark.)

29. Later historians take it seriously, although with some reservations. See, for example, Lloyd P. Gartner, *The Jewish Immigrant in England, 1870–1914* (London, 1960); Harold Pollins, *Economic History of the Jews in England* (East Brunswick, N.J., 1982); William J. Fishman, *East End 1888: Life in a London Borough Among the Laboring Poor* (Philadelphia, 1988).

30. Max Weber, *The Protestant Ethic and the Spirit of Capitalism,* trans. Talcott Parsons, ed. Anthony Giddens (New York, 1976 [1st Eng. ed., 1930]), pp. 166, 180.

31. Werner Sombart, *The Jews and Modern Capitalism,* trans. M. Epstein, ed. Bert F. Hoselitz (New York, 1962 [1st German ed., 1911; English trans., 1913]), p. 235.

32. Webb could have read them later in English, Sombart's book having been translated in 1913 and Weber's in 1930. In the three volumes of the Webbs' letters and the additional three volumes of Beatrice Webb's diaries, there is only a single passing reference to Sombart; in 1928, when he was visiting England, she regretted having seen so little of him. (*Letters of Sidney and Beatrice Webb,* III, 297 [March 19, 1928].) I have found no reference to Sombart in her other books, and only a single footnote reference to Max Weber on another subject. (Sidney and Beatrice Webb, *Methods of Social Study* [London, 1975 (1st ed., 1932)], p. 12, n. 1.)

33. Sombart, *The Jews,* pp. 235–36 and passim. In his later works, his references to Jews had an anti-Semitic tone absent from his earlier book.

34. *The Diary of Beatrice Webb,* ed. Norman and Jeanne MacKenzie (Cambridge, Mass., 1982), I, 322 (February 1, 1890).

35. Ibid., II, 63 (December 28, 1894); *The Minority Report of the Poor Law Commission,* Part II: *The Public Organization of the*

Labour Market (London, 1909), p. 302; Part I: *The Break-up of the Poor Law* (London, 1909), p. 513.

36. See, for example, E. P. Thompson, "The Moral Economy of the English Crowd in the Eighteenth Century," *Past and Present,* 1971; and a critique of Thompson by A. W. Coats, "Contrary Moralities: Plebs, Paternalists and Political Economists," *Past and Present,* 1972.

Chapter VII: The New Women and the New Men

1. Friedrich Nietzsche, *Twilight of the Idols,* in *The Portable Nietzsche,* trans. and ed. Walter Kaufmann (London, 1976 [1st ed., 1888]), pp. 515–16 ("Skirmishes of an Untimely Man," No. 5).

2. Karl Beckson, *London in the 1890s: A Cultural History* (New York, 1992), p. 252. The three-part essay by Ellis appeared in *The Savoy,* the successor to *The Yellow Book,* in 1896. It may have been inspired by the appearance the same year of the English translation of Nietzsche's books on Wagner.

3. David Rubinstein, *Before the Suffragettes: Women's Emancipation in the 1890s* (New York, 1986), p. 217.

4. Ibid.

5. *The New Woman: Women's Voices, 1880–1918,* ed. Juliet Gardiner (London, 1993), p. 15 (excerpt from a journal of January 1894).

6. Beckson, *London in the 1890s,* p. 144. This book is an excellent account of the period and I am much indebted to it, although I differ with it in some respects. Beckson, for example, sees a closer relation than I do between the old feminist and the new woman, and between the *fin de siècle* movement and modernism.

7. Ibid., p. 129.

8. Ibid., p. 134.

9. Olive Schreiner, *The Story of an African Farm* (Oxford, 1992 [1st ed., 1883]), pp. 209–10, 247.

10. See, for example, Elaine Showalter, *A Literature of Their Own:*

British Women Novelists from Brontë to Lessing (Princeton, 1977), p. 195.

11. Schreiner, *The Story of an African Farm,* Introduction by Joseph Bristow, p. xxvii.

12. Grant Allen, *The Woman Who Did* (Boston, 1926 [1st ed., 1895]), pp. 13, 41, 74–76, 138, 155, and passim.

13. Barbara Caine, *Victorian Feminists* (Oxford, 1992), p. 256.

14. Showalter, *A Literature of Their Own,* p. 185.

15. Allen, *The Woman Who Did,* pp. 187, 223.

16. George Orwell, *In Front of Your Nose, 1945–1950* (vol. IV of *The Collected Essays, Journalism and Letters of George Orwell*), ed. Sonia Orwell (New York, 1968), p. 416 (letter to Julian Symons, April 20, 1948).

17. Elaine Showalter, *Sexual Anarchy: Gender and Culture at the Fin de Siècle* (London, 1991), p. 19.

18. George Gissing, *The Odd Women* (New York, 1977 [1st ed., 1893]), p. 144.

19. Thomas Hardy, *Jude the Obscure* (Dolphin Books, New York, n.d. [1st ed., 1896]), p. 5. The novel was originally published serially from December 1894 through November 1895, which is why the publication date is sometimes given as 1895. These parts were somewhat revised for the volume published the following year.

20. Hardy, *Jude the Obscure* (London, 1951), p. x (reprint of preface to the 1912 edition).

21. Hardy, *Jude the Obscure* (Dolphin ed.), pp. 242, 260, 282, 295.

22. Ibid., pp. 224, 353, 365–66.

23. Beckson, *London in the 1890s,* p. 147.

24. Schreiner, *The Story of an African Farm,* p. xix, quoting a letter of 1895.

25. D. H. Lawrence, *Study of Thomas Hardy and Other Essays* (Cambridge, Eng., 1985), p. 109.

26. It has been said that "relationship," in this sense, is a neologism, an invention of our own times. (*Times Literary Supplement,* June 25, 1993, p. 13, quoting Harriet Harman, *The Century Gap: 20th-Century Man, 21st-Century.*) Havelock Ellis and his wife used the word exactly as it is used today. See

Ellis, *My Life* (London, 1967 [1st ed., 1940]), pp. 238–41 (letter dated June 13, 1891).

27. Ruth First and Ann Scott, *Olive Schreiner: A Biography* (New Brunswick, N.J., 1990 [1st ed., 1980]), pp. 159, 168.

28. Ruth Brandon, *The New Women and the Old Men: Love, Sex and the Woman Question* (New York, 1990), pp. 120, 131.

29. Ibid., p. 158.

30. Ibid., p. 265.

31. Brandon, *The New Woman*, p. 21, quoting H. M. Hyndman, the leader of the Social Democratic Federation.

32. Amy Levy's writings have just been reissued, with an informative introduction by the editor: *The Complete Novels and Selected Writings of Amy Levy, 1861–1889*, ed. Melvyn New (Gainesville, Fla., 1993).

33. Eleanor Marx-Aveling and Edward Aveling, *Thoughts on Women and Society*, ed. Joachim Müller and Edith Schotte (New York, 1987), pp. 13, 17, 25. This is a reprint of the pamphlet published in 1887 under the title *The Woman Question*. Bebel's book is more commonly known under its original title, *Woman and Socialism;* because of Bismarck's decrees against socialism, the title was changed for subsequent editions.

34. Ibid., pp. 27–29.

35. H. G. Wells, *Experiment in Autobiography: Discoveries and Conclusions of a Very Ordinary Brain (Since 1866)* (New York, 1934), p. 465.

36. Anthony West, *H. G. Wells: Aspects of a Life* (New York, 1984), p. 56. (Anthony West was the child of Wells and West.)

37. Gissing, *The Odd Women*, p. 145.

38. Hardy, *Jude the Obscure*, p. 381.

39. *The Later Letters of John Stuart Mill, 1849–1873*, ed. Francis E. Mineka and Dwight N. Lindley, in *Collected Works* (Toronto, 1972), IV, 1693 (February 2, 1870).

40. John Stuart Mill, *Autobiography*, ed. John Jacob Coss (New York, 1924 [1st ed., 1873]), p. 75.

41. William Godwin, *An Enquiry Concerning Political Justice, and*

Its Influence on General Virtue and Happiness (1st ed., London, 1793), II, 870–71.

42. For more details of this circle, see Gertrude Himmelfarb, *Marriage and Morals Among the Victorians* (New York, 1986), pp. 156–57.

43. Beckson, *London in the 1890s*, p. 46.

44. Some commentators regard the *fin de siècle* movement as a prelude to modernism—Pound, Yeats, Eliot. (Beckson, *London in the 1890s*, p. 69; Linda Dowling, "The Decadent and the New Woman in the 1890s," *Nineteenth-Century Fiction*, 1979, pp. 434–37, 447.) But modernism too had a gravity and sense of morality lacking in the earlier movement.

45. Oscar Wilde, *The Picture of Dorian Gray* (London, 1985 [1st ed., 1891]), p. 28. This first appeared in *Lippincott's Monthly Magazine* in July 1890, and was much revised for the publication of the volume the following year.

46. Wilde, *Dorian Gray*, p. 26.

47. Ibid., p. 214.

48. Peter Ackroyd, Introduction to *Dorian Gray*, pp. 7–8.

49. Ibid., p. 7.

50. Wilde, *Dorian Gray*, pp. 183, 185.

51. Richard Ellmann, *Oscar Wilde* (New York, 1988), p. 463.

52. Wilde, *Dorian Gray*, pp. 156, 179, 257.

53. David Cecil, *Max: A Biography* (New York, 1985 [1st ed., 1964]), p. 98.

54. Stanley Weintraub, *Beardsley* (London, 1972 [1st ed., 1967]), p. 83.

55. Jerome Hamilton Buckley, *The Victorian Temper: A Study in Literary Culture* (Cambridge, Mass., 1951), p. 232.

56. *The Yellow Book: A Selection*, ed. Cedric Ellsworth Smith (Hartford, Conn., 1928), p. 1.

57. Cecil, *Max*, p. 92.

58. Ellmann, *Oscar Wilde*, p. 583.

59. Holbrook Jackson, *The Eighteen Nineties* (London, 1950 [1st ed., 1913]), p. 18 (quoting John Davidson, *Earl Lavender*).

60. Oscar Wilde, *The Importance of Being Earnest and Related Writings*, ed. Joseph Bristow (London, 1992 [1st ed., 1899]), p. 52.

61. Gissing quoted by Showalter, *Sexual Anarchy*, p. 3.
62. Linda Dowling maintains that where today we may be more inclined to see the differences between the two groups, contemporaries were prone to identify them as "twin apostles of social apocalypse." ("The Decadent and the New Woman in the 1890's," *Nineteenth-Century Fiction*, 1979, pp. 434–37, 447.)
63. Showalter, *Sexual Anarchy*, p. 170.
64. Wilde, *Dorian Gray*, p. 72.
65. Ibid., p. 132.

Epilogue: A De-moralized Society

1. Thomas Carlyle, "Chartism," in *English and Other Critical Essays* (Everyman ed., London, n.d. [1st ed., 1839]), pp. 165–73.
2. In 1833 the British Association for the Advancement of Science established a statistical section, which was promptly followed by the founding of statistical societies in Manchester and London. The London society announced its purpose to be the compilation and elucidation of facts about the "conditions and prospects of society," including "moral and social statistics." (*Annals of the Royal Statistical Society, 1834–1934* [London, 1934], p. 22.)
3. There has been much controversy over the use of ratios (illegitimate births in proportion to all births) or rates (illegitimate births in proportion to all women of child-bearing age or to unmarried women of childbearing age). Many statisticians regard the latter as the best measure. See, for example, Peter Laslett, Introduction, *Bastardy and Its Comparative History: Studies in the History of Illegitimacy and Marital Nonconformism in Britain, France, Germany, Sweden, North America, Jamaica and Japan*, ed. Peter Laslett, Karla Oosterveen, and Richard M. Smith (Cambridge, Mass., 1980), p. 15. Charles Murray discusses the implications of the alternatives and explains why ratios are preferable in some circumstances.

("Welfare and the Family: The U.S. Experience," *Journal of Labor Economics,* 1993, pp. S240–43.) For my purposes, I believe, ratios reveal more clearly the moral and social climate in which illegitimacy takes place.

4. These figures apply to England and Wales. For statistics prior to 1841, see Laslett, Introduction, *Bastardy,* p. 14. For later statistics, see B. R. Mitchell, *British Historical Statistics* (Cambridge, Eng., 1988), pp. 42–44; Office of Population Censuses and Surveys [OPCS], *1837–1983 Birth Statistics,* pp. 19, 21; Penny Babb, "Birth Statistics 1992," *Population Trends* (OPCS), Winter 1993, pp. 8–9; *Annual Abstract of Statistics 1992,* p. 30. (1991–92 figures were provided by the staff of OPCS.) In some cases I have converted absolute numbers to percentages, and throughout I have rounded off the figures.

5. Edward Royle, *Modern Britain: A Social History, 1750–1985* (London, 1987), p. 54.

6. For the nineteenth century, there are a few estimated ratios for a few states. Massachusetts, for example, rose from less than 1% in 1860 to 2% in 1890. (Daniel Scott Smith, "The Long Cycle of American Illegitimacy and Prenuptial Pregnancy," *Bastardy,* p. 372.)

7. Etienne van de Walle, "Illegitimacy in France during the Nineteenth Century," *Bastardy,* p. 270; Jean Meyer, "Illegitimates and Foundlings in Pre-industrial France," ibid., p. 252; Laslett, Introduction, ibid., p. 46 (reproduction of a graph from a book published in 1860); Margareta R. Matovic, "Illegitimacy and Marriage in Stockholm in the Nineteenth Century," ibid., p. 336. (The figures for Paris and London are for 1860, those for Vienna and Stockholm for 1851–55.)

8. *Demographic and Social Aspects of Population Growth,* ed. Charles F. Westoff and Robert Parke, Jr. (U.S. Commission on Population Growth and the American Future, 1972), p. 383; Reports of National Center for Health Statistics.

9. Penny Babb, "Teenage Conceptions and Fertility in England and Wales, 1971–91," *Population Trends,* Winter 1993, table 5, p. 15.

10. *Demographic and Social Aspects,* p. 384; *Monthly Vital Statistics Report Supplement,* September 9, 1993, p. 31.

11. William J. Bennett, *The Index of Leading Cultural Indicators* (Washington, D.C., 1993), p. 8, citing National Center for Health Statistics and the Alan Guttmacher Institute.

12. Royle, *Modern Britain,* p. 55; Penny Babb, "Teenage Conceptions," pp. 12–13.

13. Tom W. Smith, *The Demography of Sexual Behavior* (Henry Kaiser Family Foundation, 1994), p. xiv.

14. V. A. C. Gatrell, "The Decline of Theft and Violence in Victorian and Edwardian England," in *Crime and the Law: The Social History of Crime in Western Europe since 1500,* ed. V. A. C. Gatrell, Bruce Lenman, and Geoffrey Parker (London, 1980), p. 240.

15. Mitchell, *British Historical Statistics,* pp. 776, 392–94. The statistics compiled by V. A. C. Gatrell and T. B. Hadden differ somewhat because they are based on different categories, but the trend lines are identical; see "Criminal Statistics and Their Interpretation," in E. A. Wrigley, ed., *Nineteenth-Century Society: Essays in the Use of Quantitative Methods for the Study of Social Data* (Cambridge, Eng., 1972), p. 394. Here and elsewhere I have converted absolute numbers into rates per 100,000 population.

   There are obvious methodological difficulties in compiling these statistics: the difference between recorded and actual crime rates, changes in the defining and recording of crime partly as a result of legal and administrative reforms, regional variations, and the like. The difficulties are greater earlier in the nineteenth century, but by the late 1850s, the data are more reliable, especially as they reveal trend lines. (For a comprehensive methodological discussion, see Gatrell and Hadden, "Criminal Statistics," pp. 337–86.)

16. Joseph Fletcher, "Moral and Educational Statistics of England and Wales," *Quarterly Journal of the Statistical Society of London,* 1847, p. 210. On the relation between education and crime in the nineteenth century, see also Fletcher, ibid., 1849; F. G. P. Neisen, "Statistics of Crime in England and Wales, for the

Years 1834–1844," ibid., 1848. Gatrell points out that while illiteracy had been virtually eliminated in the country at large by the end of the century, 16% of the prisoners were still illiterate in 1902. (Gatrell, "The Decline of Theft and Violence," p. 335.)

17. V. A. C. Gatrell, quoted by Ted Robert Gurr, "Historical Trends in Violent Crime: Europe and the United States," in *Violence in America* (Newbury Park, Cal., 1989), I, 31.

18. The *Criminal Statistics* (formerly entitled *Judicial Statistics*) are published by the Home Office; the population statistics by the Office of Population Censuses and Surveys. See also Mitchell, *British Historical Statistics*, pp. 776–78. The *British Crime Survey* (also published by the Home Office), unlike *Criminal Statistics*, does not rely upon reported crimes but upon its own estimates of actual crimes. Between 1981 and 1987, for example, *Criminal Statistics* reported a 41% increase in crime, whereas the *Crime Survey* gave an estimate of 30%. The difference is accounted for not by a smaller number of estimated crimes but rather by an increase in the reporting of crimes. (Pat Mayhew, David Elliott, and Lizanne Dowds, *The 1988 British Crime Survey* [London, 1989], p. 23.) According to A. Keith Bottomley and Ken Pease, more serious offenses increased less rapidly than less serious ones, but this, they suggest, may reflect the growing tendency to report slight offenses. (*Crime and Punishment: Interpreting the Data* [Milton Keynes, Eng., 1986], p. 61.)

19. James Q. Wilson and Richard J. Herrnstein, *Crime and Human Nature* (New York, 1985), p. 409; Gurr, in *Violence in America*, pp. 35–7. The violence in the mid-nineteenth century has been attributed in part to the large influx of working-class Irish immigrants. Yet a new wave of immigrants in the last decades of the century coincided with a substantial decline of violence. On the decline of drunkenness and disorderly conduct in most major cities between 1860 and 1920, see Eric H. Monkkonen, "A Disorderly People? Urban Order in the Nineteenth and Twentieth Centuries," *Journal of American History*, December 1981, p. 548.

20. Geoffrey Gorer, *Exploring English Character* (New York, 1955), p. 13.

21. U.S. Department of Justice, F.B.I., "Crime Index, 1960–1992"; U.S. Department of Justice, Bureau of Justice Statistics [B.J.S.], *Highlights from 20 Years of Surveying Crime Victims: The National Crime Victimization Survey, 1973–92* (1993), pp. 5, 7; U.S. Department of Justice, F.B.I., *Uniform Crime Reports, 1992,* table 1, p. 58. The estimated crime rates in the victimization surveys conducted by the B.J.S. are higher (and probably reflect the reality more faithfully) than the reported rates given by the F.B.I. But the trends that emerge from both studies are similar. In one respect, they seem to differ substantially. Unlike the F.B.I. figures, the B.J.S. violent crime rate in 1992 was lower than in the peak years of the late 1970s and early 1980s, but higher than in any year between 1985 and 1991. (U.S. Department of Justice, B.J.S., *Criminal Victimization 1992,* p. 3.) A more systematic study than I am attempting here would disaggregate these findings racially, regionally, and demographically. James Q. Wilson, for example, attributes the fall in the crime rate in the early 1980s to the decline in the number of teenage boys. ("What To Do About Crime," *Commentary,* September 1994, p. 26.)

22. U.S. Department of Justice, *Lifetime Likelihood of Victimization,* March 1987.

23. U.S. Department of Justice, *Highlights from 20 Years,* p. 6.

24. U.S. Department of Justice, F.B.I., *Index of Crime, United States, 1960–1992; Historical Statistics of U.S.* (1975), Part 1, p. 414; *Statistical Abstract of the United States,* 1992, table 292; U.S. Department of Justice, F.B.I., *Uniform Crime Reports, 1992,* table 1, p. 58; U.S. Department of Justice, F.B.I., *Preliminary Report,* May 1, 1994. Statistics compiled by the F.B.I. give the homicide rate in the mid-1930s as 6.5 (not 9.7, as *Historical Statistics* has it); the other figures are the same. Some sources give a higher homicide rate for the first two decades of the twentieth century; in part, this reflects the fact that automobile fatalities were often recorded as homicides. (Gurr, *Violence in America,* p. 38.)

25. Bureau of Justice Statistics, "International Crime Rates," May 1988 (citing Interpol and World Health Organization statistics).

26. Gurr, *Violence in America,* p. 40; Wilson, "What To Do About Crime," p. 26.

27. John J. DiIulio, Jr., "Saving the Children: Criminal Justice and Social Policy" (paper presented at the Conference on Social Policies for Children, Center of Domestic and Comparative Policy Studies, Woodrow Wilson School, Princeton University, May 25–26, 1994), p. 7 (quoting Barbara Allen-Hagen and Melissa Sickmund, *Juveniles and Violence: Juvenile Offending and Victimization*).

28. Ibid., p. 35.

29. Office of Population Censuses and Surveys, *Birth Statistics, 1992,* p. xxv; Charles Murray, "Underclass: The Crisis Deepens," (London) *Sunday Times,* May 22, 1994, p. 10.

30. Douglas J. Besharov and Karen N. Gardiner, "Teen Sex," *American Enterprise,* January–February 1993, p. 56.

31. See, for example, James Q. Wilson, *The Moral Sense* (New York, 1993), pp. 176–78, and notes, p. 263; Norman Dennis and George Erdos, *Families Without Fatherhood* (2d ed., London, 1993), pp. 30–54; Barbara Dafoe Whitehead, "Dan Quayle Was Right," *The Atlantic Monthly,* April 1993, pp. 47–84.

32. Charles Murray, "The Coming White Underclass," *Wall Street Journal,* October 29, 1993, p. 14.

33. Charles Murray, "Underclass: The Crisis Deepens," and "The New Victorians and the New Rabble," (London) *Sunday Times,* May 22 and 29, 1994.

34. Christie Davies, "Moralization and Demoralization: A Moral Explanation for Change in Crime, Disorder and Social Problems," in *The Loss of Virtue: Moral Confusion and Social Disorder in Britain and America,* ed. Digby Anderson (London, 1992), p. 5. See also Davies, "Crime, Bureaucracy and Equality," *Policy Review,* Winter 1983, pp. 89–105. The American criminologist Ted Robert Gurr has questioned the applicability of the U-curve to United States criminal statistics, point-

ing out that there have been three, not two, upsurges of crime in the past two centuries. But the second, in 1900, is based on dubious evidence, such as homicide rates that include automobile fatalities. (See Roger Lane, "On the Social Meaning of Homicide Trends in America," in *Violence in America,* ed. Gurr, I, 64–67.)

35. Daniel Patrick Moynihan, "Defining Deviancy Down," *The American Scholar,* Winter 1993.

36. Ted Robert Gurr, "Historical Trends in Violent Crime: Europe and the United States," in *Violence in America,* I, 24 (quoting Alfred Soman, "Deviance and Criminal Justice in Western Europe, 1300–1800," *Criminal Justice History: An International Annual,* 1980).

37. Charles Krauthammer, "Defining Deviancy Up," *The New Republic,* November 22, 1993.

38. Jose Harris, *Private Lives, Public Spirit: A Social History of Britain, 1870–1914* (Oxford, 1993), pp. 209–10n.

39. Arland Thornton, "Changing Attitudes Toward Family Issues in the United States," *Journal of Marriage and the Family,* November 1989, p. 884.

40. Dennis and Erdos, *Families Without Fatherhood,* p. 60 (citing *British Social Attitudes: Seventh Report* [1990]).

41. National Opinion Research Center, survey dated February–April 1993.

42. Myron Magnet, *The Dream and the Nightmare: The Sixties' Legacy to the Underclass* (New York, 1993), pp. 50, 231.

43. Gatrell and Hadden find a positive correlation between property offenses and downturns in the trade cycle in the early part of the nineteenth century and again in the early part of the twentieth century, but not in the last quarter of the nineteenth century. In this latter period, which included the severe depression of 1886, there was an inverse relationship. Moreover, for other kinds of crime, such as assaults against persons and drunkenness, they find no correlation with the trade cycle, in either the early or the later part of the century. (See Gatrell and Hadden, "Criminal Statistics," pp. 368–69, 379, 385; Gatrell, "Decline of Theft and Violence," pp.

310–11.) The most forceful statement denying any correlation between economic depression and crime is J. J. Tobias, *Crime and Industrial Society in the Nineteenth Century* (London, 1967).

44. Jock Young, "The Failure of Criminology: The Need for a Radical Realism," in *Confronting Crime,* ed. Roger Matthews and Jock Young (London, 1986). See also Edwin Lemert, *Human Deviance, Social Problems, and Social Control* (New Jersey, 1967); Jason Ditton, *Contrology: Beyond the New Criminology* (1979); S. Box, *Power, Crime and Mystification* (London, 1984). For a discussion of this and other interpretations of the crime statistics, see Stephen Davies, "Towards the Remoralization of Society," in Martin Loney et al., eds., *The State or the Market: Politics and Welfare in Contemporary Britain* (2d ed., London, 1987).

45. Bottomley and Pease, *Crime and Punishment,* p. 138 (quoting R. Tarling, Home Office, *Research Bulletin*).

46. Richard B. Freeman, "Crime and Unemployment," in James Q. Wilson, ed., *Crime and Public Policy* (San Francisco, 1983), pp. 96–97.

47. *Newsweek,* December 13, 1993, pp. 35, 37.

48. Richard Hoggart, "The Standards to Defend" (review of *The Loss of Virtue,* ed. Digby Anderson), *Times Literary Supplement,* March 19, 1993, p. 3.

49. Martin J. Wiener, in his very informative book *Reconstructing the Criminal: Culture, Law, and Policy in England, 1830–1914* (Cambridge, Eng., 1990), maintains that the "moralizing" agenda of penal policy gave way, in the last quarter of the nineteenth century, to an "administrative" agenda, whose effect was the "de-moralizing of criminality" (p. 215). For a critique of this book, suggesting that the de-moralizing policy was more characteristic of the Edwardian than of the late-Victorian period, see the review by Gertrude Himmelfarb, *Times Literary Supplement,* March 15, 1991, p. 7.

50. Magnet, *The Dream,* p. 19.

51. William Raspberry, "Courage to Say the Obvious," *Washington Post,* April 5, 1993, p. A21.

52. Barbara Dafoe Whitehead, "Dan Quayle Was Right," *Atlantic Monthly*, April 1993.

53. *Newsweek*, December 15, 1993, p. 35.

54. This reconsideration of conservatism (although not necessarily the criticism of Thatcherism) is evident in David Willetts, *Modern Conservatism* (London, 1992); David Green, *Reinventing Civil Society* (London, 1993); John Gray, *Beyond the New Right* (London, 1993). Shirley Letwin, in *The Anatomy of Thatcherism* (London, 1992), describes Thatcherism as a moral and social, not merely an economic system, which promoted the "vigorous virtues."

55. A. P. Herbert, quoted in *The Times* (London), August 26, 1970, p. 9.

56. Morris Ernst, quoted in *New York Times*, January 5, 1970, p. 32.

57. James Bowman, "American Notes," *Times Literary Supplement*, June 18, 1993, p. 16.

58. Martha Nussbaum, "Virtue Revived," *Times Literary Supplement*, July 3, 1992, pp. 9–11. Although her own preference is for an "ethics of virtue" that is universal as well as particularistic, she concedes that most philosophers now lean to the latter mode.

59. *Washington Post*, May 2, 1993, p. A24; *New York Times*, January 16, 1994, pp. 1, 19.

60. *Bastardy*, parts I and III.

61. The best-known statement of this theory is Daniel Bell, *The Cultural Contradictions of Capitalism* (New York, 1976).

62. Karl Marx and Friedrich Engels, *The Communist Manifesto*, ed. Samuel H. Beer (New York, 1955), p. 12.

63. *The Autobiography of William Cobbett: The Progress of a Ploughboy to a Seat in Parliament*, ed. William Reitzel (London, 1933), p. 9; Asa Briggs, *Victorian Cities* (New York, 1965), p. 92.

64. Laslett, Introduction, in *Bastardy*, p. 63; Christopher Smout, "Aspects of Sexual Behavior in Nineteenth-Century Scotland," ibid., p. 199.

65. Daniel Scott Smith, "The Long Cycle of American Illegitimacy and Prenuptial Pregnancy," ibid., p. 377.

Postscript: The "New Victorians" and the Old

1. Patrick Devlin, *The Enforcement of Morals* (Oxford, 1965), pp. 133–35.
2. The feminist Catharine MacKinnon is said to be the archetype of the New Victorian. See Gertrude Himmelfarb, " 'New Victorians' Don't Earn That Label," *Wall Street Journal,* January 12, 1994, p. 10; Pete Hamill, "Woman on the Verge of a Legal Breakdown: Feminist Catharine MacKinnon," *Playboy,* January 1993, p. 138; Stanley Kauffmann, "Dark Magic," *New Republic,* January 24, 1994, p. 40; Susan Faludi, "Whose Hype?" *Newsweek,* October 25, 1993; Calvin Woodward, "Speak No Evil," *New York Times Book Review,* January 2, 1994, p. 11; Katie Roiphe, *The Morning After* (New York, 1993), p. 66.
3. Charles Dickens, *Bleak House* (New York, 1977 [1st ed., 1853]), p. 37.
4. T. H. Green, *Lectures on the Principles of Political Obligation* (London, 1941 [1st ed., 1882]), pp. 39–40 (Nos. 17, 18), p. 218 (No. 219). (See chap. V, p. 152.)

INDEX

Acton, John E.E.D., 97
Acton, William, 73–5, 115
Addams, Jane, 156–8
Allen, Grant, 192, 204–5
Anderson, Elizabeth Garrett, 109
Aquinas, Thomas, 9, 13
Aristotle, 8, 13
Arnold, Matthew, 13, 28, 40, 114n, 118, 167
Arnold, Mrs. Matthew, 99
Arnold, Thomas, 28, 40
Asquith, Herbert, 96, 154
Asquith, Mrs. Herbert, 99
Attlee, Clement, 158
Augustine, 9, 13
Austen, Jane, 219n
Aveling, Edward, 201–3, 218

Bacon, Francis, 92n
Bagehot, Walter, 55
Bagehot, Mrs. Walter, 99
Balzac, Honoré de, 120
Banks, J. A., 122
Banks, Olive, 122
Barnett, Samuel, 150, 153, 155, 159
Baudelaire, Charles Pierre, 209, 216
Bax, Belfort, 96
Beardsley, Aubrey, 212–14
Bebel, August, 202–3
Beerbohm, Max, 212–13, 215
Beesly, Edward S., 96
Beesly, Mrs. Edward S., 99
Belloc, Hilaire, 219
Bennett, Arnold, 191, 219
Bennett, William, 17

Besant, Annie, 121–3
Besant, Walter, 158
Best, Geoffrey, 136n
Beveridge, William, 156, 158
Binney, T., 60
Blackwell, Elizabeth, 75, 109, 123
Booth, Charles, 36–8, 137n, 147, 149, 154, 160–1, 172
Booth, William, 37
Bosanquet, Helen, 83, 105, 163
Bowdler, Thomas, 6
Bradlaugh, Charles, 121–3
Brandon, Ruth, 205
Bridges, Robert, 219
Briggs, Asa, 77, 255
Bright, John, 96
Broadhurst, Henry, 97
Brontë, Anne, 106n
Brontë, Charlotte, 98, 106n
Brontë, Emily, 106n
Browning, Elizabeth Barrett, 98, 107n
Bryce, James, 96
Buchan, John, 219
Buckle, Mrs. Henry, 99
Burke, Edmund, 45, 51–2, 57, 129, 138, 246
Burns, Robert, 47
Butler, Josephine, 88, 103, 105, 114–17, 119–20
Butler, Samuel, 94n
Byron, George Gordon, 208n

Caird, Mona, 191
Camus, Albert, 24
Carlile, Richard, 121
Carlyle, Thomas, 13, 24, 26, 35, 165n, 167, 221–2
Carpenter, Edward, 199, 215
Cecil, David, 213
Chadwick, Edwin, 38
Chesterfield, Philip, 4th Earl of, 21
Chesterton, G. K., 57, 66, 219
Churchill, Lady Randolph, 99
Churchill, Winston, 171
Clinton, Hillary Rodham, 251
Clinton, William J., 4–5, 246
Clough, Arthur Hugh, 107
Cobbe, Frances, 88, 120
Cobbett, William, 71, 127, 255
Coke, Edward, 54
Coleridge, Samuel Taylor, 72
Colley, Linda, 104
Comte, Auguste, 90n, 184
Conrad, Joseph, 219
Cook, Eliza, 107n
Craik, Dinah, 46n
Cross, John, 23

Darwin, Charles, 26–7
Davies, Christie, 234
Davies, Emily, 88, 103, 105, 110
Dennis, Norman, 245
Devlin, Patrick, 259

Dicey, A. V., 113, 154
Dickens, Charles, 13–14, 24, 56, 133, 148, 261
Dilke, Charles, 120
Disraeli, Benjamin, 55–6, 133, 158
Douglas, Alfred, 211, 214n
Doyle, Arthur Conan, 210, 219
Drysdale, George, 121

Edgeworth, Maria, 107n
Eldon, John, 133
Eliot, George, 23–4, 26–7, 98, 106n, 109, 167, 188, 201, 219n
Ellis, Edith, 215
Ellis, Havelock, 19, 189, 199
Emerson, Ralph Waldo, 71
Erdos, George, 245
Ernst, Morris, 249

Fawcett, Millicent, 88, 98, 100, 120, 123–4, 193
Foucault, Michel, 51
Freud, Sigmund, 199n
Froude, James Anthony, 58–9

Galsworthy, John, 219
Gaskell, Elizabeth, 98, 107n
Geddes, Patrick, 65
George III, 6, 55
George IV, 48
George, Henry, 139

Gibbon, Edward, 6
Gissing, George, 94, 194, 206, 213, 215
Gladstone, William, 24–6, 59, 70, 96–7, 192
Godwin, William, 57–8n, 208n
Gorer, Geoffrey, 226n
Goschen, Mrs. George, 99
Grand, Sarah, 190–1
Gray, John, 214n
Green, Mrs. J. R., 99
Green, T. H., 20, 151–3, 158, 164, 187, 262
Green, Mrs. T. H., 99

Haldane, Richard, 154
Halévy, Elie, 54
Hanway, Jonas, 145
Harcourt, William, 96
Hardy, Thomas, 112n, 195–8
Harris, Jose, 235n
Harrison, Frederic, 58, 63–4, 96, 99, 109
Harrison, Mrs. Frederic, 99
Henry VIII, 114n
Herbert, A. P., 248
Hill, Octavia, 103, 105, 162
Hobbes, Thomas, 22, 29, 52
Hoggart, Richard, 241
Howard, John, 145
Housman, A. E., 219
Hunter, John, 47
Huysmans, Joris Karl, 209, 212n
Huxley, Thomas Henry, 67–8

Huxley, Mrs. Thomas
Henry, 99
Hyndman, H. M., 96, 172

James I, 45
James, Henry, 212–13, 219
Jones, Inigo, 47
Joyce, James, 249

Keats, John, 47
King, Martin Luther, Jr., 4
Kingsley, Charles, 66, 94
Kingsley, Mary, 107n
Kinnock, Neil, 13
Kipling, Rudyard, 219
Knowlton, Charles, 121
Krauthammer, Charles,
235–6

La Rochefoucauld, François,
23
Lancaster, Joseph, 47
Lawrence, D. H., 198n
Levy, Amy, 202n, 215
Lewes, George Henry, 23
Linton, Eliza Lynn, 99
Lovett, William, 43
Lowe, Robert, 96

Macmillan, Harold, 170
Machiavelli, Niccolò, 52
Magnet, Myron, 237, 244
Mallarmé, Stéphane, 209

Malthus, Thomas Robert,
120, 127, 129–30, 138
Mann, Thomas, 17
Mann, Tom, 154
Marshall, Alfred, 49,
109–10, 139
Marshall, Mary, 109
Martineau, Harriet, 103, 107n
Marx, Eleanor, 201–4, 218
Marx, Karl, 11, 53, 77,
180–2, 201, 254
Matsys, Quentyn, 47
Mayhew, Henry, 37, 117
Melbourne, William, 25
Meredith, George, 107n, 219
Meynell, Alice, 61
Mill, James, 207
Mill, John Stuart, 24, 26,
89–96, 98–9, 111, 115, 121,
152, 165n, 167, 196, 207–8
Milner, Isaac, 47
Milton, John, 21
Mitford, Mary Russell, 107n
Montaigne, Michel de, 50, 72
Montefiore, Moses, 177
Montesquieu, Charles Louis
de Secondat de, 9
More, Hannah, 145
Morley, John, 96, 98
Morris, William, 13, 70
Moynihan, Daniel Patrick,
232–5
Murray, Charles, 233

Newman, John Henry, 25–6n
Nicholson, Adela, 202n

Nietzsche, Friedrich, 10–11, 19, 51, 188–9, 211, 214–15, 220
Nightingale, Florence, 98–9, 102, 105, 114
Nisbet, Edith (Edith Bland), 205
Nussbaum, Martha, 250–1

Oliphant, Margaret, 98, 107n, 198
Orwell, George, 194, 263
Ouida (Louise Ramé), 190
Owen, Robert, 57–8n

Paget, James, 75
Palmerston, Henry, 25
Parnell, Charles, 120
Pater, Walter, 209
Patmore, Coventry, 61, 66
Pearson, Karl, 96, 199–200
Perceval, Spencer, 71
Perkin, Joan, 82n
Petronius, 25
Pitt, William, 128
Plato, 8, 13
Potter, Richard, 172, 181

Quayle, Dan, 245–6

Rabelais, François, 120
Raspberry, William, 245
Ricardo, David, 179, 181n, 185

Rimbaud, Arthur, 209
Roberts, Elizabeth, 78–86
Rothschild, Nathan, 177
Rosebery, Archibald, 96
Rossetti, Christina, 98–9, 107n
Rowntree, Seebohm, 147
Ruskin, John, 13, 24, 56, 64–6, 96, 109

Schreiner, Olive, 106n, 191–2, 198–201, 215
Shakespeare, William, 66, 203
Shaftesbury, Anthony, 7th Earl of, 57, 119
Shaw, George Bernard, 19, 46, 219
Shelley, Mary, 107n
Shelley, Percy Bysshe, 203, 208n
Showalter, Elaine, 193
Sidgwick, Arthur, 154
Sidgwick, Henry, 110, 154
Smiles, Samuel, 47–8, 50, 52, 72, 86, 165–8
Smith, Adam, 127, 166, 181n, 246, 256
Smith, Sydney, 38
Solomon, Samuel, 75–6
Sombart, Werner, 184
Somerville, Mary, 107n
Stead, W. T., 118–19
Stephen, Leslie, 27, 154
Stephen, Mrs. Leslie, 99
Stevenson, Robert Louis, 219

Strauss, Leo, 15
Symons, Arthur, 212

Taine, Hippolyte, 27–8, 39, 45, 71–3, 135, 145–6
Taylor, Harriet (Mrs. J. S. Mill), 24, 89n, 90n, 92n
Tennyson, Alfred, 61–2, 64, 66, 69–71, 109, 118
Ternan, Ellen, 24
Thackeray, William, 22, 47–8
Thatcher, Margaret, 3, 5, 8, 12–14, 16, 22–3, 33, 143, 170–1, 221, 247
Thomas, William I., 19
Thompson, F. M. L., 36
Thomson, J. Arthur, 65
Tocqueville, Alexis de, 40, 125–7, 187, 247
Toynbee, Arnold, 150–1, 153, 159
Toynbee, Mrs. Arnold, 99
Treitschke, Heinrich, 35
Trollope, Anthony, 13, 49, 108
Trollope, Frances, 107n

Victoria, Queen, 6, 27–8, 55, 59, 69, 71, 75

Walter, John, 133–4
Ward, Mrs. Humphry, 99, 103, 107n, 154

Watt, James, 47
Webb, Beatrice, 66–7, 96, 99, 100–3, 105, 107n, 118, 146–7, 149, 157, 170–87
Webb, Sidney, 96, 171, 185
Weber, Max, 10–11, 19–20, 143, 184
Wedgwood, Josiah, 47
Wells, H. G., 204–5, 213
Wesley, John, 33, 143–4, 157
West, Rebecca, 204–5
Whitehead, Barbara Dafoe, 245
Wilberforce, William, 105n
Wilde, Jane, 31
Wilde, Oscar, 24, 31, 154, 209–16, 219
Wilson, Dover, 40
Wilson, Harold, 16
Wilson, James Q., 16
Wollstonecraft, Mary, 57, 208n
Woolf, Virginia, 68–9n
Wykeham, William of, 21

Yeats, William Butler, 209, 213
Yonge, Charlotte, 98, 107n
Young, G. M., 59

Znaniecki, Florian, 19
Zola, Emile, 120